Project Editor: Agnès Saint-Laurent
Proofreader: Elizabeth Lewis
Designer: Johanne Lemay

Cover informations: François Daxhelex

EXCLUSIVE DISTRIBUTOR:

For Canada and the United States:
Simon & Schuster Canada
166 King Street East, Suite 300
Toronto, ON M5A 1J3
phone: (647) 427-8882
         1-800-387-0446
Fax: (647) 430-ƒEszt9446
simonandschuster.ca

Bibliothèque et Archives nationales du Québec
and Library and Archives Canada cataloguing in
publication

Caine, Alex

   Befriend and betray 2 : more stories from the
legendary DEA, FBI and RCMP infiltrator

   ISBN 978-1-9880022-0-0

   1. Caine, Alex. 2. Gangs - North America.
3. Organized crime - North America. 4. Terrorism
- North America. 5.Undercover operations - North
America. 6. Informers - Canada - Biography.
I. Perreault, François, 1950-   . II. Title.
III. Befriend and betray two.

HV8080.U5C342 2016   363.2'32092
C2016-940825-6

Poland Fears Its Judas Files, first published in
The Tablet on August 7, 1999, is reproduced
on pages 141-146 of this book with the permission
of the original publisher, thetablet.co.uk.

08-16

Conseil des Arts   Canada Council
du Canada   for the Arts

We gratefully acknowledge the support of the
Canada Council for the Arts for its publishing
program.

We acknowledge the financial support of the
Government of Canada through the Canada Book
Fund for our publishing activities.

Befriend and Betray
PART II

Collaboration : François Perreault

LES ÉDITIONS DE
L'HOMME

Une société de Québecor Média

A man that flies from fear may find that he has only taken a shortcut to meet it.

J. R. R. Tolkien,
The Children of Hurin

In writing my first book, *Befriend and Betray*, decisions were made to include only a certain number of cases for the sake of length and clarity. In this second collection, I recount my involvement in national security issues, unexplored or barely mentioned previously.

TABLE OF CONTENTS

PROLOGUE

Back in California—I never thought I'd be here again. With all the gangsters I had run into while working the West Coast, it wasn't a safe place for me. The feds had wanted to bring me in under escort, with all the bells and whistles that a man with my background requires. Were they really that worried about my safety? Not a chance—they just didn't want me getting whacked in their backyard.

If this gives you the impression that I was somebody important, don't be fooled. I was just a guy hired to do a job, and a relatively simple job at that. When I was notified through my rabbi (slang for a liason officer: my boss on the police end) that my presence was required for an inquiry into the circumstances of an ongoing case, I said that I'd make my own way there and would call them the night before the hearing for details and instructions. That probably freaked them out—being unable to control my movement. But my rabbi knew me pretty well by then, and hung up without forcing the issue.

So I got there on my own the night before my day in court. I parked my rental car at the edge of Balboa Park, looking over the beach and at the breakers, watching the sun set. Some might think the scene was loaded with meaning, but I've never looked at things that way. You make your choices and deal with the consequences, good or bad. If things go your way, you're a hero, if only for a brief moment. If things go badly, well—you end up at Balboa Park, watching the sunset.

My presence had been requested by an organization whose history can be traced back to the Office of Special Investigations. The OSI was once a powerful and highly influential arm of American law enforcement. Simon Wiesenthal, the famous Nazi hunter, was instrumental in creating the organization, and its original mandate was very different than it is today. Its goal had been to ferret out Nazis living in the U.S., strip them of their citizenship and deport them. As the years passed, though, most of the Nazis ended up either caught or dead, and fewer people were still around to testify against them. Consequently, the OSI tried to extend their mandate to include war criminals from states with more contemporary conflicts—Bosnia, Serbia and a few African nations, for instance—but only a small number of the people involved in these conflicts ever made it to the U.S. What's more, their crimes, as horrific as they were, just didn't evoke the same outrage and sympathy for the victims as those of the Nazis. Their crimes against humanity didn't elicit the same popular and political indignation as the crimes related to the Holocaust, which will forever loom large.

So, the bulk of the OSI's mandate was eventually handed over to the International Court of Justice in The Hague: a huge machine with a vast budget but no real focus. As for what remained of the OSI in the U.S., it splintered into different areas of expertise when it was dismantled. The U.S. Air Force assumed the mainstay of the operation and became the visible face of the organization. The remaining layers of investigation departments sank into the shadows where they could operate freely. It was one of the shadiest and least known of these departments that had summoned me.

The AAA (American Agents Abroad) kept track of all the cases handled or sponsored by the U.S. They had insider knowledge on all the secrets and dirty tricks involved in U.S. foreign relations reaching all the way back to the Vietnam War. Obviously that's no small amount of stuff. The AAA also had the ability to dispatch discreet clean-up crews or to make vehicles, passports or large amounts of cash appear in an instant—whatever agents might need in a hurry. They're also equipped to handle other special "problems" that come along. I was becoming one of these problems—which was not an especially comfortable place to be. Over the years, I had accumulated my own fair share of secrets. I'd even became one myself. If that was problematic for the organizations that worked with me, it was just as problematic in my own life. My secret life made me close myself off from others too often—especially from my wives. And of course, I was sure to blame every one of them for not understanding my situation. But let's face it: how could they have understood when we never really talked?

My career had been underway for almost twenty years by the time I took the case that brought me to the hearing in California. My credibility and professionalism had never been called into question—not to my face at least. I had walked pretty much unharmed out of situations of great danger—and some others involved hadn't been as lucky as me. I knew the agency thought I was good. The truth is, I was mostly lucky. Either way, I was still alive and had a reputation for success that I believed to be unshakeable. I considered myself one of the best infiltrators in the business. There wasn't a criminal group I couldn't get into. I'd almost developed a prima donna attitude based on my victories.

Over time, though, the scenery had gradually changed, and I had failed to change with it. The line between crime and politics had started to blur. In the old days, crooks were crooks, and politics didn't come into play unless they were required to profit the criminal activity. Now the balance had shifted, and crime had become a means to advance and finance politic goals. President Nixon famously crossed that line, using thug tactics to firm up his hold on power. Closer to home, there never seems to be a shortage of scandal involving collusion between organized crime and all levels of governments.

The shift has led to great confusion in the formerly separate worlds of law enforcement and politics. The criminal mind is beyond the traditional purview of political analysts, and on the other side of the coin, criminals don't always grasp the subtleties of political manoeuvring. And politics and crime make an especially dirty mix. When mistakes occur, people can die. Look at my own experience: I had blundered once, and two people were dead. I knew I had to answer for that, and if I thought my experience and past accomplishments would carry me through, I was wrong. I was just another piece on the board: expendable for the interests of those in charge. And for someone who's seen a lot, it's important to remember the cliché that dead men make poor witnesses.

Now back to the matter at hand on the glorious West Coast. As far as I was concerned, I was extending this group a courtesy by appearing for the inquiry. I didn't owe them anything; I answered only to my rabbi and CSIS, the Canadian Security Intelligence Service. The U.S. was merely a client I'd been assigned to. I had to wonder, though, what power they held over my superiors to make them offer my services. The waters seemed extremely murky. Well, for better or worse, I had made it out there. Nothing to do but adopt a wait-and-see attitude.

I checked into the hotel, entered my room. I made a telephone call and received my instructions. The following morning, I was to go to the fifth floor of the courthouse, where I would be given a room number; I was to wait there until I was called. At nine o'clock the next morning, I sat in the courthouse, trying to look composed, on a cold wooden bench that reminded me of a church pew. I felt a mixture of curiosity and nervousness. Being called into the inner sanctum of what remained of the OSI was like being called to the principal's office—except that the principal was capable of dispensing capital punishment should it be deemed appropriate. Finally the door opened, and a woman emerged. "They" would see me now.

I almost expected to enter a darkened room with shadowy figures in a semi-circle around a folding chair placed under a glaring light bulb. I'd probably seen too many movies. Instead, I found myself in a tastefully decorated room with a large conference table in the center. There were three people at the table: two men and a woman. Another man was setting up a recording machine in the corner. They looked at me fairly pleasantly, but their eyes were penetrating and cold. I skipped the normal pleasantries, took a seat and waited. My rabbi had only given me one simple piece of advice: "Do not take these folks lightly. They could finish your ass with the stroke of the pen."

After a short, tense silence, the woman spoke. Their role, she told me, was not to judge, but to assess the situation and recommend whether future action was needed. "We want to hear your version of events," added one of the men.

My version? This was a twist. Who ever said there was more than one version?

I told them I would need to see written permission from the various agencies involved before I could discuss the particulars of the case. I probably sounded slightly confrontational. Maybe I was trying to look good, or maybe I was just stalling for time—I'm not really sure. Silence followed, making me feel defensive.

After looking at me hard, the man took a document from the file. They had secured the authorization.

The score so far: Panel: 1, guy from Quebec: 0.

I started recounting the events of the case, then paused. I found it hard to get to the heart of it, of what I had experienced. Everything I said sounded flimsy and trite. It was like trying to explain something by text message.

One of my interlocutors suggested that I start from the beginning, and they would interject questions as I went.

I started over, warming up to the crucial parts. As I talked and talked, I realized it would be a very long day. In a slow and, I hoped, dispassionate voice I began to tell the story of the twists and turns that had had such an impact on my life, and that had ended the lives of two friends. It was heavy material. I probably sounded cold and matter-of-fact, like I could handle anything. Trying to stay calm was the only strategy I had, my only way to keep from getting swept away. It was merely a false front. In truth, I was like a duck—floating serenely while paddling like hell under the surface of the water.

Eventually, the woman cut in. "It's getting late in the day," she said. "I propose we get our notes together and reconvene in the morning. We'll meet tomorrow at nine o'clock."

Clearly we all felt drained. The group started gathering their papers and I headed back to my room at the Hilton to unwind for the night. I had no energy left to explore the city. I simply shut out the memories and tried to settle into sleep.

My mind kept drifting to my last conversation with the feds in Vancouver, when Bonnie's unit—who I knew first as "Aunt Bonnie," as you'll find out later—had offered me a job as a consultant—an agent in charge (AIC), in fact. It was another job working alone: No matter how used to it you are, it still feels strange at times. It seemed like so long ago now. But for Bonnie, it was literally a lifetime away.

I arrived the next day, punctual as usual. I had a quick smoke outside, and went into the meeting room. We hadn't got very far in our conversation when an assistant walked in and whispered something to the woman from the previous day. The latter politely excused herself for the interruption, and the two of them went out into the hall. I was excused for a break; we would reconvene in thirty minutes.

I went outside to have another smoke, and sat on the stairs thinking about how things were going. I didn't feel that I was handling the situation correctly. Once you start talking, it's hard to stop. Interrogation training methods dictate that you get the subject talking; you should let him craft his story without interruption. The more he talks, the more you have to work with. What interrogators hate the most is when someone won't give an inch. *Nada.* There's nothing to work with, nothing to contradict.

I went back inside and joined the two male agents. Barely two minutes later, the woman returned with some surprising news: The inquiry was being postponed. No more stories and no more questions. She thanked me for coming, and kindly reminded me to keep all my receipts for reimbursement. I was free to go, with their thanks. I had things to say but I wouldn't get the chance to say them, at least for now. No date was set, but she said they would let me know.

The funny thing is, I felt a little cheated. But that was just a matter of personal satisfaction. What stuck out like a sore thumb was the obvious question: Who had had me pulled out of the questioning? Whoever it was, they had a lot of clout, and little concern for the time and effort of the group I'd met with. It was just another question mark in a career that had been full of them.

Bear with me: All will be explained. But before clarifying these mysteries, take a step back in time with me, to get a glimpse of where I came from and how I ended up leading the life I led.

CHAPTER ONE

Somewhere, Somehow

In my hometown, people always seemed to think I was different—a "ne'er-do-well," in fact. I guess in some ways that was true, but there was more to me than that. Whatever I was, I wasn't made from the standard mold. Most of my friends never even left the neighborhood. They met a local girl, got married too young and ended up working at the mill. They usually had too many kids, drank too much, smoked like chimneys and left this mortal coil without leaving much of a mark.

Such were the 1950s in a blue-collar Quebec town like Hull, just across the river from Ottawa. Two mills formed the lifeblood of Hull: E.B. Eddy (known for manufacturing matches), and the Canadian International Paper (CIP) mill, which was right next door. Men of the neighborhood were hardworking and hard-playing: They belonged to the Moose Lodge or the Knights of Columbus, and joined bowling, soft-ball, hockey and curling leagues. Outward affection was at a premium, generally considered a sign of weakness. Women had their roles laid out for them: child rearing and house-keeping, with sewing circles and church events for social en-gagement. Priorities were vastly different then; above all, achieving a sense of stability was the goal. Coming off years of war and deprivation, a boring life was to be cherished. Safe and unchanging was good enough. Surprise and adventure had little appeal for a generation that had been through so much.

We kids who were brought up in the post-war era couldn't really grasp what our parents had gone through. Inevitably, your dad, and your mom, for that matter, would use the fact of their service to their country to drive a point—any point—home. But no matter what they said, it just didn't register with us. Kids live in the present, and we had our own battles to deal with. It must have hurt them to know that we were bored by tales of the biggest event of their lives. But the fault was partly theirs. Lectures always began with, "Before the war..." or "During the war..." We were numb to it, and it only distanced us from the event. Bridging that gap of experience is probably the goal of every parent, and ours weren't the first to confront it.

Unless there were inescapable chores at hand, we spent all the time we could outside of our homes, fighting our own wars with our enemies. A typical Saturday morning looked like this: a bowl of oatmeal, toast, a glass of milk, then out the door. Most of the boys in the area would congregate at the local *terrain de jeu*, playgrounds maintained by the city. Every neighborhood had one. The focal point of the *terrain de jeu* was the baseball field, which we used constantly. Beside the field was a cabin equipped with a small counter to buy coveted cokes, chocolate bars and packaged cakes. During the cold months, the field became a skating rink. That's when the cabin went from being a luxury to a necessity. With a wood stove in the corner, it was a cozy shelter where we could put on our skates.

At lunchtime, everybody headed home. Then, after running our errands, we'd spend our afternoons hanging around at "Marcil pool hall." We were keen on dancing—well, we were keen on girls, and they congregated at dances. Each parish held a school dance in their gym. It was called a "school dance" not because particular schools were the hosts, it just referred to the location. One of our favorite dances was held at Sacred Hearts High. The appeal was offset by a number of problems, however. We lived two turfs away from the dance, which meant we had to pass two street gangs on our way there. The first was the Kent Street Gangsters, who used a restaurant called Chez Michael as their base. Dealing with the Kent Street Gangsters put me in an awkward position. I knew and got along with most of the members; still, I would fight them if it came down to it. We simply belonged to a different parish, and the lines had been drawn before we came along. It's ironic, of course, that for us the concept of a parish (a word used by the Catholic Church meaning an area of influence with a church and two priests) was primarily a way to distinguish gang affiliation.

If you got through the Kent boys, you'd be in the Dare Devils' stronghold: This was a group that was a little older and better organized. They even had cars and motorcycles and wore a one-piece patch. (Interesting fact: The Dare Devils later became the Prophets of Hell, which was later taken over by the Popeyes, which then moved to Montreal to eventually become a chapter of the Hells Angels.)

The important thing about all this is really the effect it had on me. That whole environment, with its separate tribes, its protocols and boundaries, formed the base of experience that made me good at my job. It taught me about levels of power and affiliation. After all, we were all greasers with one common enemy from across the bridge into Ontario: the *Anglos*. We had to protect our turf against the gangs from the other bank, which meant we had to fight together.

At the time, I hadn't the slightest inkling of what my future would hold. But when my future employers put me on biker cases, the knowledge I'd gained helped me fit in with those characters perfectly. So much that I often risked getting lost in my role, and possibly crossing the line. The thugs and roughnecks were like me in so many ways. The stakes were bigger, but it was still the same game.

When you look back on things, you tend to see the significance of events on the home front. No one at the time seemed to pay any attention to the seeds that were being planted in young psyches in towns and cities all over the country.

When Canadians were called to fight abroad, the men enlisted, and with a tin hat and a gun, off they went. These same men would never have ventured out of their hometowns under normal circumstances. After spending years overseas, fighting for their very lives, their former values were long gone. They came of age in a time of upheaval. For their part, the women were called on to work in factories and so on, an exciting change from the life of drudgery they had known before. Thus the seeds of change were sowed in the fertile ground of dissatisfaction. Our parents were tired and needed to get back to what they remembered life to be. Their offspring left home in droves for colleges and universities all over the country. They became the protesters and hippies, rebelling against just about everything. So was I such an oddity or more in tune with my generation than I thought?

There's another factor I should mention that helped shape the man and agent I would become. While my father was Québécois to his very core, my mother was part Irish and part Aboriginal. Native persons were not looked on with favor, or even sympathy, at the time. "They're all alcoholics, savages, godless," was a common refrain. These harsh prejudices left a lasting mark on my childhood.

Throughout my life, it seemed as though I was fated to be different from both my parents and my peers, from the older generation that cared only for post-war stability, and from my own social group that didn't seem overly interested in seeing the world beyond our neighborhood streets. But the world was changing outside of our town, and maybe my story makes sense in terms of the spirit of the times. No one would ever mistake me for a hippie, but I was definitely rebellious in my fashion. Maybe, in a strange way, my own path paralleled that of the hippie generation. They grew their hair, protested and left their home towns for university campuses. My own rejection of the world I had known was wildly different, but the shift was probably just as extreme.

We are what our life experience makes us. Within the parameters of my rebellion I did more than just go around getting high and protesting. I was too ambitious, too much of a schemer. I had to do it the hard way. Today, when I think back on the choices I made, I see big mistakes and small victories.

All in all, the past can't be changed, and the future remains paved with good intentions. The "now" is all we have, and hopefully it's enough to carry us forward. Sometimes we move so fast that we don't even take notice of the casualties we leave behind. Those people you brushed away while thinking only of yourself—those who trusted you, be they wives, a girlfriends, or worse, your own kids. Later in life, you come back hat in hand, looking for a rapprochement, hoping for their understanding despite their anger and pain.

CHAPTER TWO

The Burial

A few days after Shannon's murder, she was laid to rest, with no known relatives to claim her. It was left to the agency to take care of the arrangements. I resolved to go to the graveyard by myself. With the service and all its obligations, I hadn't had a private moment to say goodbye.

A continuous stream of folks from the office and neighborhood showed up to the reception at her house. One by one, they paid their respects and left, until finally it was over. I had made arrangements for the leftover food to be sent to a soup kitchen. Shannon's Aunt Bonnie loaded the last of it in her car and drove off. Exhausted, I locked the door behind her and climbed the stairs to the bedroom.

Heavy drapes blocked the light of day. The bedside lamps provided the room with a sterile light, feebly illuminating the carefully washed baseboards and dim corners. Two pillows, one large, and another small and thin, sat undisturbed on Shannon's favorite comforter; the small, thin one was mine. Though all of it was familiar, I felt like a stranger, as though I had entered someone's private space, uninvited.

The air was dry and warm, with the light scent of burning that you get in closed rooms on scorching summer days. A lack of life and feeling of abandonment pervaded the space. I opened the drapes and the window, welcoming the flood of fresh air.

I couldn't feel her anymore. This was no longer Shannon's place, I realized—no longer our place. I left the room, closing the door behind me, and walked downstairs. Turning the ringer off on the phone, I lay down on the couch and awaited a sleep brought on by exhaustion and despair. Tomorrow I would say goodbye to Shannon, call J.P., my rabbi, and simply, almost magically, become someone else for a few months. More than welcome, it was irresistible: It would give me a chance to heal.

J.P. expressed true sympathy on the phone the next day when I called him. I knew he meant every word. I was glad for that. I told him I wanted a short job, something that would immerse me in work and help me forget for a while. He wondered aloud if maybe I should hold off and deal with grief before making any decisions.

"That's not what I want to do," I told him firmly. "I can't stay here. I need to get away."

"I'm not sure that's the best idea right now," he pressed on. Clearly he felt strongly that I shouldn't return to action. He could have ordered me to step back for a time, to wait until he felt I was ready for an assignment, but he didn't. Maybe that was his mistake. There were certainly enough mistakes to go around. J.P. knew that I was serious. He promised to look into it and see what was available and to get back to me.

"Look," he added, giving it one last shot. "I still think you should just lay low for a while, work through your grief— maybe get some help, find someone to talk to."

But that just wasn't my way. I would do what I always did in these situations: I would run away. It was a habit that was tied to my job. When things start going bad on a case, you pull out, jettison your identity and cease to exist. In that sense I had definitely become my work. I was always running, never stopping long enough to take on responsibility, not caring about whatever collateral damage I might cause—kids left without a father, mothers without a son. It was a ruthless game, with its winners and losers. Winners went home, and losers went missing. It was the only way I knew. I was ready to take off again, to get outside of myself and leave it all be-hind.

But first I had to go back to the graveyard one last time.

The road to the graveyard took a long incline, ending at a gate that resembled a dark, gaping mouth edged with stony teeth. Shannon's plot was deep inside the grounds, where the small sandy pathways ended. The section hadn't been land-scaped, so I stumbled along narrow footpaths between green mounds, graves long abandoned and forgotten. This part of the cemetery was ancient. Certainly no ancestors were left to pay to maintain the headstones, which were spread out in no visible order, tilting in every direction, green with moss. On some graves the large heavy stones seemed to be crushing the people underneath—killing them all over again.

Sunlight poured down as I walked into a section with newer graves, well-groomed and standing proud. I approached Shannon's tombstone and sat on a small bench. Her grave was clean and had been decorated with flowers; signs of love. How long would it be, I wondered, before her marker decayed and crumbled, became moss-covered like the rest? Despite the promises I had made to myself, I knew that I would never come back to this place.

Before I left, I willed her to give me a sign that she was here with me. But nothing happened. I was seized with a desperate need to get close to her one last time, to feel her essence, to give both of us peace. But I was also swept away by a very different need: for closure and revenge. The feeling burned inside me, overwhelmed me. I would find her killer, I promised, whoever he was. I would make him pay for what he had done.

I'm not a religious man by any stretch of the imagination. I'd seen too much of man's depravity to believe in that kind of thing. But at times like this, one tends to revert back to the teachings of one's youth. In this case, it was a Bible verse that came to mind: "I saw a pale horse and on him rode death and hell followed with him" (Rev. 6:8)

They say revenge can destroy you. They also say it won't bring back the dead. But it was all I had left; it would have to be enough. It meant I had a mission, a reason to keep going and a new sense of purpose.

As I walked away it occurred to me that perhaps Shannon had given me a sign after all—filling me with rage that was like a weapon I could use to avenge her death. It continued to well up inside me and wouldn't abate. The only remedy was to find who was responsible and destroy them. Through two years infiltrating biker gangs, I had survived by my ability to stay focused, to provoke fear in those around me, and to keep my inner core carefully hidden. All of that would serve me well in what lay ahead.

It took two days for J.P. to get back to me. While I was waiting, I prepared for my departure. I cleaned out the fridge—some things in there were beyond recognition. I opened an old takeout container; it looked like chicken, but I couldn't be sure. I made a reservation at the kennel for my cat, T.C., and packed my bag.

I also called Aunt Bonnie and asked her to come over. Aunt Bonnie was a motherly figure in Shannon's life, someone who would check in, water our plants, have a cup of tea—that sort of thing. In time her closeness with Shannon expanded to include me, and I was happy about that.

We worked things out over a drink. She would empty Shannon's apartment and put everything in storage. I would go through the contents when I returned. Meanwhile, she would pick up my mail, pay the rent, and do all the other necessary chores.

I told her how I felt, that I needed to get closure and I had to do it my way. She was upset about my plans and concerned about my safety, that was clear, but she didn't object. Maybe she knew that nothing would change my mind. And maybe, deep inside, she felt the same need as me—she wanted Shannon avenged.

That evening I sat alone for hours watching the fire, compartmentalizing my thoughts and feelings. That was something I was good at. It meant pushing the painful stuff down until it was shelved in a place that was almost too hard to access. It was a temporary solution, but it was the only way I could cope.

From then on, time would be measured in *before Shannon* and *after Shannon*. I knew that none of this was healthy for me, but I couldn't help myself. Maybe over time that would change, but it wouldn't be any time soon.

I wished I could go back to a normal life where spy stories were only on TV series and in movies.

It all stemmed from one decision. You can't always know the impact your choices will make on the people around you.

CHAPTER THREE

The Chinese Connection

It was a few days later in Vancouver. The morning was colder than I'd expected. I parked my car on the East block parkades and walked toward Hastings, hunching my shoulders against the wind. I was only a couple of blocks from the noble stone building that houses Vancouver's City Hall, but I might as well have entered another world. Princess Street, which runs through the lower east side of the city, was lined on both sides with four- to five-story buildings, with stores and other businesses at street level. Laundry hung from lines strung between fire escapes. Half the shops were grocery stores, mostly displaying Chinese fruits and vegetables that were unrecognizable to me. As I threaded my way through busy sidewalks, I was met with no smiles, no nods, no movements to stand aside.

I stepped into the street to avoid a pack of tough-looking teenagers. One of them grabbed my arm and yanked me back onto the sidewalk, an instant before a speeding cab would have run me down.

"Watch it, man!" the kid said. "You want to get yourself killed?"

"Thanks," I muttered a bit sheepishly. The kid and his friends were already on their way, rejoining the city's blanket of noise.

I reached my destination and stood looking up at an old brick and wood building. The place was so familiar, and I wondered why I had come back here, like some psychotic homing pigeon. It certainly wasn't a safe place to be—and it seemed a pointless place to be as well. I leaned against the building to watch the drug addicts and homeless scurrying around in the small park across the street. What a hard life: sleeping anywhere you can, eating thanks to the generosity of others, collecting spare change handed over out of pity.

The nondescript building before me offered no indication that it was in fact one of the most prestigious martial arts studio in the city. There had never been a sign. But the place was legendary. During my years of intense training, I constantly heard stories of Wong-Ha's School of Choy-Li-Kung-Fu. I didn't know much about it at the time; just that admittance was by invitation only and membership was almost exclusively Chinese. Its students never seemed to participate in local tournaments, which helped give the place an almost mythical reputation.

I thought of Wong-Ha, the school's namesake. I remembered him well. I'd met him the first time I visited the school. Wooden *Wing-Chun* dummies lined the hall, along with ancient spears and lances. In the corner was a shrine, with candles and incense burning before a portrait of an elderly man.

Not knowing what to do, I stood around aimlessly, watching people work out. An elderly man quietly walked up next to me. He must have been eighty. He wore an ornate Chinese coat fastened with a wide red sash, baggy black pants and black canvas shoes. His thinning grey hair was brushed back, accentuating his goatee. His eyes, sharp and penetrating behind plain, thick, round glasses, seemed to measure and assess everything they saw. He carried an old umbrella held shut with black electrician tape.

After looking me up and down, he poked me in the chest and said, "You Caine?" I bowed in reply. Those would be the only English words I heard from him for a full year.

I was nothing if not persistent. I went to the school almost every day. Mostly I was taught by senior students. I should probably point out that it wasn't like some 80s Hollywood movie, with the determined white guy earning the begrudging respect of the locals. They taught me because they were told to do so—it was as simple as that. I didn't understand their language, so they kept me at arm's length.

Wong-Ha would walk among the group, stopping to watch for a few moments before moving on. Sometimes he would give recommendations to the instructor. Then one day, he finally spoke to me again in English. I'd waited all that time, completed all that training, and wondered what words would eventually pass between us. Those words ended up being fairly to-the-point.

"You go now!" he said. He shooed me away with his hand, like one would gesture to a child. It was delivered with no malice—it sounded almost like an afterthought. There was certainly no room for discussion or debate. Then he simply turned his back and walked away.

There had been no welcome at my arrival and no farewell at my departure, just a bare acknowledgment of my existence each time. My training was done and my time there had simply come to an end. I left, as I was expected to do, and I'd never returned since.

That had been years ago. Now, standing on the same sidewalk, I wasn't even sure that the school was still operating. I felt a sense of loss—until I saw a Chinese man enter, carrying a tote gym bag. Clearly Wong-Ha's school was alive and well.

I crossed the street and sat on a bench. Why had I come back? What was I expecting to find? I had no idea, but I was reluctant to walk away. My visit to the club left me feeling sad, unsettled. Mostly because it brought back memories of the "Hobo" Mah case and chasing after Asian triads, a hunt that had taken me to Taiwan, Hong Kong and mainland China in the late 1970s.

When you're inside a case you don't really notice how things spin around you.

The "Hobo" Mah case has been pivotal in my life and my career. It was my first operation, the job that ushered me into the shadowy world of infiltration. It was the beginning of a life of danger and intrigue that I never would've imagined. And it wasn't an easy start—more like diving in the deep end than wading into the water gradually. As it unfolded I never knew where I would end up—or if I would even make it to the next job.

In most ways, Hobo and I couldn't have been more different. We were about the same height, but it ended there: He was built like a fire hydrant, and had about seventy pounds on me. I met him in my days of martial arts tournaments. After a couple of months we started meeting for coffee or drinks. He became a friend of sorts. The more time I spent with him, the more he told me about his business. The secrets started piling up. I started to get the feeling I was being groomed for something. Otherwise there was no way he would have told me so much—unless it was all talk, just a lot of bluster and showmanship. What I didn't know was that before we had become pals, he had been checking me out. He must have liked what he heard, and after a while he had felt he could trust me. I had no idea how it would all pan out.

The day he finally made his move, we met at Bino's, a Denny's-type restaurant on the edge of Chinatown. Right off the bat, he told me he was a member of the Sun Yee On triad. It failed to impress me; I knew nothing of triads, secret Asian criminal organizations, at the time. My blank expression didn't faze him, and he proceeded to tell me he wanted me to be part of his business expansion into eastern Canada and the West Coast reaching down to L.A. Since I was French-speaking, my turf would be Quebec and Ontario. He didn't mention whom he had picked to work the South.

I made a point of showing clearly that I had no interest in getting involved in death-dealing, which was presumably part of the job. Hobo was obviously displeased. He offered me a day to think about it. "You're either with me or you're against me," he warned me. "There's no gray area."

As quickly as that, I had entered a kind of trap. My life was starting to look a lot more complicated for the foreseeable future.

The safest thing for me to do, as someone who never wanted to be involved but had found himself caught in a dangerous situation, was to call the cops—Sergeant Kilgore, from the police drug unit. Of course, they were more than interested in my story. They plied me for details, then met me again for further information. Before I knew it I had agreed to find out more about Hobo and his activities. By that time I was thoroughly involved. When the cops asked me to actively help them take Hobo down, I accepted. In for a penny, in for a pound.

I phoned Hobo and told him I was in, but I wanted more territory down East. I knew it was promising to be a good beginning for a sting—but I didn't realize quite how good. If I followed it through, we could get a partner to come in and pose as my accomplice. The partner would help push the deals forward. This would create an ideal scenario in court: not one but two witnesses to testify on behalf of the Crown. Of course, all that was far beyond the scope of my knowledge at the time. Chalk it up to beginner's luck.

As exciting as it seemed, I felt I was getting in over my head. A dire end for me seemed to hover over the proceedings. Sooner or later, Hobo would ask me to do something that was beyond my scope: the classic "bargain you can't refuse." I would have to say no, and I sensed that Hobo didn't like to hear "no." Though he was overweight with a jovial round face, he was fast and mean in a fight and had a surprising ability to move in on a guy in seconds. A fight between him and me would be close, and only one of us would walk away.

To be honest, I didn't even know exactly why I kept pushing further into his dark world. I wasn't a cop—I was something else. Perhaps something lurked deep inside me, some unrecognized desire. Maybe on some level I felt tempted by that world. Not for the drugs, certainly. Just for the lifestyle. But I do know that if it happened again, I would pack up and drop the whole thing. I had a lot to learn about the brutal realities of crime.

Kilgore phoned me a week later. He and his team wanted to meet that same day in a nearby hotel. They grilled me extensively, going over every detail I gave them, and making me dig deeper. It was effective; I would suddenly think of things I hadn't even thought I'd noticed because they seemed so unimportant. Details about Hobo's personal life, events and names he had mentioned.

We also discussed my fees. I told them the truth: I was working with my father-in-law, doing renovations. It was agreed that they would pick up all my lost wages and pay my expenses. That was it. I told them I was earning twenty dollars an hour—in truth, it was only fifteen (that's in 1978 dollars). I figured the 25% bonus could be considered hazard pay. What I didn't realize was that the trifling amount was nowhere near enough to compensate me for a life that would be turned upside-down forever. That twenty dollars an hour bought a one-way ticket—there would be no way back.

———————

Hobo wasted no time in getting me started with some serious crime. I would go to Hong Kong to purchase a sample of heroin. A contact there would front the cash for me. The suppliers in Hong Kong were Rocky Chui, a high-ranking member of Sun Yee On, and Davey Mah, a close friend of Hobo's who had lived in Canada for ten years before being deported for drug charges. Davey and Hobo were the middlemen, one would get the money, the other the drugs. The risk to them was zero.

Was this entrapment? If it hadn't been for me, the deal wouldn't have gone down. The problem bothered me, and I mentioned it to my handler. His answer was typical. "If they didn't make the deal with you, they would have found someone else. But they didn't, because they had us."

You might think entrapment is a simple matter, but I've never found it cut-and-dried. But, here's an example: A certain barfly—let's call him Johnny—frequents a certain shady bar. Over the years, Johnny has met a lot of unsavory characters and got to know some of the local drug suppliers. Enter our operative. He hangs around the bar, trying to approach a particular dealer who spends time there. But he can't make contact with no one vouching for him. That's when our affable friend Johnny gets roped in. The operative uses him to get an introduction, to gain a foothold socially. In my experience, guys like Johnny tend to be pretty harmless and overly trusting. They also talk too much for their own good. If they trust the wrong person—like our operative—they may have to pay dearly for their mistake.

This kind of concern was just an inkling at the beginning of my career.

Anyway, things were moving forward at an alarming pace and I didn't have a lot of time to contemplate the subtleties of police ethics as I tried to keep my head above water. Hong Kong was a long way from Hull, Quebec. I hoped it would be worth the ride.

Another undercover agent named Pineault was brought in. He would be acting as my brother. It was also decided that our team would have two handlers and a dozen of guys to tail and cover us. What a number! It was practically a junket. I pictured the throng making its way through the endless back alleys of Hong Kong. How could we not attract attention?

But it wasn't my job to point that out. The project had become a joint operation between the RCMP and the Royal Hong Kong constabulary (this was before the island was given back to mainland China). The ball was rolling and picking up speed.

After we got to Hong Kong, adjacent hotel rooms were booked for Pineault and me. We spent the day getting organized. The plan was to buy half a pound of heroin as a sample, and then to go back for more. The details didn't seem too bad, really, for a Mountie plan. The main flaw was one that undermines many of the best-laid plans: It was overly rigid, leaving no room for error.

On our second day in Hong Kong, I made my call to Davey. He spoke to me as if we were old friends; I almost sensed that he was trying to impress someone in the room with him. I responded in kind.

Before we made the deal, he wanted us to join him for a car ride. I could see no way to decline the offer. We met him downstairs in our hotel. Things quickly took a different turn when we embarked on a terrifyingly fast ride that twisted and turned through the narrow streets of Hong Kong. There was no way our backup could have kept up; we were on our own.

The drive ended in the district of Kowloon, in an elevated area away from the city. We pulled into a sandy parking area. No houses, nothing: a perfect spot to get whacked. Trying to sound confident, I told my partner to be ready. But I was deeply scared. Who wouldn't be? Pineault, for his part, was visibly petrified. Speaking in French as I had done, he whispered that we should make a break for it and run.

"And go where?" I demanded. I told him to calm down. We exited the car and set off on a narrow footpath. Pineault followed Rocky, behind Pineault was Davey, and I brought up the rear.

Then, seemingly out of nowhere, two men joined our troop. My heart sank; it was looking very bad. We had no guns, and I started figuring our odds if it came down to hand-to-hand combat. We arrived at a clearing, where four men stood, leaning on shovels. In front of them were two large holes dug in the ground.

By now my partner was having difficulty putting one foot in front of the other. I couldn't blame him. As we neared the men, I entered a state of intense focus, driven by the horrible possibility that lay before us. Amazingly, Rocky didn't even slow down; he walked right past the workers without a word. Following his lead, we all continued on. The threatening scene was a message

We stopped at the top of the hill and sat down to work out numbers, delivery details and time between shipments. We argued for a better price—that's what real criminals would do. Both sides gave concessions, and finally we reached an agreement.

On the way back, there was no sign of anyone; even the holes had been filled. It had sent a pretty powerful message. I wonder if Rocky ever found out how close he came to ending the whole project. As we walked past, I thought about how foolish we had been, and how lucky. The smart move would have been to refuse to walk down that pathway, but we had called his bluff and survived.

Rocky drove us back to the hotel. There we called our handler, who met us in our room. We sat down and wrote down every detail, down to what they were wearing, in the notebooks the handler gave us. This might seem like the most boring part of the job. But come court time, that notebook was all you had to jar your memory. And in cases such as this one there would be several different trials, since the defendants would probably opt to be tried separately to avoid being painted with the same brush.

The stage had been set for the delivery. Davey must have thought it unsafe to give us a delivery time via our hotel; instead we would be informed by the end of the week. In the meantime, he would be coming to pick up the payment for the sample.

You may have noticed the strategy previously: The drugs and the money were never to be found in the same place. With Rocky only speaking Mandarin and the money and drugs being kept separate, gathering enough evidence to prosecute him would be a challenge. Davey, on the other hand, was dead in the water.

Two days later there was a knock on the door, so soft that I barely heard it. A pretty Chinese girl stood there with a stuffed manila envelope, looking at the ground. I accepted the package, and she took off without a word. I felt a surge of pity for her: so young and scared, caught up in something much bigger than her. I thought of the cameras we'd had installed in the hallways, right up to my door. She would probably get caught in the sweep that was to come. I vowed to go easy on her when I took the stand. It wouldn't be a stretch: I hadn't seen her face or heard her voice. It all just made me that much more determined to catch the real criminals—and especially to bust Rocky.

Back in Canada, another problem was emerging. Hobo would certainly want to see the drug shipments and control their movement. If he didn't get the goods that he had been promised, he could become a serious problem, even a dangerous one. There was no way we could allow that to happen. We already had him on conspiracy to import for the purpose of trafficking—a serious charge to be sure, one we didn't want to let slip. It was getting sticky, but the cops found a simple solution. Hobo was already on probation—they simply pulled his papers for review. Hobo would end up in the slammer and our trip to Hong Kong could move forward with one less complication.

Of course, even with Hobo behind bars, we had to keep him from getting suspicious. If he suspected anything, he could send word to Hong Kong and I could be lured into a trap. I was one phone call away from another life-threatening situation.

Hobo was being detained at the Okalla prison in Burnaby, a city next to Vancouver. Dealing with him directly fell on my shoulders, so I went to visit him. In the visiting room, there was a glass wall between prisoners and visitors. I waited for a little while and Hobo appeared. The prison couldn't have been too bad: He seemed relaxed. He sauntered down the row of chairs with his usual big smile, sat down and picked up the phone. I did the same.

Hobo said he had heard from his father that the trip had been successful. He assumed I was there to get instructions for his end of the deal. We exchanged jokes and he opened his left hand. On the palm was written a name, Al Lim, and a phone number. Hobo wanted me to get Al to move the product. He had it all figured out and was confident that he would be a free man before long. However, I knew better.

As I was leaving, he asked me for money for the jail canteen. I dropped five hundred dollars into his jail account on my way out. Maybe I did it out of guilt. I knew what heroin did to people, of course, and I knew I was on the right side of the game. But that didn't mean I always felt good about it. Befriend and betray—the wrong thing for the right reasons. No matter how long you've been in the business, it can be hard to remember that you're on the good side.

I called the number and we set up a meeting with Al Lim, who was one of Hobo's close friends. I was ready with a list of explanations as to why I had not yet come up with any drugs or money for Hobo. At the time, we were just fishing to see who else we could get from Hobo's social circle. During the call, Al told me he would be bringing someone along to our meeting at Bino's. I wasn't impressed: That's a faux pas for first meeting. I told him I needed a name or the guy could stay home. Al didn't argue, told me his friend was Phillip Yu. I would give the name to my guys, of course—but there was no time before the meeting to find out anything.

Having no idea how things would go, we opted for close-range cover: two guys inside the restaurant and a sniper in the parking lot across the street. It felt precarious. I had no background with these guys.

As usual, things turned out differently than planned. Al Lim showed up alone. That was fine with us, since it gave us more time to run down the new man before meeting him. The name of Phillip Yu didn't ring any bells. A computer search, though, gave us an expansive picture of his activities. Yu was triad and a soldier in Tommy Fung's crew. He was suspected of being involved in homicide, extortion, drugs, guns—the whole nine yards. He had no convictions. We were beside ourselves at this stroke of luck. This guy was the real deal.

It was hard not to be skeptical of Al Lim, however, when he showed up. Picture your conventional nerd and you'll pretty much get Al Lim. He was five foot ten, maybe 150 pounds, wore black-rimmed eyeglasses and had short hair parted on the side. He sported black pants, a white open-collar shirt and a light blue vinyl windbreaker. All he needed to top off the look was a pocket protector and an umbrella.

Once we were settled, I told my partner Pineault, in French, not to denigrate Hobo or say anything bad about him. These guys obviously had a plan we needed to hear.

Al Lim started talking. In no time I could see there was a sharp mind behind those glasses—he wasn't what he seemed. In short, he told us that his boss (Tommy, I assumed) had decided that we were to stay away from Hobo: He was a heat score, and they had to write him off for now. We were not to worry about taking care of him. They would be responsible for that. So Hobo's friends turned out to be more self-serving than we thought. I didn't believe what he told me for a second, but I kept my mouth shut.

So we were looking at a new deal with new players. I wondered if Rocky and Davey Mah in Hong Kong would still be our suppliers. We agreed to meet with Al Lim again in two days, and we insisted that we needed to meet Phillip Yu. It was decided that the Night & Day restaurant would be the spot. It was a family diner-type of place, but definitely rough around the edges, situated on the edge of Chinatown and a well-known hangout for outlaws.

One thing was clear right off the bat at the next meeting: Yu was definitely a gangster. Hair slicked back, leather coat—he had the complete look. Al wasn't interested in the deal with Hobo. He and his friend wanted to strike a totally new deal using a different supplier. We were more than ready to accept that. Yu said he was going to Hong Kong the following day to make the arrangements, and we were to meet him over there a week later. Perfect. More encounters meant a longer suspect list. It was all falling into our laps at this point. I couldn't resist asking again about Hobo. Again they said that they would take care of him in time, and we shouldn't worry about it. It irked me a little; these guys were obviously stiffing their friend in order to deal with us directly. But it wasn't my concern; I had a hidden agenda of my own.

Still, we had to play it safe. I asked for some kind of assurance that they were on the level that we could trust them to come through. Phil nodded to Al, who took a small bag from his pocket and passed it to my partner under the table. Sure enough, it was an ounce of heroin. The quality was tested later—the drugs were pure. Only serious dealers could provide such a high-quality sample. We had to do these guys.

At the end of the project, we had over twenty triad dealers and fourteen million dollars' worth of high-grade heroin. It was the biggest takedown Canadian law enforcement had ever done.

Before the busts, I ended up doing several more trips to Hong Kong, for this case and others as well. Word spread quickly that I was a solid guy to deal with. The success of the Hobo Mah case would lead me to visit places and deal with people I'd never dreamed I'd encounter.

But in the immediate aftermath of the job, I wasn't savoring my victory; instead, I came swiftly crashing down from the high I'd been on. I soon became bored. I lost any interest in doing home renovation work. I tried to burn up my excess energy by working out—but it wasn't enough. How can an adventure like that not change you?

In 1979, just as I was starting to get over my depression, I got a call from Scotty Paterson, one of the handlers for the triad cases. He wanted to meet for coffee. I agreed. We met at the food court in the Brentwood mall. I knew Scott had some kind of an offer to make. My game plan in meetings like that is simple: Keep quiet and listen very carefully.

He made a point of asking how I was doing. I told him I was great. I said it to put myself in a good position—the better I was doing, the more I could demand for a new assignment. Still, to give him a chance to make his pitch, I told him I was missing sneaking around alleyways in the dead of the night and that I'd like to get back to work.

He dropped the small talk and got down to business. He had been approached by the FBI. They wanted me to talk to them at their Seattle office. I won't deny it: I was impressed. The Bureau, requesting my services! It was the opportunity I'd been waiting for. I couldn't wait for my marching orders.

I called them and arranged a meeting in Seattle. When I arrived, I was greeted with great respect and briefed thoroughly—they treated me like one of their special agents.

The FBI had received a tip that members of a Thai Airlines flight crew were bringing quantities of high-grade heroin, obtained from Pakistani and Afghan suppliers, into the U.S. The case (later known as the Thai Pilot Project) was weak. All they had so far was the name of the hotel in Seattle where the flight crew from Thai Airlines spent their overnights once a week. Whatever else they had was either material they weren't ready to share with me, or sheer speculation. My job was to check out the story and confirm their suspicions or put the case to rest.

The FBI wanting my help was exciting—an ego boost. No more would I have to worry about the boredom I now found in everyday life. Still, I should have turned them down and walked away. I shouldn't have jumped into a new identity, without having settled back into my own first. But that's what I did.

———————

I got a room at the same hotel as the Thai pilots. It wasn't a four-star affair—more Motel Six than the Ritz. But the rooms were clean and it seemed basically well-run. Anyway, I wasn't there on vacation. I had just one day a week to win the pilots' confidence, so it promised to be a challenge.

By the fourth week, I had a plan.

I noticed that the pilots and other male members of the crew had female visitors—"working girls"—in their rooms while they stayed overnight. Clearly they were prostitutes. It offered me a way in. I knew better than to suggest recruiting female police officers to play that role. That left me with one option: I had to find girls on my own. I asked my FBI handler if he had any sources connected with strippers or escorts, and he came up with a name. To avoid blowing my cover, he had to be indirect in introducing me. He told his source that I was a Canadian criminal and that the Bureau wanted him to keep an eye on me.

That same night, I sat alone at the hotel bar, and the Bureau's source approached me (let's call him Fred). We introduced ourselves, and in less than an hour we were in my car on our way to the Pussycat Club.

The Pussycat Club was a small converted house. The entry fee was a whole five bucks. The club took up the entire ground floor, and the girls it employed occasionally guided "friends" upstairs for more private encounters. The place was sleazy at best.

There was no alcohol, but soft drinks were available—at five dollars a glass. The club was divided into a small living room, with a drinks table in the corner, adjacent to a middle room where the action was taking place—very; it was really dark except for the stage. Then there was the strangest room: the kitchen, in the back. A shower had been installed against one wall. In it, a dancer was getting personal with a back sponge. Let's just leave it at that.

The place was expected to close before long because of pressure from the Ghost Riders, a biker club and a prospect club for the Bandidos. The Ghost Riders didn't tolerate competition unless a tax was paid. The owner of the Pussycat Club, however, was not the type to bend. But I had little interest in local politics if it didn't affect my case.

Before too long, I had convinced three of the four women working at the Pussycat to visit my hotel once a week in the evening, to play pool and hang out, to develop their trust. Eventually I had 250 business cards made up, calling my venture "Elite Escorts" and offering special services "for oriental gentlemen of discerning tastes." I added my room and phone number, and I was in business.

I told the girls they could keep any money they made. All I wanted was an introduction to their Asian clients. I would pay $250 to the first girl who would make introductions for me. The girls were fine with the deal; they assumed I was a drug dealer or some other kind of crook looking for new contacts.

In the second week, Rachael (a lovely young woman with a true heart of gold) told me her "new friend" had agreed to meet me to discuss a business proposition. The friend was one of the Thai pilots. Thanks to the women of the Elite Escort Agency, I had my shot.

On the day of the meeting, I brought several women to the game room of the hotel. In a way, it was a farewell party to commemorate the end of the short-lived Elite Escort Agency. It had served its purpose.

The pilot's name was Niran. He accepted my invitation to go to a donut shop nearby to discuss business. I didn't have to dig; soon he was eagerly explaining the whole scheme. The pilots brought in samples, and facilitated deals in terms of payment and shipment. It was up to the clients to work out those details.

Niran was able to provide me with a name and phone number to make a deal of my own, based on my own arrangements. I told him that was fine. When he gave me the number, i noted that it was local. That would make things much easier than dealing with somebody on the other side of the Pacific.

It was all going so smoothly. I figured I would have this sucker wrapped up in a week. I was so very wrong.

The next day at the FBI office, I set up a meeting with the contact Niran had given me. The man I spoke to was short on details. He simply asked me if I had a passport and told me to call him back in two days, when he would have made arrangements for me. I hung up. As we say in our line of work, at times like these, I smelled jet fuel. I hoped the destination would be somewhere warm. Now I can appreciate the proverb about being careful what you wish for.

Over the next two days, I caught up on my notes and checked out of the hotel and into another one that was closer to the FBI office. Meanwhile, no one seemed to know what to do with my information. A short time later, I got another call from the same unnamed voice giving me a new name and phone number. The number was strange: It had only five digits aside from the country code and a 051 area code.

The name was very foreign to me too: It was something like Mohammad Halem Rasika. I was to meet him in ten days in Islamabad, Pakistan. If I didn't make contact within ten days, I was told, he would refuse to acknowledge me. Just like that, a path was laid for me to the Middle East.

Meanwhile, I was advised to go home and get some rest. Three days later, I was called to a meeting at the Bureau. An agent confirmed that I was indeed going to Pakistan and told me I would be accompanied by two other operatives. My knowledge of Pakistan at the time was limited to fourth-grade geography: Basically, I knew it was somewhere near India. Other than that, there was an ocean of ignorance between me and my destination.

The choice was very much mine, of course. I could've forgotten the whole thing, if I liked. It wouldn't affect their view of me—that's what they said, at least. If I did decide to go, however, I would have to sign a waiver releasing the FBI of any responsibility for my safety. "There's really nothing to worry about," one of the agents told me. "We'll always be nearby, watching your back." The vague statement didn't make me feel any better.

But of course I agreed to go. I spent the next four days in the library, reading everything I could find about Pakistan. If

I'd thought it might make me feel better, I was wrong. The more I read about the country, the less I liked. Still, I was excited about the trip, and that was enough to override my fears.

Before we left, I was told not to acknowledge the presence of the FBI agents on the same flight as me in any way: I was to give every appearance of being a solo traveller. I saw the agents for the first time on board my flight to Karachi. As instructed, we never spoke to each other or gave any sign of recognition.

I had no intention, however, of staring out the window for the entire flight. My idea was that I would board a plane in Seattle, enchant the pretty flight attendants with incredible tales from my life of danger and adventure, have some snacks and sip a martini or two (shaken, not stirred), take a nap, and step off the plane in Pakistan ready to rock n' roll.

Once again, I was very wrong. I was in the air for more than 30 hours, but not comfortably: I flew from Seattle to Washington, DC, then had a stopover in Frankfurt, Germany, where I changed planes to fly to Dubai, in the United Arab Emirates. Then I switched planes again for the two-hour flight to Karachi. On that last leg of the flight, the attendant's name was Abdul (really not the pretty stewardess I'd dreamed of), and the only choice of drink was coffee, tea or water. There were other things that surprised me, too. Everyone around me was a man—there wasn't a woman in sight. That's because the passenger areas were not split between first-class and economy (the peasants, in other words). On this flight, the women were in the front and the men in the back.

I didn't have a lot of expectations, but my short experience with Dubai was pretty positive. It was an Islamic country that seemed very progressive. At that time, the airport had only two large terminals and there were all kinds of shops on the concourse. Women were dressed conservatively, but they gave the impression of being independent, and the place was spotless to boot. As I walked I reflected that based on what I saw, the books I had read criticizing Islamic societies seemed way off base. All this Muslim stuff didn't seem so bad. The trek to Pakistan started to seem like it could end up being a positive experience for me. Of course, I didn't have a lot to base my feeling on—I was just changing planes, and never left the terminal building. That also means I didn't experience the outside temperature: a brutal 38°C (100°F).

I didn't spot my guardian angels on the final stretch, the flight to Karachi. Aside from that, the flight was uneventful and upon landing I was granted a tourist visa. As I waited in line at customs, I saw a man holding a sign with my name. I identified myself, and he drove me to a hotel. I took in as much of the city as I could on the drive. It appeared to be similar to any modern North American city: clean here, dirty there, and not incredibly interesting or unusual anywhere.

At my hotel, I found a message waiting for me in my room. I was to go to another room, where my two FBI "buddies" were waiting, along with a Pakistani man named Abu. Not much taller than me but more wiry, Abu wore a scarf that reminded me of a gigham tablecloth. He had short hair and a small raggedy goatee. His eyes kept shifting as though there was something or somebody in the room we didn't know about. Maybe we made him nervous, but overall he didn't inspire a strong feeling of confidence. Nonetheless, the agents and I still agreed to use Abu as our go-between; meeting openly in Islamabad, where we would be flying the next day, would be too dangerous. Dead tired from the journey, I went back to my room and fell immediately asleep. The next day, I flew to Islamabad.

———————

Islamabad is the only planned city in Asia. It was founded in 1960 and built from scratch, which gives it a very modern appearance, with an abundance of space and perspectives. I liked that. The weather was accommodating, too. Abu travelled with me, sticking to me like glue and helping to negotiate taxi fares and doling out the tips, or *baksheesh*.

We checked into the Marriott Hotel, set up the recorder, and made our first phone call. A man with a thick accent told me I would have to go to the post office in Chitral to speak to him in person. I assumed he was talking about a part of town or a hotel or something close by, but when I told Abu our destination he clearly wasn't happy.

Reaching the Chitral district meant taking a hair-raising trip on the infamous jeep road into the mountain areas of the then-named North West Frontier Province. Our goal was a visit with a warlord, who had a heroin-refining laboratory that was under constant threat by bandits and by Soviets, who were fighting in Afghanistan at the time. Chitral is a forbidding land, impenetrable in winter and sometimes in summer, accessible only by four-wheel drive or airplane, weather permitting. The forecasts were not favorable to flying, so we had to take the jeep route—a decision that did not thrill Abu in the least. I had spent years on the west coast of Canada and had driven through the Rockies more times than I cared to remember. I knew how bad mountain travel could be, but I believed we could manage it.

None of this calmed Abu. Finally I agreed to hire a jeep with a professional driver—attempting the drive myself would have been crazy. I made the arrangements from the hotel, and the next morning we were picked up by two jeeps: one for us and our driver, we were told, and the other to carry tents and survival gear. I had ordered one jeep, and I suspected this was a scam to gouge the dumb foreigner. Why would we need all that gear when the trip was only about 250 miles? Even on bad roads, I thought we would get there in six hours at the outside.

Eight hours of pure terror later, we reached the summit of the Lowari Pass, which was the halfway point to our destination. I desperately needed to get out and stretch—and to calm my frazzled nerves. We had been travelling on a two-lane road, sometimes paved like a highway, sometimes rutted like a cattle trail. On one side was sheer rock rising straight up; on the other side was sheer rock dropping straight down. I admit, I was scared—can you blame me?—and Abu clearly felt vindicated, looking at me repeatedly with an expression that said, "See?"

The final 100 miles would be entirely downhill. As we descended, I cursed the FBI and anybody else I could think of. Then another break. We sat around resting, working up our nerve to finish the trip, until the drivers began to get impatient and off we went again. I'll spare you the nightmare that was the last stretch of our journey, except to mention the suspension bridge that crossed over two hundred feet of absolutely nothing. I refused to look down.

The terrain began to level off as we neared the Kalash Valley; the road became wider, and I started to relax. When I looked back at the mountains we had crossed, I told myself I didn't care how long it would take to get a seat or how much it would cost: I would be flying back to Islamabad.

As we entered Chitral, Abu took command once again, yelling at the drivers and issuing instructions. The sun was going down, and I told Abu I was concerned about where we would be staying for the night. He said he knew of a hotel where we would be safe. "Define 'safe'," I demanded. "If local people do not decide to rob us," he said, "if bandits in the area don't hear of our presence, and if Russian MiGs from the Wakhan Corridor aren't aware of us, then we are quite safe." After the drive through the mountains, this sounded fine to me.

When Abu had paid the drivers, they pulled a U-turn and disappeared, leaving us in front of the Park Hotel. The rooms weren't as bad as expected, and I calmed down a little, until Abu pulled a revolver from his robe. He told me he was off to make arrangements for the meeting and that I should keep the gun, "Just in case."

"In case of what?" I demanded, but he had disappeared out the door.

It was dark when he returned. He woke me up to tell me we were to meet our guy at eight the next morning. I went back to sleep, and woke at about six a.m. Abu had spent the night in a chair facing the door, the revolver in his hand. I woke him up and we went down to the café for a breakfast of fruit and unleavened bread. Over the meal, he gave me a background on the man we were to meet. He was a member of the Kafir-Kalash, known as "Wearers of the black robes," a primitive pagan tribe about four thousand strong. Legend has it that deserters of Alexander the Great's army had settled in the area and married locals, resulting in a line of people with unusual blue eyes and blond hair.

"When you meet him" he said, "you must not shake his hand. Nod your head to acknowledge his presence. Do not assume that he does not understand English—and do not say anything at all that might cast doubt on his honor," he added seriously.

"Or what?" I asked, thinking Abu was getting overly dramatic again.

"Or he will kill the both of us on the spot."

As I considered this piece of advice, Abu continued to brief me. He instructed me to give him money immediately upon sitting down.

"How much money?" I asked.

"About 500 U.S. dollars" Abu answered.

"For what?" I demanded.

"For taking the time to talk with us," he said matter-of-factly.

Now that seemed crazy. If anyone should be compensated it should be us, for making it through those godforsaken mountains to get there!

I spotted our man as soon as we approached the post office. I had to say, he looked very cool, dressed almost entirely in black, with a black turban and a dark gray smock under his black robe. He looked a bit like Omar Sharif in "Lawrence of Arabia."

We sat at tables outside the post office. I immediately took $500 from my pocket and handed it to him. He took it without a word and it disappeared inside his robe. Then Abu and our contact—let's just call him "Omar"—had a lively discussion in their own language. Finally Abu informed me that I could buy a sample pound for $6,000, to be delivered to me in the U.S. I could have haggled, but I thought of what Abu had told me about honor, and I agreed. I would pay the Islamabad contact and return home to wait the shipment. The guys from the Bureau wouldn't like that arrangement, but they weren't facing this guy. He was clearly a serious man, not someone likely to get ripped off.

Then Abu and Omar chatted on in their Pakistani dialect. It was as though I wasn't even there. Finally Abu stood up and told me we had to go: Our plane was leaving in about an hour to take us back to Islamabad.

I stood up, nodded in Omar's direction and turned to leave, when I heard a voice say in perfect English, "That is in U.S. dollars, of course." Looking back, I saw a trace of a smile on Omar's face. His command of English was surprising; even more surprising was his awareness that I wasn't American.

"Of course," I said. Then gave him another bow and left with Abu for the airport.

The flight out of Chitral was a six-seat Fokker. I gazed out my window at the mountains, a panoramic and mesmerizing view.

———————

The one-pound sample arrived in Seattle as planned, and the FBI promptly arrested the two pilots. They ran into problems, though, when they tried to get to the suppliers outside the U.S. The reason I was told: The geo-politics were not favorable. The warlord had good contacts within the Pakistani government. The Americans were eager to hold onto any influential friends they might have in the country—anything to counterbalance the weight of the Soviet occupation in the region—and they didn't want to risk making waves. The case was eventually dropped, and the pilots were given a free get-out-of-jail card and a ride back home.

All I could do was shake my head. I'd risked my life, and the case hadn't gone as far as anyone had hoped. But I was okay with Omar getting away. He seemed too noble to be in jail.

———————

Back in Seattle, the agent in charge of my debriefing was a woman. And, I have to say, *what* a woman.

She sat across from me, with my notes laid out on the steel table between us. Her hair was in a bun and her glasses rested at the tip of her nose. She wore a crisp business suit that showed enough leg to tempt my eyes, yet remained within the bounds of professionalism.

The meeting was pretty straightforward, but when we finished the unexpected happened.

"I guess you'll be going out on the town for your last night here?" she said, putting her papers in a file.

"I'm not the party type," I said. "I'll go to my hotel, have a drink and bite to eat, and call it an early night."

"Well, it's early," she said with a smile. "Do you want some company?"

You could have knocked me over with a feather. Does a kid want candy? It was almost too good to be true. I have gotten my fair share of dates but usually from somewhere other than the office—and my dates don't usually carry a badge and a gun.

The wake-up call rang incessantly, demanding attention. When I finally answered, I realized I was alone in the room. So this is how it feels to be the victim of a discreet getaway, I thought. I made a mental note never to do that to a woman again; it didn't feel too good.

A note lay on the nightstand. It read: "Thanks for the lovely time. I'll call you in a few days."

And at the bottom, the signature: *Shannon*.

Before long I was on a plane back to Vancouver. I had a meeting with J.P.—something was up. That meant no time to wallow in memories, old or new. That suited me fine.

So, my last case had left me with a sense of unfinished business. That happens sometimes, and all you can do is brush it aside and move on. In retrospect, I have the feeling J.P. knew I had to find a foxhole to lay low in. It was a way of protecting me.

The new job was a lot closer to home: bikers. It would involve a total commitment that would last two whole years, leaving the memories of my brief but powerful encounter with Shannon just a vague recollection.

I had no idea then that my posing as a biker and my involvement in this case would take me off the grid. None of the characters on previous cases would be able to locate me. So, I guess I was hiding in plain sight, blissfully unaware that people were turning over stones for clues to my whereabouts. It's strange how things have come to be so interconnected in my history—it almost seems supernatural. This case, and later the Mann deal, plus the Chitral affair, were literally worlds apart but for one common link: Henry (much more on him later). Add to that my encounter with Shannon. It was all very strange. If I were a believer in karma I'd be a little spooked by now.

In the first book of *Befriend and Betray*, I told the story of the Bandidos case. It's an incredible saga, covering the years 1982 to 1984, and there's more to it than I could ever cover in one book. Many readers have written me to ask me to expand on this or that part of the story, to give a better picture of the gang, to show how they operated and to paint a fuller picture of my involvement. So here I'll delve a little deeper into their history and my involvement in the Club.

While I was writing the first book, the Shedden massacre occurred: Eight people were found dead in a field in Ontario in April 2006, and the Bandidos were involved. The Bandidos Club was back on the front page. Not everyone who read about that famous case is familiar with my participation: So off we go again down memory lane.

The whole biker thing seemed pretty far-fetched when I first went down to Blaine, Washington. I had many reasons why I couldn't or shouldn't take on a case that involved posing as a biker. The primary reason was that I had never been on a motorcycle in my life. I had been a passenger a couple of times, but that's pretty different. And there was another reason I didn't want to take the Bandidos case: At the time, I was still wrapped up in another case, and waiting for a deal to go down in Bangkok. Sgt. Gary Kilgore had been transferred there for that case, and before he left we went out for lunch. He explained how he wanted to make a big slash when he was settled in—and I would be the point of his spear—approximately three months after his arrival.

But in the meantime, the Blaine guys had a good spiel, one that was hard to turn down. All they wanted was ninety days in which I was to give them the goods to demonstrate that the bikers' chapter there was moving drugs and guns. My role was to get the team in Blaine the necessary information so they could build up a file that would get upstairs approval for more serious action. They had the gun; my job was to help get them the bullets.

I don't really want to go in depth on this case here; but it was such a turning point for me, it's hard to ignore. Considering the circumstances and the lack of tools I had then to conceal my identity, it proved to be my biggest accomplishment—and yet, is was also my greatest downfall.

When I say I wasn't ready for that job, that's putting it mildly. I did my best, and it took a lot. It was enough to get the job done. My success in the new agent role can be put in a nutshell: I became a full member of the club. But it left little room for my true self.

Blaine is a small town just over the border. Its income is from Canadians cross-border shopping for cheap gas and stuff like that. The DEA's office there had just three agents and a secretary. They worked closely with Immigration on seizures. When I settled in to Blaine, I was posing as a crook and border runner. It was the only plausible reason I could think of for being in that one-street farm town. I moved into a trailer, which fit nicely with my story The trailer park I picked was right near the interstate, perfect for my purported line of work.

The local chapter of the Bandidos wore a patch that named Bellingham as their location, but they were actually based in the small hamlet of Ferndale, right between Blaine and the city of Bellingham. It was so far off the highway that a stranger hanging around was an unlikely sight, sure to be the subject of gossip—especially a stranger driving a flashy muscle car. My lodging place also gave me a good excuse to hang out there. The place had two bars, one for the locals, the other for the bikers. I had learned that after their Tuesday "church" (their weekly meeting), they all went to bar called the Pioneer.

I remember my first meeting with the Bandidos. I was naive, sure, but I must also have been crazy. And I took dangerous missteps from the very start. Since they would only meet on every Tuesday, going there on Wednesdays would have been a waste of time. Biker bars usually have parking reserved for the gang's bikes right at the front door. Being completely unaware of that fact, I arrived at about eight o'clock on a Tuesday and parked—you guessed it—right outside the front door.

No one was there except the barmaid. I don't drink—a preference that on the whole hasn't made my work any easier—so I ordered a coke and waited. It didn't take long until they started coming in in twos and threes. Not a word was spoken to me—but if looks could kill, I'd have been murdered many times over. Within an hour there were a dozen of them in the bar, and me.

My miniature-John-Wayne impression could easily have gotten me beat up, or worse. I don't know if I'd have the guts to do it again. One thing I had going for me was that I didn't know what these guys were like or the extensive damage they could bestow on my person. Having said that, I had no street cred with them. For all they knew I was some guy stopping for a beer before moving on. Had I been challenged, I would have been in serious trouble. Maybe I could have done all right one-on-one, but that's not how bikers fight—I could have gotten myself in serious trouble. Even if I won, I would have lost. That, so early on in the job, would have made me persona non grata.

I was unscathed thus far, but it had gone far enough, and their response had been clear. I decided not to push my luck and slowly walked out of the place.

I had survived a first attempt, and it had obviously been too direct. I switched to showing up during the other days of the week, like Wednesdays when they had a turkey shoot pool tournament. I was meeting the wannabes and the hangers-on. But once in a while, a few of them would come in—small groups that were much more manageable.

It was a long process to get accepted enough to start buying drugs, guns and anything else that came up. Here again in our story is the moral question about acting in the capacity of a buyer and pushing guys into doing things they wouldn't normally do. The method: I was always hanging around, and always ready with some cash. I wasn't a member yet, so I paid a little more than I would as a member—I effectively became a cash cow. Here's how the deals typically worked. Biker one is broke. He goes to see biker two, and gets an ounce of coke fronted to him (given to him on credit) for, say, $2,500. He could take it directly to me and sell it for $3,000; then go back to his brother, biker two, to pay off the $2,500. In a matter of hours, he has made $500, plus a couple of grams for himself by cutting the product with a few grams of mix. What I was aiming to do with the coke was my business, but I let them know that I would be selling it to my "invisible" clients in Canada.

Many things were accomplished with this system. Biker two sold quantity without leaving his house. Biker one made money later on the resale. I looked good to my bosses, and they looked good to their whole departments. Plus, we were racking up charges against patched members of the club. The process continued, and in the end ninety members of the club were charged in nine states: a very successful operation by anyone's standards. We could have gotten more, but after almost two years undercover, I was fried. They had to pull the plug. Unfortunately, for me the damage was already done— more subtle this time than the boredom and depression I'd experienced at the end of the triad cases.

When I reread about my incursion into the Bandidos, it sounds like I thought the whole thing was a piece of cake. That the roughnecks just weren't up to my wit and savoir-faire. But that's not even close to the truth. It wasn't a fiction movie, and they weren't an "over-the-hill gang."

After all these years and other events that came into play, I want to put the record straight. I don't really know why it's so important to me, but strangely enough, it is. The Bandidos were not a bunch of clowns terrorizing society with no rhyme or reason.

As I mentioned, the notorious Shedden massacre took place after I wrote at length about my infiltration of the Bandidos. Between my time with the gang and that terrible event, things had apparently changed for the gang. In my time, they had no presence in Canada whatsoever: they were strictly American. Another thing I realized was that the members involved in the shooting were not among the higher-ups in the organization. To be frank, some of them seemed to be as dumb as soup. They would never have been accepted in my time, or even considered for membership.

I was drawn into the Shedden massacre court case. The Crown's prosecutors asked me to testify as an expert witness on biker gangs in general and the Bandidos in particular. Acting as an expert witness takes guts and composure. It's comparable to turning the last page, closing the book on an affair—even though you can never be quite sure when things are really over.

The trial took place in the small city of Guelph, Ontario. While there, I met a lawyer defending one of the accused—I'll call him Gardner. Gardner had no money and was supported by legal aid. The lawyer told me that his client had an unfair disadvantage: He was up against the unlimited means of the government and its squad of investigators. The lawyer wanted to hire me to work as part of a legal aid team. My job would be to poke around, track down missing witnesses and shed light on some of the testimonies.

It didn't take long, though, for me to realize that Gardner's story was full of holes. It looked more and more like he was indeed guilty. In good faith, I withdrew from that obligation. Still, against all odds, I heard they won their motion for appeal a couple of years later.

So how did it all end for most of the Bandidos? On September 15, 2014, they were back on center stage in the Court of Appeal. It was impressive; although first-degree murder convictions come with a right to appeal, the Bandidos had to overcome a mountain of Crown evidence and testimony, including that of a turncoat. As I write these lines, no decision has been rendered.

After the biker case I had to work on a small Toronto file. Scott Paterson told me that I should phone a staff sergeant in Ontario. I called that evening. The sergeant, whose name was Tom, told me that an East Indian crew was flooding the streets with black tar heroin. The sketchy quality of the drug was causing junkies to drop like flies. Addicts who were used to taking five caps a day just couldn't understand the caution that was now necessary: With this new stuff, a miniscule amount could have the same effect as what they were used to. Black tar is a horrible substance, poorly refined and unpredictable in its potency—scary shit.

Tom told me they hung out at the MacDonald's on the lower side of Danforth Street. A real bunch of desperados. I looked at some pictures and was on my way. Just like that, I was back to work, with a straightforward job: Take them down, with a side of fries.

CHAPTER FOUR

TO CATCH A COP

A very unusual job happened to come at a difficult time for me. A time when I was a little shakier than usual—more than a little. I had just buried two people in my life. First my mom, a few months back. More recently: Shannon.

As for my grieving my mother, they actually didn't have reason to worry. I wasn't very close to her. She and my Dad had sort of lived in their own bubble; their lives didn't really seem to include my brothers and me. You can't go on caring for people who just don't respond; eventually you stop waiting and caring about the answer. It was like they had had a secret existence. First my Dad took their secrets to the grave, and then she did.

But Shannon was another story. Though she was dead, I still hadn't had any real resolution. The darkness of it followed me around like a storm cloud. I wasn't myself. It gave J.P. and a lot of the brass reason to be concerned. It wasn't that they cared deeply about my well-being—they needed to know that I was still able to function and do my job properly.

The little I knew about the job was that it would require six weeks of infiltration in Vancouver: It was basically an intelligence-gathering operation. It looked perfect to me, short and sweet, no follow-up, no court appearances. The money was good—almost too good for the mission. I left a message with J.P. asking him to call me back and fill me in.

The first order of business was my cat. A big ball of fur that spent his days sleeping, waking up only to eat and use the litter, T.C. wasn't the most thrilling of companions. Still, for the last ten years he had been a source of constancy in my life. I dug up the bottle of duty-free brandy I had in my bag and went next door to collect him—he often spent the night at my neighbor's, visiting their cat. It didn't bother them, and it was always nice to see him again.

T.C. had showed up on my window ledge ten years ago and I had let him in. He was full grown then, but skinny and more than a little mangy. I had put up a few posters and an ad in the community paper seeking the owner, but no response came, so I hung on to him. He was alone and just wanted a warm home. I could relate to that.

With T.C. home again, I had phone calls to make and emails to respond to, but evening found me in my favorite chair looking at the fire with Billie Holiday in the background. I drifted off to sleep with a warm peaceful feeling—a rare moment for me. The next morning, T.C. woke me up by brushing past my face, telling me it was time for breakfast—he had some internal clock when it came to food. I felt good, although it was strange that J.P. hadn't called me back about the case.

When J.P. finally called, it turned out my hunch had been right. Something unusual was going down: There was no official request for my services after all. Instead, a twist. It seemed that a member of the police squad had been busted with dope, and his squad was out to clear him. But the squad had been ordered by Internal Affairs (IA) to back off, not to get involved. The cops' hands were tied. Needing someone to take over the job, my name came up.

At least, that was the explanation the cops were giving. On the other hand, the officer in question might be guilty, and maybe they needed me as a fall guy. Either way, it was trouble. I would have no protection and there were no definitive good guys. I asked J.P. what he thought. Unsurprisingly, he said I should stay out of it.

But I've always been as curious as a cat, and I thought it was worth checking out. I called Aunt Bonnie to ask for a ride to the airport and to ask her to take care of things while I was gone. While we drove, she seemed to be speaking in tongues—I had no idea what she meant.

"I thought I picked up two rabbits—one when we left— and then the change of the eye was clumsy," she said.

"What?" I asked. I was baffled. "What are you talking about?"

She answered simply, "Alex, things are not always what they seem."

My thoughts got confused. In normal circumstances I would have had her pull over and got satisfaction for the nagging in my head. Not today, I was too self-absorbed to care about anything that didn't concern the case at hand. Clearly, that didn't concern me.

When I settled in my Vancouver hotel room, there was a message on my answering machine, instructing me to call Billy: a man who'd been on my backup team for a case I had worked several years prior. The message was entirely unexpected.

Instead I decided to called J.P. to see if there was anything I should know. It was a breach of protocol for Billy to reach out to me directly, before the details of the job were worked out. We certainly weren't friends. He should have gone through CISC (the Criminal Intelligence Service of Canada), and my rabbi, to square it with him first. But on top of that, how did he even know what hotel I was staying at? It was a little disturbing: Obviously they were already keeping tabs on me. I hoped J.P. would have some answers.

I'm always edgier than normal on my first days in a new town. It usually takes me about a week to unwind, and this was all getting sketchy too soon. I felt like I was being pressured, and I didn't like it. I felt the presence of risk; but then, risk is always a part of the game. I'd been around long enough to know that security is just something you strive for, not something you can fully achieve. You create diversions, surround yourself with protection, and keep your fingers crossed that luck will be on your side.

When I finally spoke to J.P., he still had no idea what the job might really involve. He asked if I could hold off another day while he checked it out. Fine with me; I would use that time to work on the long list of things I had to do. I called Dana, an old friend and a fellow martial artist, and Chris, a security man who was also into martial arts. I was happy to reach them; they were guys I could count on if the shit hit the fan.

When J.P. called me back later, he had some interesting information. He thought the suspected cop had been set up. Something bigger was going on. I asked who the target was.

"A cop named Mann," he told me.

"Mann," I said. "I never trusted him. But I didn't know he was dirty."

"Well, if you want to check it out, I can give you a week off. But I want daily progress reports and a copy of your notes. If the case blows up on you, I'll need those to save your ass," he said.

"Deal."

J.P. never showed the slightest trepidation or uncertainty in his voice. The guy was like an oak. So the hesitation he was showing this time certainly didn't give me confidence.

I phoned and made arrangements for a car rental. I also picked up a burner phone and had it activated under a different name. I didn't want to advertise that I was on their turf.

Then I finally called Billy. He wouldn't say anything on the phone—not that I expected him to. We made arrangements to meet in the covered parking at the Starlight Casino in New Westminster, a city next to Vancouver, the next day at noon. The casino's parking lot was next to the river and had an underground section with only two entrances. It offered great cover.

I drove through town and headed for the Westminster Quay, and drove into the underground parking at river level. I spotted the cops immediately. I parked at one end and walked over to the other end of the parking lot where they were waiting.

I hadn't seen these guys in a while, but no one was in the mood for small talk. Billy's partner, Jason, was especially quiet. He assessed me coldly and had a predatory look.

The vibe was bad. I felt like I was talking to gangsters rather than cops. I saw that I needed to show them that I wouldn't be intimidated, that I was under no one's control.

They started to tell me the details of the matter, what they were after. I listened as I watched a small tugboat moving sluggishly down the Fraser River, towing an incredible load of logs behind it.

"It'll have to be done my way," I said without turning around, when they were through.

"Understood," said Jason. I knew immediately he wouldn't be good for his word on that point.

"It's important you understand why I'm even considering this," I told him. The question just hung in the air and he felt he had to say something.

"No it's not. We all have our demons, Alex. I don't give a rat's ass why you do anything. My friend needs help."

I turned away from the river and studied him carefully. "Who's paying the bill?"

"The whole squad is chipping in," he said. "How much are we looking at?"

"I'll let you know in a couple of days," I told him, "when I tell you whether I'm in."

I pulled out a business card that had a few different numbers. "Fax me his personal information, home address, the type of car and details of the seizures—where in the car the stuff was found. And anything else you think is relevant. And make sure I have a copy of the lead investigator's notes."

Jason looked down nervously. "You know I can't do that," he said.

I was in no mood to be played with. "Don't start with me, man," I warned him "I want that stuff today."

Jason sighed in resignation. "You'll have it," he said. "Anything else?" he added.

I ignored the sarcasm. "Arrange a visit with Sergeant Mann for me. Tomorrow evening, at his house."

I walked back to my car and thought things over. Maybe it was the long flight, or the situation I was getting myself into, which I highly suspected was a messy one—whatever the cause, I could feel a headache coming on. I decided to go back to the hotel to take a nap and to grab some pain medication. I knew I had to stay sharp on this one.

In my rearview mirror, I could see Jason watching me as I started to drive away. There was something he wasn't telling me. Then he got back in his vehicle; Billy, his partner of several years, had stayed in the car. Despite the distance, I could see that the two men were not happy—were agitated, in fact. As I drove off, my imagination started working, picturing what their argument might have been.

"*This isn't right, Jay,*" I imagined Billy saying.

"*Don't start on me, Billy. Don't you think I know that?*" Jay would say, with his voice rising. "*It isn't our decision!*"

My suspicion was that these cops were merely pawns in the game. But the question remained: If Mann was being framed, who was behind it all?

There was an envelope waiting for me at the front desk of my hotel, sent by express courier. I opened it in my room, and found a B.C. driver's license and Canadian passport; everything looked perfect, even my photo. I spent the next half hour going over the documents in the file. My guy had done a great job of research, as usual. The history provided for my cover went all the way back to a grandfather emigrating from Russia eighty years earlier. I emptied my wallet of all Alex Caine ID, except for my driver's license, which I could need to prove my identity when dealing with the cops. I resealed the envelope. It would be mailed to a post office box a few miles away in Burnaby. After a quick shower, I lay down and immediately went to sleep. My last thought was for Sergeant Mann. I should let him rot, I thought—crooked cops are even worse than crooks, in my opinion. I knew I wouldn't just let him swing; but I wasn't above letting him dangle a bit.

I woke later from a nap to find that Jason had been true to his word and had sent the information I had asked for. A good start, I thought.The first place I wanted to see was Mann's house. If the drugs had been planted that was the only place it could have happened. Maybe the bad guys had made a mistake, left something behind.

Mann's bail hearing wasn't till the next day. There was little doubt he would make bail; the crown was almost sure not to object to his release. I pulled up at Mann's house, already knowing that the coast was clear—his wife had gone to her mother's, and no one else was home. I parked across the street on a quiet cul-de-sac. The first thing I noticed was an old lady peering at me from her window next door. Not long after, a man walking his dog took out a pen and paper and jotted down my plate number. Apparently this was no place to sit in a car without drawing attention. But no one knew exactly when Mann was coming home, and someone had to keep watch. But from where? Open carport? No, he'd be seen when Mann pulled in the driveway. The yard? Maybe, but unlikely.

I decided to check out the premises. As I approached, an outside light turned on in the carport. I walked along the five-foot hedge that separated the yard from the house next door, and something caught my attention: a cigarette butt. I picked it up and put it in a small plastic bag for collecting evidence. Then I went back to the car and got my flashlight. I went back to the hedge and crawled on all fours, looking for anything at all. It didn't take long. Under broken branches I found six or seven more butts. That meant someone had been sitting between the hedge and the garage keeping watch. I bagged them and got back in my car.

I called Jason and asked him whether Mann was a smoker. I knew the answer would be no. I told him I'd left them a little gift in a plastic bag; they should check for DNA or fingerprints. Jason was at a loss for words. He started to ask where I was at the moment, but I hung up. No need to start with the small talk now.

I went back to the hotel and pored over the notes and case file Jason had sent me. Aside from some obviously shabby police work, there wasn't much that stood out. I decided to review what I did know.

On the evening of March 2, Mann had left his house in his personal car. He made it just two blocks before a uniformed cop stopped him for a broken taillight. The officer's notes stated that Mann was acting suspicious; consequently the officer asked him to step out of the car. Another patrol car arrived and they searched Mann's car. They found twenty kilos of cocaine in the trunk. Mann was put under arrest, and the vehicle was impounded. When they checked his bank accounts, investigators found suspicious transactions that Mann swore he knew nothing about.

It seemed pretty cut and dry—and maybe a little bit too neat. It started to look a little thin under the light. For instance, why didn't Mann flash his badge when the cop pulled him over? If he had, he almost certainly would have been able to drive away. And how exactly was Mann acting "suspicious?" And why wasn't the second cop named on the arrest sheet?

I decided I had one more place to go before calling it a night. I knew that vehicles under investigation weren't always taken into the police impound lot; occasionally they were kept overnight in an unguarded underground parking lot in Gastown. All I needed was gloves, lock picks and a flashlight—and my pocket knife for good measure. I loaded a few things into a backpack and set out.

I was only two or three blocks away when I caught on to the tail. Seeing them switch the watching eye tipped me off. Here's how it works: The target is called the "rabbit," and one "eye" (a single car) follows at a time. The team then follows the eye, with units alternating regularly as necessary to follow the eye's movements. It's a good technique, and provides maximum protection for the team. But of course, it depends on the eye not being detected.

Rabbits, eyes—ring a bell? Maybe Bonnie's ramblings on our drive to the airport had a little more meaning than one might think.

I pressed the speed dial on my cell to call Sue, an old friend. A guy like me has friends like her in cities all over the world. It gives you someone to visit when you're away from home, someone to count on. You keep in touch when you can, and solidify a platonic friendship. You always play it straight with them—no games. You help them out a bit with money and entertainment, or just good company. It's nice for you both: You have someone to talk to, someone to listen to your tales of exotic places and wild adventures while you enjoy expensive (expense account) dinners. It helps if you keep a list of birthdays and other events that matter to them and their kids. Try to send a card, make a call, order gifts at Christmas, that sort of things. There's something bigger at stake for you, too. Sooner or later you might need a safe place to go or some timely help.

Today it was Sue's turn to help me out. The call was totally unexpected, but she wasn't at all surprised. They never are.
I came and went unpredictably—like a case of the flu, but
hopefully a lot less painful.

I had her full attention on the other end of the line. Any
request would be treated implicitly as an instruction, so long
as it was something she could manage. "I need to trade cars
with you for a couple of days," I told her, without further ado.

"Where are you?" she said.

"Not far," I told her. "Open your garage door and leave the
keys under the sun visor. Make sure you close the door after I
leave. I'll call you later."

She agreed without asking any more questions. It showed
she knew better: The less she knew, the better she'd sleep. I
headed for the east end and Pender Street. On the way, I kept
an eye on the tail. I made a sudden turn down the alley behind Pender Street. I knew they would switch the eye and pick
the chase at the other end of the alley. The car behind me
would have to race around to assume his position. Halfway
down the alley, I pulled into Sue's open garage. I found Sue's
keys under the visor and backed out. Pulling down my ball
cap, I headed back the way I had come, leaving the lights off.
I drove across the street and continued driving in the alley for
two blocks. Then I turned the lights on, hung a right and
merged with traffic onto Hastings Street. It worked like a
charm—the tail was lost.

———————————

Who knows what was happening at the police station
then. My guess? Something like this:

"*What do you mean he disappeared?*"

"*I'm telling you, he never came out of the alley. We had it covered, both ends!*"

"*I want a full report on my desk, do you understand me?*"

"Yes, Sir!"

Deputy-Chief Moore slammed the phone receiver down on the cradle. This thing could easily could go sideways, and there'd be hell to pay if it did. He opened the side drawer and took out his antacid pills. He had to call Jerry and let him know—but not from his office phone. Too many ears. At the beginning, he had been against bringing Alex in. The man had over twenty years of experience, a potential danger if he happened to luck out with his mission. Definitely not a risk to take. But he had finally given up.

"After all," he thought, leaning back in his chair. "Alex would make the perfect patsy for the events to come."

I arrived in Gastown and pulled into the garage. Picking the door opener was child's play; I had the door up in no time and drove in to look for Mann's car. I found it on the second lower level. I used my Slim Jim to open the doors and popped the trunk. It was empty. But I did find that all the car's lights seemed to be working perfectly. I even checked the turn signals: no problems there.

I got into the car and sat in the driver's seat to think. Almost as an afterthought, I popped the glove compartment and took out the paperwork. The plates, the name and address—everything jibed. Then I got out and looked in the door jam to compare the vehicle registration number with the one in the papers. Bingo: They didn't match. That would be normal for an undercover car, but this was supposed to be Mann's personal car. It was clear: This wasn't really his car.

On the way out of Gastown, I phoned J.P. I gave him the name and badge number of the arresting officer and the car's VIN number. He said I would get my answers by the next morning. I also considered calling Jason to give him the new information, but I decided against it. It seemed wise to play things close to the vest, at least until I felt I had some solid footing.

When I got back to the hotel, I parked in the back and went in through the rear entrance, taking the service elevator to get to my room. I would need a little time in the morning so I called Jason and left a message on his machine. "Hey man, it's me," I said. "I'll meet you at the station about 9 a.m."

I knew that would lead them to wait until I showed up before putting the tail back on me. Someone was obviously spending a lot of money and going to a lot of trouble on this deal. I decided the situation warranted shadow notes. On any case, you have to keep notes that are given to your handler at the end of each day. But in cases that feel uncertain or sketchy, you keep shadow notes and send them to another party. They're also known as CYA notes: CYA meaning "cover your ass."

The phone started to wail at 6:05 a.m. It was J.P., and he got right to the point.

"The arresting cop wasn't one of ours," he told me—meaning RCMP. "He's with CSIS. And the VIN number you gave me is a reserved government number. What the hell is going on over there?"

"I don't know, man. I really don't know," I admitted.

"Phone me every couple of days," he told me, "And watch yourself! Send your CYAs on a secure ISP. And Alex—you may want to consider walking away." He hung up.

After those comforting words, I ordered room service and watched the news. At around 8:30, Jason called.

"I've made arrangements for a meeting at three o'clock this afternoon," he said.

"Sounds good, where?" I answered. I knew that it wouldn't be Mann's house at that hour.

"You know where Westminster Abbey is?"

'Yeah, just past Abbotsford up the road to the left—it's on the hill."

"Right. He'll meet you in the parking lot."

"I'll be there." Click.

It was actually a good spot. The parking lot overlooked both the highway and the road into the abbey. It was quiet and we would be able to talk uninterrupted.

I placed a call—a number I hadn't used in a while. I hoped it was still active. An answering machine picked up on the second ring and I left a message:

"Hey, it's the Dog. Is Roscoe around? I'm here till the ninth, Room 217 at the Delta. Call me."

Two hours later, there was a knock on the door. When I opened it, an Asian woman handed me a small package and left in silence. Just once, I would have liked to exchange a few words with one of these delivery people! When she was gone, I opened the parcel. It contained a single key for a locker at the bus depot.

On my way out I walked around the building a few times, looking for signs of a tail. When my mind was at ease, I headed to the bus depot, found the locker, and pulled out a 9 mm pistol with two extra clips. On the way back to the hotel I dropped by a bank and made a $1,000 deposit into a numbered account.

Back in my hotel room, I turned on the radio, and was hit with some news.

And here are our top stories. Police are tight-lipped about the body of a man found near the Abbotsford medium-security correctional facility. At approximately five o'clock this afternoon, two young men were walking in a field and stumbled on the lifeless body. Sources say the victim may have been a police officer. The area has been cordoned off, and members of the Major Crime Unit are still on the scene. Police have not said whether foul play is suspected.

J.P. called me moments later. He didn't waste any time getting to the heart of it.

"Who do you think he is?" he asked me.

"I don't know," I answered, "but I don't think he's a cop. At least not from around here."

"Get the photos from the internet, maybe they'll be able to place him," he said.

"Already done," I answered.

"You're out, as of now!" he said with finality. "You are to cease all communication with anyone tied to this case. If they want your services, they will have to go through the proper channels. Take the rest of the week off and unwind. I'll be in touch."

That settled that. I gave Sue a call and thanked her for her help. Then I gathered my things, left the hotel, returned the car and headed for home. J.P. was almost always right about this kind of thing. I didn't mind when he, and only he, talked to me in that tone, like he was giving me orders—I'd learned to trust him implicitly. When he said something, you just did it and looked for answers after the fact.

Besides, cop killings are a sign of a very messy situation. This thing was clearly much bigger than it seemed, and who knows how high up it went. Just in case, I decided to keep the gun for a little while longer.

CHAPTER FIVE

Shannon's Role

The abrupt ending to the Mann case left me in a state I'd hoped to avoid for a while: aimless. I had emerged unscathed after playing with fire. But I knew the luck that had kept me safe from disaster—from crooked cops, psychopathic killers and ruthless criminals—could fail me at any time. Just like it had failed Shannon, as I was soon to learn.

Back in 2005, after the biker case, I had taken three months off to recalibrate. When I returned home, I learned that Shannon had been transferred to Vancouver. We picked up where we had left off in Seattle, and what I thought had been a one-night stand turned into something more. I couldn't have been happier.

Shannon was working with Canada's National Security and Transnational Criminal Investigations (NSTC). The NSTC targets national and international crime, and had become more active than ever, having its hands full with the spread of Eastern European organized crime.

For years, Eastern European organized crime (sometimes shortened to EEOC) had been downplayed or ignored outright. In places like Vancouver, it had been considered a small-time matter: shoplifters and pawn shop owners who trafficked in stolen goods. Busting a shoplifting ring had no media value. The real budgets were spent on bikers and illegal immigration. Add to that the cops' total ignorance of the structure of EEOC and you ended up with fertile breeding ground for Russian criminals in Canada. The bad guys were able to hunker down and develop their strategies without anyone taking much notice. Before long, their days of stealing jeans from department stores were behind them; they had moved on to BMWs from the lot, or right off the street.

But things were changing—better late than never—and EEOC had definitely come to the attention of the federal authorities. A struggle was looming.

Knowing what was happening on the street was always a part of my business, and I never liked what I heard about the Russian mafia. Their methods were brutal, and they seemed to have a total disregard for the public at large, and even for their own people. This made them different from the Italian mafia. The Italians operated in the shadows and left innocent people and families alone whenever possible. With the Russians it was a different story. They seemed to have no limits. Entering a house and killing everyone inside, for instance, was no big deal—just another day at the office. It may have helped them gain power on the streets, but it had a downside. The viciousness of their approach meant that the authorities began to take a keen interest in shutting them down.

As far as I knew, Shannon's role with the police involved debriefing and other matters on the administrative end. Nothing risky. But I was dead wrong. She also did some second line incursion investigations—something I would find out about much too late.

One of her specialties was playing the role of a decoy. From what I heard later, she was very good at it. Her specialty was what's known as the sister act.

Here's how it works: The decoy has to be an attractive woman—a real showstopper. Pick a bad guy, and determine what bar he likes to frequent. (They all have one.) The decoy hangs around the bar, checking her watch every few minutes making it obvious she's waiting for someone. The bad guy spots her and eventually makes a move, starts chatting her up hopefully. The decoy's story is that she's waiting for her brother to arrive; she's in town visiting and they had made plans for a goodbye drink before she leaves.

She and the bad guy have a drink together while she waits. The brother (another agent) arrives late; the decoy introduces him to the bad guy. They all hang out, but not for too long, and make sure to exchange email addresses or phone numbers. Then the decoy and the brother say goodbye.

A week goes by. Then, at a moment when the bad guy is in bar, the brother comes in by himself. He walks past the bad guy and makes no acknowledgment. Eighty-five percent of the time, the bad guy will greet him and enquire about his sister. Voila: The infiltrator now has an in. The "sister" is kept in reserve, in case things go wrong. It might sound too easy, but it really works.

For a further level of involvement, the sister keeps loosely in touch with the bad guy and starts telling him that she's worried about her brother. Eventually she tells him that he's a criminal, and mentions that he's involved with the bad guy's acquaintances. At some point she asks for his help.

Shannon was known as one of the best decoys around. Still, if I had known at the time that she was involved in taking down the Russian mob, I would have voiced my concerns. No matter how skilled and smart she was, the potential dangers were great, especially if the brother bungled his side of the job. Unfortunately, I knew nothing about it. That was because while we were a couple, Shannon and I had an agreement: We didn't take our work home. I kept my cases to myself, and she did the same. It seemed safer that way, and it made our time together our own.

After she went missing, I went to her office every day demanding information and rattling cages. No one would tell me anything; the official line was simply that she was AWOL.

But I'd been around long enough to know that I should assume the worse. I was a wreck, and I needed answers. I could feel it hanging in the air: Shannon wouldn't be coming back.

Finally, J.P. told me he wanted to meet with me. I knew this would be a hard conversation and that I would get the answers I feared but needed to hear. We decided to do lunch at Denny's: lots of windows, low backrests, easy to scan for dubious characters. Maximizing safety just becomes second nature when you're in this line of work. After a quick check around us, he began to talk.

"How much do you know about Shannon's work?" he asked me.

"Not much," I told him. "We kept our work separate, and to tell you the truth, I thought she was mostly admin. But now I'm not sure I got the whole story."

"That's far from the truth," he agreed quietly. He was clearly struggling to tell me something, or dreading my reaction. I told him to tell it to me straight.

"Aside from her admin work," he said, "her job was exactly the same as yours."

I was stunned. "Are you her rabbi?" I asked.

"No," he said with a sad smile. "I only get the ugly ones, like you."

I spent the next hour listening to him, taking it all in, reshaping my memory of the Shannon I thought I had known. Little things that had nagged me in the months before were suddenly making sense. But still I had a thousand questions. For one, the idea that Bonnie—*Aunt* Bonnie—was her *rabbi*—it was almost too much for me to believe. A portly older woman, Bonnie seemed made to be in the kitchen baking cookies, not running major crime cases, packing a gun and leading swat squads on dangerous busts. But she must have been good. Really good. If she could fool me, she could fool anyone.

But most of all, it was clear that J.P. knew that Shannon was gone. That's why he was telling me this now; something had gone wrong, something terrible. But I couldn't get the full story out of him.

Bonnie, he told me, was the one I should talk to.

Two nights later, I was mulling over food options at the local watering hole when in walked Aunt Bonnie, unannounced.

"How'd you know I was here?" I asked her as she took a seat beside me.

"I know a great deal about many things," she said with a slight smile.

"Well, I don't," I said flatly. "So how much can you tell me?"

With that, Aunt Bonnie came out of the kitchen: She was all business. Shannon, she told me, had been trying to help infiltrate the Russian mob before she disappeared. She had been working on a decoy intro with a crooked cop—a cop whose name was very familiar to me. His name was Mann. I was stunned as I tried to take that in, but there was no time to digest it. Bonnie had more to tell me.

The decoy intro had gone very wrong.

I looked straight at Bonnie, without seeing her, without seeing anything at all, as she confirmed my worst fears. Shannon had been murdered.

My sense of foreboding about the Mann case had proved to be more accurate than I could have imagined. But it turned out it wasn't my own safety that was the problem. It was the safety—and the life—of the woman I loved.

Every Tuesday, without fail, Mann had gone to the Odessa Social Club to meet up with a Russian gangster he had dealings with. He may or may not have been set up for the drug bust, but he was far from squeaky clean as a cop—which came as no surprise to me at all. Shannon was aiming to establish a connection with some of these gangsters. Plans were made and she went into the bar. She never came out.

What Bonnie told me next was almost too much to bear. Several days later, she said, the office had received a box. Inside was a barely recognizable female head.

Why had I been put on the Mann case? Had Bonnie known about that? She did, she told me. But she didn't explain why the decision was made. I decided not to pursue the question for the moment. I just hoped it would become clear later.

"Was Billy involved with the Russian mob, along with Mann?" I asked. "Or Billy's partner?" The facts behind the mess with that Vancouver squad were still so unclear.

"No, we don't think so," she answered. "They wanted to clear Mann. But Internal Affairs told them not to touch it. So they decided to go through you to find out the truth."

So their story had been true. I tried to make sense of it all—those tangled connections. But it was hard to focus. Part of me was just so furious that this had happened, that they had allowed it to happen. I couldn't hold it in.

"Where was her support crew?" I demanded. "You don't just send someone into the lion's den without back-up."

She gave me a look that told me I wouldn't be getting the answer anytime soon. Instead, she shifted the conversation to something that she was sure would interest me.

"Alex," she said, "I'm going to offer you Shannon's caseload. If you want to pick up where she left off—the EEOC project is yours."

I didn't see that coming. There was no way I was going to say no.

"I'll have to talk to J.P. about it first. He would need to know." I said.

"I have his approval as of tomorrow. You'll be a special consultant for the NSTC," she said.

With no further ado, I accepted. I told Bonnie I wanted access to Shannon's case files and assignment diaries, and she agreed. She told me to report to her office in the morning for a crash course on the EEOC and our targets.

With that, a new direction was set for me. A path that would lead me who knows where, a search that would go on for years. I was emotionally spent—depleted to the very core. I left Bonnie's office and went home.

That evening I did my own research about Russian organized crime online. Any scrap of information about that type of criminal could prove crucial. What I read was far from encouraging. The reality of the Russian mafia was truly nightmarish. As I searched, the stories piled up—drug trafficking, prostitution, homicide. To a man, they seemed to be killers without a conscience.

It was during this time that I heard some news that I didn't expect: Abu, my former guide in Pakistan, had been killed. Corky Cochrane, a contact of mine in the FBI, had heard about it a full two years after the fact. Abu had been killed by a Russian sniper in the Kalasha Valley. According to the FBI, the killing had nothing to do with me or my case. I didn't know quite what to do with the information. I had only worked with him briefly and I really didn't know him. But one thing I did know: Deaths seemed to be piling up around me.

It was cold like only October in Vancouver can be. After a week of rain, the streetlights reflected off the pavement with a false promise of comfort. The part of town where I lived then wasn't picturesque, but its drab anonymity and sparse traffic made it as good a choice as any for a safe and invisible place to stay from time to time. I settled into a chair with the huge file Bonnie had given me. I knew this was the start of a job that would take me deep—maybe deeper than ever before. I thought back to Shannon's funeral. I had a new motivation, a mission that was intensely personal: revenge. I would do whatever it took to make her killers pay. I could barely contain it—I almost felt a sensation of vertigo, like I was losing a part of myself. But I was fine with that. At the moment, being someone else seemed pretty appealing.

The next day I went to the NSTC office. I was stopped at the turnstile; I told them about my appointment, and they called Bonnie down. She looked so professional in this setting. Gone was the persona of the doting old lady I was used to—she was all business. She led me to a conference room with a large TV at one end and a long rectangle table in the center. Several people were already seated around the table, so I took a seat and waited with them. Finally an older man entered, set up a chalkboard, and laid a large folder on the table.

"Your all new to this task force," he began in a monotone, "so I'll assume that you know nothing about the enemy. Those who already do know, please bear with me. You're about to get a crash course on the Russian mob."

The audience dutifully began to take out their pens and notebooks. It felt exactly like a college lecture hall. The poor man began to ramble and ramble. He obviously wasn't a field agent—and he had the bedside manner of a hockey puck. He probably did important work behind the scenes, analyzing and parsing data in front of a screen—not a job I envied, but over the years I had come to understand that his kind of work was crucial for what I do. In this case, though, most of his material I had already found online. I left my notebook untouched. There wasn't really anything highly strategic for me, that would help me on my quest, and any information I needed later wouldn't be hard to find.

For those of you who were unable to attend EEOC 101, here's an overview: Russian organized crime groups have been in Canada for a long time, and include as many as twenty thousand soldiers. Most of the groups are fairly disorganized: merely local gangs that prey on their own communities. There are, however, several hundred more highly structured gangs that operate with a hierarchical leadership. These are the groups to worry about. They pull in massive amounts of money and have thousands of soldiers to draw on.

What's more, they are hard to break. One reason for that is that North American prisons are almost country homes to them. Their prisons back home barely resemble our own; over there, being locked up means you're really doing hard time. The only thing they don't want, legally at least, is to be deported. Many of them have dangerous loose ends and lingering problems with the cops or with other gangsters back in Russia.

How can you identify a member of an Eastern European gang? It's not easy. On the streets of Canada they tend to look pretty normal, in a blue collar sort of way. They often drive trucks that advertise electrician work or some other trade on the side. In other words, you don't even see them. They blend right in, which helps them make deep inroads into our society.

Many of those involved in these organizations, especially at the higher levels, are former KGB agents and officers. With contacts in the government and connections with spy networks in Europe and overseas, they can get thoroughly established fast making their mark in the criminal world. However, links between gangs are tightly limited. The U.S. Financial Crimes Enforcement Network identified a structural model the groups use in the U.S. and Canada. They found that the basic principle is to minimize contact with other cells that could lead to the identification of the entire organization.

Each of the many cells of the Russian mafia specializes in its own type of criminal activities. Each cell also feeds a portion of its income upstairs to the Pakhan—basically a God-father. The Pakhan has life-or-death power over four cells. Most of the ground-level gangsters don't even know who works for any other cell; only the Pakhan knows. It seems extreme, but it effectively ensures that one bust can't bring down the whole organization. The Pakhan operates through a sort of underboss, called a Brigadier. Usually the Pakhan also has a spy in each cell to ensure loyalty and minimize skimming. Of course, at the bottom of the heap is the soldier, the one who does the dirty work; and soldiers are allowed to bring in non-Russians—throwaways, they're often called—when necessary. As in the Italian Mafia, there is a ceremony each time a man is "made."

Today, Russian organized crime groups in the U.S. and Canada are thriving. Once limited mostly to theft and small drug operations, they have formed a vast, vicious and powerful criminal enterprise whose reach spans the continent. Groups operating on the East Coast cooperate and trade with their West Coast counterparts. U.S. groups also deal continuously with the mob in Russia; over 200 of Russia's 6,000 gangs operate with U.S. partners in 17 cities in 14 states.

According to intelligence reports, members of criminal groups in Russia are sent regularly to North America to secure and consolidate their business links. At times, Russian gangsters may also be sent over to our shores to perform a particular task, such as a murder or extortion. The disturbing truth is that Canada has become an entry spot for these criminals. Things are much safer for them here. For some, the trip is a chance to escape pressures in Russia and avoid threats from authorities.

Here's some specific history, for a fuller picture: According to law enforcement sources, a Russian organized crime leader named Vyacheslav Ivankov (known as Yaponchik, which translates as "Little Japanese"), moved to the U.S. in the 1990s. It is believed that his aim was to establish links on behalf of groups in Russia. Ivankov was high-ranking in his world, an organized crime leader or "thief in law" well known in Russia and the U.S. He was arrested in Brooklyn on June 8, 1995, for trying to extort $3.5 million from a Wall Street investment firm.

As a result of Ivankov's intensive networking, there are hundreds of cells between the Bay Area and Los Angeles alone. Money has to be coming in constantly to support them, so the groups stay busy, working through different street gangs and with associates from Eastern Europe and frequently teaming up with Armenians.

Normally, such activities would make it easy to infiltrate an organization—unfortunately, that's not the case here. An agent attempting to get inside would have to have a story about where he's from. By tapping in to a vast intelligence web maintained within Russian organized crime, the gang can check the story out by making a single phone call. If the information turns out to be false, your agent is as good as dead. Newcomers in that world don't gain the organization's trust right away; it takes a long time. The problem this creates for law enforcers is that there's no way around working undercover for that long without committing a major crime.

In the class, the "college professor" went on and on, serving up stale information. I was getting no wiser than when I had walked in—and worse, I was getting thoroughly bored. I'm definitely more of a street guy than anything else. It's my experience that office meetings never really accomplish much, other than handing down some decision that's already been made to the rank and file. For me, the question was what to do next.

After lunch, Bonnie and I went into her office and she closed the door. I suspected I was about to get the real lesson of the day, and I was right.

"Your target is Major Jivco," she told me. "He's ex-KGB, now a major crime figure in charge of North American expansion for the Russian mob. His underboss is a man by the name of Henry Cludd. Shannon's mission was to get to Jivco through Henry. She was getting close, when…," she paused for a moment, then resumed, "…Henry Cludd was almost certainly the man who killed Shannon or had her killed."

A wave of emotion hit me. It was a wave that would continue hitting me whenever Shannon's name came up.

"Mann was on Henry's payroll." she continued. "He told Henry everything about our operation. This office leaks like an old pipe"—her faced tensed angrily—"and thanks to Mann and others like him, we have no absolute secrets. Which is why we do most of our talking outside this building."

But it turned out it wasn't Mann who had caused Shannon's death.

"You infiltrators always talk about that 'five percent,'" Bonnie said. "The five percent margin that you can never fully cover—the part you don't know about till it's too late."

I knew exactly what she meant. It can be the littlest thing: You could be walking your dog when out of the blue someone drives by and recognizes you. Maybe that person tells someone else; or maybe they simply follow you home then and there. Your case is closed, permanently, before you even know something's gone wrong. There's no guaranteed protection against that.

In Shannon's case, it turns out that one of the bad guys had visited the federal building and happened to see her: The badge around her neck couldn't have been clearer. This was long before she got involved in the Jivco case, but she was such a stunner that he never forgot her face.

"When she went to the Social Club to make the intro with Mann," Bonnie said, "she was already made and she had no idea." We looked at each other silently for a moment. "No one likes to see an agent killed and have it end there. That's why I'm putting the case in your hands."

I took the file she gave me and got to work. As I sat at the temporary desk I'd been given, I thought about Henry, trying to imagine what he might be like. I stared at his picture, looking for some clue—his face was as unreadable as granite. But his number was up, though he didn't know it. I had no intention of arresting him, no matter what instructions I had from Bonnie or anyone else. I wanted him to pay, not with a trial and prison sentence, but my way. The direct approach, with permanent results.

The next day, I had expected to meet with Bonnie to continue our discussion of the Henry case. Instead I was directed to the conference room. In it were six people, none of them smiling. A cloud of tension hung over them like smog over a Chinese city. All eyes were on me.

"Henry Cludd is on your radar, isn't he?" asked one of them.

I told them it was a name on my case file; I didn't want to give them too much until I saw where this was going.

The man glanced at his colleagues and followed with another question—one that completely bowled me over. "What do you know about nukes," he asked, "and groups that get could their hands on one?"

Their sources had discovered that Russian mobsters were having dealings with local extremists who were planning an act of terror: an attack along the lines of 9/11.

I was pretty much speechless. This was new territory for me. I asked the first question that came to mind.

"Why would the EEOC get involved? What's in it for them?" I said.

"Money," he answered gruffly. "The EEOC sells weapons to third-world countries. A war with the U.S. would mean millions in weapon sales. And there's a side benefit: a major disruption in the U.S. would ease the pressure on EEOC groups here. The U.S. would have its hands full with other problems."

From what I knew, that made sense. The U.S. is very target-oriented, tending to take an all-or-nothing approach. When it comes to fighting terrorist activities, there's no limit to the funds that can get swallowed up. An attack of this magnitude would surely take the air out of other anti-crime projects.

What I was hearing seemed vague, and I wasn't being given much in the way of solid intelligence. But if it got all these suits in one room, the threat had to be real. When the top guys came to me, it meant they needed confirmation of what they already knew. This wasn't the time for me to ask questions.

They filled me on what my role would be, and told me Bonnie would be my immediate handler. With that I was dismissed.

My mind raced for the next half hour or so. One thing bothered me most: Why had they mentioned Henry? When Bonnie arrived, I couldn't hold back.

"I don't think any of this has anything to do with Henry or the Russians," I told her. "I think they threw that in because they know why I'm here. Because I'm out to find Henry." I stared her down, but she didn't even blink. I was amazed. Clearly it would take me some time to get used to the real Bonnie.

"I won't say you're wrong," she said, "and I won't play games. But I will tell you this: You solve this case and you'll be able to write your own ticket. You'll be a golden boy. That means you would have carte blanche in your hunt for Henry." She clearly knew exactly what I wanted to hear.

"I'm in," I said. "I know Henry will still be out there after I'm done with this."

"Yes," said Bonnie gravely. "But the question is: Will we?"

It was time to head home to Vancouver. I went back to my hotel and got my stuff together. I also called Dana, my old martial artist buddy, and arranged to be picked up when I got back. I needed some regular life, just for a little while. We had dinner and spent some time doing nothing in particular, and I took a cab home.

Bonnie had obviously made it back safe and sound, too. I found her sitting in her car in front of my house. "We need to talk as soon as possible," she said when I approached.

"I had a wonderful flight back, thanks for asking," I said drily.

She ignored the sarcasm. "Just be at my office tomorrow morning." With that, she left.

I felt out of my element. There were too many players in the game, and my role was unclear. But I knew that things would start to make sense and I had to play along for the time being. I was in the big leagues, but that didn't mean I was in good hands. On the contrary. No individual agent is crucial in this kind of case. Others are always waiting in the wings. There's so much riding on a case like this that getting involved can make or break your career—or cost you your life.

This new assignment put my previous jobs in a whole new light for me. I realized that the Pakistan case and the Mann case had been a kind of test. Now I was in new territory, and on top of that I was handling two cases at once. The learning curve would be steep, but I had climbed mountains before.

CHAPTER SIX

The Terrorist Misadventure

Al-Qaeda and the Taliban are all too familiar to us these days. The names bring to mind fanatics bent on violence and capable of anything. My new role was a gig like any other, but at the same time it felt extra meaningful: Doing a job on those who operate by terror felt like a bonus. I truly would have done the job for free.

The case developed gradually, but on May 8, 2002, we got a break. A U.S. born man named José Padilla (aka Abdullah al-Muhajir) was arrested while attempting to re-enter the country on suspicion of plotting an attack with a dirty bomb—an explosive that spreads radioactive material. Padilla had gotten involved with extremist Islamic groups, including Al-Qaeda. The info that led to his arrest had come from his own people. Not surprisingly, under interrogation he told the U.S. everything he knew.

Padilla gave us the information about a planned strike: The target was Manhattan. We didn't take his word for it. Another prisoner, Binyam Mohammed, backed up his account of the dirty bomb attack. Under the name of Dhiren Barot, Mohammed had been trying to board a flight back to London, where he lived, when he was profiled and arrested for questioning.

Between the two of them, we managed to compile a list of targets: They included the New York Stock Exchange and the Citigroup Center. If they pulled it off, the attack would be a disaster of enormous proportions, a horrifying follow-up to 9/11 that would devastate a still traumatized city.

After we had gotten everything we could from Padillo at Guantanamo, we offered him a way out. I was it. He would be released on a technicality, on the condition that he would introduce me to players in his world and vouch for me. Obviously, for my protection, Padillo wasn't given my real identity. In fact, he was told that I was another suspect: The story was that I was leader of a homegrown gang of anarchists, a dangerous character, and he was told to find out what I was up to.

An FBI report leaked in 2009 described the results of a search of the Maine home of James Cummings, a white supremacist who had been shot and killed by his wife. Investigators found a treasure trove of weapon ingredients: hydrogen peroxide, uranium, thorium, lithium metal, aluminum powder, beryllium, boron, black iron oxide and magnesium, as well as literature on how to build dirty bombs and information about radioactive materials. Officials confirmed the veracity of the report but said that the public was never at risk. That's no surprise: Do you think they would admit if there was a risk? When people know they're in danger, they always demand explanations, even when there are none to give. To the intelligence agencies, the public is considered to be a nuisance to be placated with lies or a paternal pat on the head. It's one side of a problem that is truly systemic. This same mistrusting attitude leads to a lack of good intelligence and redundancy, with different agencies unwittingly seeking the same information.

Another case: In April 2009, the Security Service of Ukraine announced the arrest of a legislator and two businessmen from Ternopil Oblast. Seized in the undercover sting operation was 3.7 kilograms of what was claimed by the suspects during the sale as plutonium-239, used mostly in nuclear reactors and nuclear weapons, but was determined by experts to be probably americium, a "widely used" radioactive material which is commonly used in amounts of less than one milligram in smoke detectors, but can also be used in a dirty bomb. The suspects reportedly wanted US $10 million for the material, which the Security Service determined was produced in Russia during the era of the Soviet Union and smuggled into Ukraine through a neighbouring country.

And to finish the frightening picture, a little background about dirty bombs: Little Boy, the bomb dropped on Nagasaki had an efficiency of only 1.4%. Fat Man, the bomb on Hiroshima which used a different design and a different fissile material, had an efficiency of 14% (not a big percentage). Thus, they tended to disperse large amounts of unused fissile material and fission products, which are on average much more dangerous, in the form of nuclear fallout. During the 1950s, there was considerable debate over whether "clean" bombs could be produced and these were often contrasted with "dirty" bombs. Clean bombs were often a stated goal, and scientists and administrators said that high-efficiency nuclear weapon design could create explosions that generated almost all of their energy in the form of nuclear fusion, which do not create harmful fission products.

However clean weapons have their proponents. Other theorists note that one can make a nuclear weapon intentionally dirty by "salting" it with a material that generates large amounts of long-lasting fallout when irradiated by the weapon core. These are known as salted bombs; a specific subtype often noted is a cobalt bomb[1].

If there was any doubt that the first terrorist case I was put on was a big one, it doesn't take much research, like that above, to open your eyes. It helped to justify the secrets being

---

1. For more inofrmation on Little Boy and Fat Man – Dirty bombs https://en.wikipedia.org/wiki/Dirty_bomb

kept, the way the store was being run. The people I worked with seemed extremely tense and on edge—and I could see why. They had an incredible amount at stake.

Screwing up one of their cases meant many would die. Under the circumstances, I made sure to get serious real quick.

――――――

My location was the Mile-End neighbourhood of Mont-real. I had put the word out on the street that I was the one to talk to for illegal papers. The cops knew the bad guys could probably get papers already, including passports, but only a few at a time. I would be there to offer them an easy solution to that problem. If the papers came from us, we could at least follow the movements of terrorists entering and exiting Can-ada and the U.S. It made sense—but I wondered if it was too little too late.

It didn't take long for me to start getting nods of recogni-tion, from a coffee shop owner or a person on the street. I got around on the subway—called the *metro*, in Montreal—rather than by car, since it was easier. It was on the metro that I was first approached by a man whom I had seen around whose name I later learned was Mohammed. I was relieved that I'd finally connected; I was beginning to get discouraged. The Arab area of town had over 100,000 inhabitants, so looking for those involved in extremism, rather than regular Muslims, was like trying to find a needle in a haystack.

"Assalamu Alaikum," he said tentatively.

So I look him straight in the eye and gave the proper re-sponse: "Wa-Alaikum-Salaam."

He relaxed slightly. "We will get off and go for a coffee, yes?" he asked.

"Fine with me," I replied.

From that moment on, he didn't so much as look in my direction, clearly giving the impression that he didn't know me. I certainly had no problem pressing the locator in my pocket. Wherever we ended up, my squad would have the place covered within a half hour.

We arrived at our stop, a metro station two stories underground. As soon as the doors opened, he was off like a shot. To keep up with him I would have almost had to run. Instead, I decided to do it my way; I couldn't give him control. I leisurely exited the metro and headed for the stairs. By the time I got up to the street and stepped into the warm afternoon sun, I had no idea where he was. I spotted him sitting on a stone bench near the street. He didn't look pleased.

"Are you coming or what?" he asked sternly.

"I don't run for anything or anybody," I told him. "And that includes you."

We entered a small Turkish coffee shop. I sat saying nothing for a while, just watching people walk by. I could see from his expression that he was bursting at the seams to get to the point. Finally, Mohammed asked me whether I could get him some IDs: ten sets of passports and driver's licenses or government IDs. I told him it was no problem, but that I didn't want money in return. I handed him a list: On it were the parts needed to build a dirty bomb. He took some time reading through the list, and then said he would have to check with some people before getting back to me. His measured response told me he was taking it seriously. If he had said "Sure," just like that, I would have dismissed him outright.

I gave him a phone number and told him to call me. Then I got up and left without another word. As I headed for the metro station, I felt sure he had someone watching me, so I stayed cool. I'd given him the bait and he took it—now I had to reel him in.

It felt like I was right back in the game of making contacts and buying drugs. The same cat-and-mouse routine. The higher-ups incharge of the case were thrilled and called a meeting—the kind guys like me never get invited to. Then the U.S.

rep decided one of their agents should go undercover with me. It may come as no surprise to you that I tend to disagree when such decisions come down. The gap in experience is too great. The powers just don't understand how sensitive it is on the ground, how easily things can go wrong when you throw a new ingredient into the mix. Generally I try to hold them off for as long as I can, but they always win in the end, and I end up with some cop to worry about—worst case scenario, a rookie cop. But this time there was no room to stall for time. It was an order, not a request. I wasn't thrilled, but I just hoped my partner had some street experience.

The guys upstairs also decided we should have some time to get to know each other. I was in the office talking to Bonnie when the boss walked in with my new partner, George. When he extended his hand, I declined, telling him I don't do that. It's true, I hate shaking hands; it may sound rude, but it's just one of my pet peeves, and he might as well find out right away. Still, it did nothing to diffuse the tension, and I felt a little bad for him, being put on the spot and all.

We were to spend the day getting to know each other, so off we went. But I had really no intention of spending the day icebreaking. When we got outside, I called to George, "See you!" and headed for my car.

"But we're supposed to stay together!" he called after me.

That's not my problem, I thought. I saw it as a day off.

I had barely reached my car when my beeper went off. It was my new contact, and he had left a number for me to call. I headed straight back into the office so we could record the conversation.

He told me he wanted me to meet him in New York where his friends would like to speak in person. I told him I needed to ask him some questions first. We arranged to meet for a discussion in the same cafe as last time.

George came to the meeting, and I had to admit, he did pretty well. He sat and didn't say much, which is perfect.

Along with George and myself, we had a team of four out-side, just in case. Mohammed had brought two men with him. One clearly had a higher rank, judging by the way the others deferred to him. Again they told us they wanted to pay for the papers in cash—a straight deal. I firmly told him we had all the cash we needed; we wanted the ingredi-ents on the list. George produced the copy of the list we had brought, and pushed it across the table. They told me the same thing as Mohammed had said last time: They would see if it was possible. We were no further along than before.

Over the following months, we met up another half-dozen times, always with the same results. At a certain point we were becoming very tired of the game being played. It was time to force their hand.

At the close of one meeting, I finally told them I had had enough.

"I can't be coming down here every other day to have you waste my time," I practically yelled at them. "You have my number. Call me if something changes."

I knew George would be surprised, but he said nothing. That was to his credit; he understood that I was playing good cop/bad cop. Back at the office, I got a lot of support for my move. It had gone on long enough, and everyone was tired of getting the runaround.

It took five days for them to call me again. As usual, they wanted to meet. I said that if I had to go all that way for noth-ing, I would be extremely pissed off. I was assured that I wouldn't be disappointed.

When meeting time came, we had the place blanketed with agents. A decision had been made in the higher ranks. If it turned out to be more stalling, we were to get enough audio on tape to arrest them for conspiracy for the passports, and possibly the terrorism angle, too. One of them would almost definitely break under questioning, and we would pick it up from there. But my contact surprised us all with some astonishing information. Not only did they have the ingredients for bombs, they actually had bombs ready to blow. The reason? They were planning an attack on Manhattan. And the attack was imminent.

What could I say to that? I tried to keep my cool. I could only ask the obvious question: Where in Manhattan?

"Not 'where,'" was his reply. "The whole thing." Their plan was to pull off a strike on the heart of Manhattan, a strike that would make 9/11 seem like child's play. I couldn't believe my ears. Calmly, I asked him where we fit in—what the papers had to do with it. He told me they had an escape plan—no suicide ending for these guys—and the passports were a necessary part of that. And then there was the matter of my request. They had three bombs set up in three white cargo vans. He would sell us one of them, he said, for a million dollars—they could spare it, having more than enough to carry out their mission. I agreed without hesitating.

He stared at me hard, and I returned his gaze. "I'll tell you one thing, my friend," he said, summoning the most gravity he could muster. "You better be on the level, or I swear I'll fuck you up."

"D-day" was to be Monday, five days later, with no room for discussion. He told me I was to go to a hotel and page him at 3:30 on Sunday morning. Then I was to meet him to take a look at the merchandise, whereupon he would hand over the keys to one of the vans and I would give him the keys to the hotel room with the money. Then, he suggested, I should probably hightail it out of New York.

After the meeting I made some of the most careful, detailed notes of my career. I thought about the decisions that had to be made, and for once I was glad it wasn't me that had to make them. Then George and I sat in an empty office playing gin. From time to time, one agent or another would come in and ask a question. Finally we were given the OK to go home. It had been a long day.

I was used to the tense build-up to a bust. Poor George, however, could barely sit still. I told him to calm down, but I could understand his stress. At that point, things could easily change at a moment's notice. The cops may insist on adding some new demand that you have to make palatable to the bad guys. Or, of course, the crooks may be planning to rip you off. That's something you have to try to gauge at the crucial moment of the exchange, by judging how they stand, the way they speak, whether they're looking at the door. But for now there was nothing we could do but wait. We would deal with whatever happens when the time came.

The plan for the bust was based on something called the Mexican standoff. The technique was used by the DEA for drug deals. It works like this: Two men are in one room with the drugs, two are in a room with the cash, and two are downstairs having a coffee. The two pairs of guys upstairs exchange room keys. Then one guy phones upstairs for confirmation that the drugs are there, and the other guy (that's you, by the way) phones to your room to confirm that the money is there. Then everybody goes their separate ways. It's a great method for cops because everything stays in their control. Our deal for the bomb would operate on the same principle, except we were dealing with a mobile target, and a very dangerous one: a truck loaded with explosives.

When it came time to do the deal, however, things fell apart quickly. An argument started downstairs. They wanted the money before they gave up the location of the truck. It was too dangerous to let anyone go, so the deal was squashed entirely. We received word that we were to move the money to the adjacent room, and our contacts were arrested.

It turned out that whoever was in charge of the bad guys' crew prepared well. My guy didn't know where the three trucks were. To reduce risk, the information had been shared among them on a need-to-know basis, and he didn't need to know. The sounds coming out of the interrogation room convinced me that he wasn't lying.

Still, between them, we managed to get the general location—not the exact alley, but pretty close. The key was that they were able to track where their phone calls went. With that information, we were able to hone in on a pretty small area. The spot was well chosen, mainly occupied by old and abandoned warehouses.

Unfortunately, our biggest fear was confirmed. Each truck had a manual detonator. If the police tried to stop them, the drivers had been ordered to lead them as close as possible to the middle of downtown and hit the button to cause maximum destruction. That meant we had to get them before they started the vans.

Once the intelligence was secured, we lost no time in getting to the suspected location of the trucks. It was decided that our team would split up. I would be with George. As we warily made our way down the typical vacant Manhattan alley, I couldn't help thinking how similar this was to countless scenes in Hollywood movies—but this felt nothing like entertainment. Then we heard something. George spotted the men first and froze. Using his hands, he indicated to me that they were just beyond the dumpster. I edged forward until I saw four of them standing in a group near a loading ramp. Clearly they were waiting for something or someone.

George sent the rest of the team our location. But right after that, it started to go down. The guy they had been waiting for came out of the building from the back door. Then he started handing out keys.

I had a good spot to wait for the troops, and I was in no mood to be a hero.

But my window of safety was quickly closing. I knew one thing for sure: I couldn't let them leave. Once on the road, their orders were simple: Drive to the target, abandon the trucks, leave the island, then *boom*. Should they be stopped en route and have no way out, they would use the detonator in the truck, settling for as much damage as possible. The single explosion would make it even easier for the other two trucks to avoid obstacles, since it would draw the attention of the entire city.

I knew what I had to do, but that didn't make it easy. The Lord hates a coward, I told myself, trying to gather courage. I didn't think I would survive this fight if it went on long. They were too many and they were probably armed. I wish I could say I thought of my kids or looked back on my life, but in truth, my mind was blank. I said a short prayer to the Great Spirit—not to win, but just to stay on my feet for about 15 minutes. After all, I knew they couldn't leave in the vans until I was down.

I crouched down and crept alongside the ramp, getting as close as I could. Then, in a flash, I landed in the midst of them. Strangely enough, I suddenly felt fine: My fears had vanished. I was in the middle of a fight, and as a trained fighter I was in my element.

I focused on what I knew, which is that everyone I hit had to go down and stay down. When you're fighting for your life, you don't want to pay for the same real estate twice. It's hard to gauge time in a fight, but it seemed that my feet had barely touched the ground when one of their heads exploded. Did I mention George was a crack shot? With the fracas and the targets moving so fast—and me caught in the middle of it—it took a real marksman to pull off that shot.

I needed to stay low and move around constantly to make it hard for them to have a clear shot at me. By the time a guy gets a bead on you with a gun, you have to be somewhere else already. Then I heard the siren. My focus changed in that very second, and the thought flashed through my mind that I might live through this thing. Unfortunately, changing your focus in the middle of a scrap is not a good thing. I never saw the blow that laid me out.

I woke up in the hospital. I was a little worse for wear—a mild concussion, and my head hurt—but aside from that I was fine. George had gotten out unscathed. The nurses came by and hooked me up to an IV, and I was asleep again in minutes.

I spent the next day writing notes. In the event of my death, the video would serve as testimony. A day later I was on my way home, with a well-deserved month off in front of me. Two of the bad guys were dead, one was in care down the hallway, and the other was in custody. I couldn't be anything but happy about how it turned out. Only one truck had actually contained a bomb; the others were duds. That one bomb was real, though, and definitely powerful enough to make their mission a grisly success.

This type of case was a lot more rewarding than a regular drug case, but it was similar enough that I was able to rely on my experience to get me through. Best of all, I knew I had done some real good in the world. I felt the way I did in the old days.

Still, if it was a success it was a measured one. The threat of terrorism didn't stop with that group, and it won't stop with the next one that makes the news. Their web is so vast and their reach so long, they will keep coming, again and again. If people knew about the numerous terrorist attacks attempted since 9/11, they wouldn't sleep so soundly.

CHAPTER SEVEN

As Close as the Enemy Can Get

I t was June 2002. The Manhattan terrorism case had interrupted the Hells Angels case I was working on in San Diego (to find out more, read the first *Befriend and Betray*). Developments in that case while I was absent meant we had to make several changes in our approach. We needed to improve my standing with the club and get even closer to those members who had accepted me into their social circle. But the other cases had gotten so involved that I wondered if I could really get my head back into the biker case. Cases like these are all or nothing, and it isn't so easy to change tracks again and again.

With or without me, there were surely countless meetings going on daily within the five different police forces involved. You might think that all that manpower would mean the project ran like clockwork. You'd be wrong. Each organization had its own agenda and vied to get the biggest accolades after the take-down. Then there was the matter of running every decision by the bean counters to determine who would pay for what.

Of course, no part of our caper had leaked to the press. It remained another secret in a long list of them. I wondered how much of U.S. law enforcement even knew about that threat, how close they were to disaster. None of that involved me directly, of course, and I was just glad to take some time off. I returned to my hometown to wait it out.

As it turned out, I was about to get tangled up in a case not through my handler or usual bosses, but through someone much closer to me. So much for a holiday.

My son had moved to my childhood home of Hull, which is next to Ottawa, to attend university. I used that as an excuse to park there for a little while. Since we'd been living apart, my lackluster attempts to reconnect with him had failed. Of course I blamed everyone else around me, unable to handle the guilt. But deep down I knew the burden should fall on my shoulders. I hoped my time in Hull would change that, would bring us closer together. I also had friends there and was well liked, making it a comfortable place to hang my hat for a while. The fact that everyone I knew from the old days skirted on the edges of criminal activity, if not participating in it full-on, made it feel natural, strangely enough. Between growing up with those working outside the law and now working with the cops to bust serious criminals, it seemed that this was the kind of environment I'd been destined for.

I was staying in my son's apartment temporarily. My two sisters lived across the bridge from Hull in downtown Ottawa. I hadn't seen them in a while, and it was nice to have family around again, so I started going there almost every day—never for long, but consistently.

One day I arrived to find a stranger sitting in the kitchen. He was a friend of Danny's, my sister's son. Danny wasn't at the top of my list of favorite people. He was a racist skinhead who had travelled a lot, living in Texas for a while and then Toronto.

I don't know exactly where Danny had picked up his hatred for non-whites. I knew his dad, Johnny, his uncle, Co-Co, and everyone else in his family. They were crooks, to be sure, but not racists. Johnny was part of the crew of kids I grew up with, and he ended up marrying my sister. After I'd hit the road, pursuing my relationships and my career, I'd really left that whole world behind. Johnny was dead now, as was Co-Co, murdered. One day, Co-Co was hanging out at Chez Henri, the bar we used to while away the hours in, when some Anglophone guy insulted him. Co-Co didn't say much in response, so the guy got up and headed out. He returned with a sawed-off shotgun and blew Co-Co out of his chair, killing him instantly. Others in the bar opened fire on the Anglo, killing him in a hail of bullets. With that the bar cleared and the bartender was left to call the cops. No one was ever charged for any of it, because of course no one had seen anything.

That's just the type of town I was raised in, and Danny too. But, violent or not, it doesn't jibe with the way Danny turned out. I could see him hating *Anglophones*; that would be more rooted in history.

My sister, Louise, had shown me a VHS tape of a small riot on Bank Street, in Ottawa's Glebe neighbourhood, just south of downtown. There was Danny, attacking a guy from India with a chain. He had been arrested with some of his skinhead friends, but the charges were dropped. They were all proud of the whole thing, and had taped the CBC report.

Anyway, Danny's friend needed a ride to the Ottawa-Carleton detention center to visit Danny, who was finishing up a three-month sentence for assault. I agreed to take him out there, and took the opportunity to visit with my not-so-darling nephew. On the drive there and back, Danny's friend told me all about their organization, the Heritage Front, a Canadian neo-Nazi group connected to Toronto and reaching down to the States. Listening to him kind of stirred the investigator in me, but I blew it aside. I abide by a concrete rule: Never work in your own backyard—and certainly don't do cases on people you know. Doing so would make me an informer, as opposed to an agent. The difference between the two is huge in my eyes.

Still, I couldn't help mentioning what I'd heard in one of my regular phone calls to my rabbi, J.P. He suggested that I start keeping notes on all my encounters and conversations with the skinheads. I was surprised at his interest—to me they were just a gang of idiots, not worth crossing the street for. But my policy was to follow J.P.'s instructions without question.

Danny called me about a week later. He was back on the street and said he wanted to see me, so we met for lunch.

At lunch, he quickly launched into a convoluted story. His group had been hired by two men, a Japanese and an Arab, to cause a disturbance that would create a diversion. Danny and his friends would be paid $1,000 each. That brought him to why he wanted to talk to me. They needed another man, and Danny wanted to know if I was interested. In spite of everything, I was. But not in the way he'd hoped, of course. I'd been in my line of work for so long that it was almost beyond my control: I couldn't say no to a good lead. A case was clearly developing, and I wasn't happy about it. On top of everything else, I was on holidays!

He suggested I go down and meet some of his gang and then decide. I was glad to have some time to think. I dropped him off at his mom's place and went home. I wrote my notes and called J.P. to give him a report. He said he'd make a few calls and get back to me.

After a few days of quiet, I got a call from a Mountie who had gotten my number from J.P. He wanted to speak to me. I met him and his partner for a coffee—well, they had coffee; I don't drink coffee, so I had a coke. They told me they were from INSET, the Integrated National Security Enforcement Team. It was starting to look like this crazy scheme was pretty serious.

The Mounties told me an anti-globalization movement protest was planned to take place in Calgary in June during the G8 summit in nearby Kananaskis.

A parallel protest known as "Take the Capital!" would take place in Ottawa on the same day, an option for the protesters who could not make it out West. As for the disruption planned to be made by Danny and his crew, the feds had pieced together several possibilities. They believed the skinheads would attack the protesters in order to cause a riot, which would probably only intensify when the cops moved in to break it up. That's as much as they knew, and they needed more details. The main question was *why*. It was the end of May, so I had a month. I agreed to look into it.

Every time I talked to Danny or one of his buddies, more details of the plan came to light. It was like they were getting it a piece at a time. Then the pieces suddenly started to form a clear picture, and I realized the feds seemed to have no idea what we were really facing. Once again, the best reference point is 9/11. We were looking at a similar attack, right in the nation's capital.

Things began to crystalize when, without much notice, Danny and his friends were asked to go to Toronto for an important meeting. I phoned this news in as soon as I heard. Whether INSET followed them to Toronto I don't know. Danny and his gang returned in three days, and I knew that something drastic must have happened in Ontario. Things had changed and the tone was much more serious. The cops quit joking around, too. I found out the real story after Danny phoned me and arranged a meeting at the tattoo shop one of his friends ran on Rideau Street in downtown Ottawa. When I pulled up outside the shop, Danny jumped in in a hurry. Followed by another car, he had me drive to a building on Elgin Street across from the police station. We parked on a side street and then walked into an underground parking lot. I followed Danny as he looked through the entire lot.

"It would help if I knew what the hell we were looking for," I told him.

"I'll explain later," he said.

On the way back Danny gave me a fuller picture. The role of his gang was now much more serious than disrupting a protest march. They were now supposed to detonate explosives. There were to be five men involved: a driver, a guy on-site to protect an optimal parking space, and the remaining three parked at different locations to come pick the driver and spotter up once they had abandoned their vehicle. I was supposed to drive the van, and Danny was to be the spotter and would also hold a second detonator in case the first one failed. His detonator was simple: a throwaway phone, which he would use to call a pager connected to the explosives. After the mission was accomplished, we were supposed to meet at the tattoo shop to collect our pay.

The plan was insane. Not only was I appalled that Danny would resort to aiding terrorism, but on a practical level, I knew from experience that Danny's crew would likely not make it out. With thousands of protestors, it was impossible to plan an ideal route for escape. I knew it already, but the shoddy plan reconfirmed that Danny's crew was just following someone else's instructions.

Once I got home, I called in the new information. No opinion, just the facts, which of course was enough to call for immediate action.

The next morning the cops and I met at a hotel.

It was a tense meeting. The first thing they told me was to discuss the case with no one—not even J.P. The fact that they mentioned him by name threw me off guard. That just wasn't going to fly. I owed too much to J.P. and had too much respect for the work he'd done as my rabbi to leave him out of the loop. He had gotten me out of so many jams—I owed him the truth on that basis alone. If something went wrong, I knew he could be trusted to stand up for me.

Rather than being settled during the meeting, the case seemed to be getting bigger and more complex, reaching up to higher places. This was one time when I really would have liked to hear what the brass was saying. The one thing that was clear was that they really didn't know how to handle it. I would get some instructions and try to follow them, but before I was finished I would get new orders contradicting the previous ones. I was worried that things would remain in flux until it was too late.

To be safe, I devised a Plan B of my own. I decided that whatever happened, there was no way I would drive that van to the parking spot, as per the plan Danny had told me—it was too risky. I decided that if no other plan had been formed,

I would drive the van as far from the city as possible on the Queensway, a four-lane highway passing through Ottawa. Fifteen minutes would be enough time to get far enough to minimize the damage. It wasn't much of a plan, but it was better than nothing.

As it turned out, the chief of the Ottawa police had his own plan—it was about as basic as police work can be. He simply arrested the entire group, myself included. I wasn't held for long, of course, just long enough to provide me with plausible deniability. The rest of the group was held for a couple of days. The date planned for the attack came and went without incident. It was over.

No charges were laid in the end, which surprised me. I would have liked to see them charged with conspiracy at the very least, but it wasn't my call.

Even though I'd been arrested, the truth about my role got out somehow. I had done the unthinkable: I had worked where I lived. Word spread quickly that I was a cop. My sister, Danny's mom, was furious, as of course was Danny. I had committed the biggest sin, and there was no going back. My home was no longer a haven for me.

But soon, opportunity knocked. Within a few weeks, I was told that the Americans wanted me down there for a case. I was happy to get back to work. Then I was told that I would have a partner. As you know by now, I hate that—really hate it. It's always the same: You follow every rule, but still they treat you like a kid who needs a babysitter. It feels like you're being treated like one of the bad guys, not a valuable part of their team. I have enough to worry about when I'm infiltrating a dangerous group. With a partner you can't trust, anything can go wrong. One night you're at a party and you lose track of them. What do they end up saying to two, three other people? Will it diverge from the track you've already laid down? Only you can really know all the backstories and keep the "facts" straight. But the cops just don't care; it's great for them to have two people to testify at the end of a case rather than one. It also keeps control in the hands of the higher-ups. But it does not build cohesiveness, trust and loyalty among agents.

It could have been worse, though: My partner would again be George. Bonnie informed us that for this case a polygraph test would be administrated after every outing. No problem there. When I worked the Bandidos case, their leader, George Wegers, was famous for having a private eye give his men lie detector tests. My partner George, on the other hand, seemed none too pleased about it, and I didn't really blame him.

I'm going to digress here and give you my take on lie detectors. Bear with me. I swear to tell the whole truth.

It's a big issue and I don't want to get into every aspect. Suffice to say, the polygraph test doesn't work. There are too many variables. These include the mood of the subject, their health, and the skill of the person administering the test. If you want to get technical, the test-giver is the real liar in the process. From the minute you walk in till the minute you leave, he uses tricks and deception to manipulate the testee.

Also consider that taking the test can cause tremendous anxiety in people, even those who have nothing to hide. If you take the test, you only stand to lose and have nothing to gain. That's because a favorable result on a polygraph test has no value in court. They are trying to find evidence of lying, but absence of evidence is not evidence of absence.

Then there's the possibility of error. If the machine misreads your answers, the test-giver will interpret that as a lie. Another reason the system is far from perfect.

I firmly believe that your best option, should you be asked to take a polygraph, is simply to refuse. Unfortunately, that's not always an option; for instance, your job may depend on it. So if you can't avoid the test, here are a few tips.

Above all, remember that the tester is not your friend. The polygrapher may try to convince you that he is on your side and will help you out if you'll just be truthful. That's garbage; don't buy it. You're not the one paying his salary. He has one objective: to show that you're lying. And what are his credentials? A fourteen-week course, most of which focuses on two things: running and maintaining the machine and learning the tricks of the trade. He's no scientific genius.

Here's an example of how bogus the testing situation is. They usually perform a card trick at the beginning. The pretext is to calibrate the machine, but the real reason is to make you feel unsettled. The test-giver will usually take five cards out of a deck. Pick a card, he says; look at it, but don't tell him what it is. Then he tells you he will guess the card and he instructs you to say no, regardless of whether his guess is correct. He guesses correctly, and you answer no, as instructed. The machine reads you as having lied. What the polygrapher doesn't tell you is that all the cards were identical. It's clearly about making the test subject feel vulnerable. Of course, you're not going to object; your position means you fear that the test-giver may fail you simply because he doesn't like you.

There are three basic types of questions you will be asked: relevant, irrelevant and countercheck questions. Irrelevant questions are those that are obvious, such as "What is your name?" or "Are the lights on in this room?" Relevant questions are the important ones, like "Did you leak that memo to the media?" "Have you ever stolen money from an employer?" or "Have you ever sold drugs?" What you need to watch out for is questions that start with "Have you ever." They are meant to throw you off, when in fact they have no purpose.

Say only what you need to. Yes or no answers should be sufficent for most of the test. Resist the temptation to explain your answers or to go into detail, although the polygrapher may encourage you to do so. Be courteous and cooperative, but don't offer any more information than is absolutely necessary. Your job is to control your levels. Answer questions firmly, seriously and without hesitation. This is no time to joke around or try to be crafty. You want to appear earnest, cooperative and resolute. A good strategy is to lightly jam your tongue against your side teeth, just enough to cause a little discomfort. When the polygrapher marks the sheet with a pencil, he's separating the questions. Keep the pressure on your teeth until he marks the spot so as not to cause movement from the bottom line. Also, you might not know it, but there's likely a sensor built into the chair you're sitting on. The polygraphers may ask you if you were holding something back after the wires have already been taken off. Just one last attempt to trick you.

Above all, don't admit anything that may incriminate you. No matter what the lines on the chart look like, nothing is more damaging than a confession. The polygrapher may well try to convince you that he or she can "see" a lie on your polygraph, even if there's nothing abnormal there. He may say something persuasive, like "I feel you're holding something back." Don't fall for it. Because that's the whole point: The job of polygraphs is really to extract confessions. The whole exam process is a complex ruse to make you confess to something.

The point of my telling you all this is not to show bad guys how to beat the machine. Polygraphs are a fixed game, and they can be used against anyone. The subject may seem to be lying because of embarrassment about something personal— something that's no one else's business. Or the subject might be the type of person who gets anxiety attacks when under stress. It's just not fair. The problem isn't that the test works. It's that it's believed to work.

The best policy is to politely refuse to take any test that isn't required by the courts. But I leave that up to you. Many people are too intimidated to say no. It can make it look like you have something to hide. Ask your lawyer whether you should take the test. If the lawyer says no, let him or her deal with defending your decision.

CHAPTER EIGHT

Arbeit Macht Frei
("Freedom through work"
sign on concentration camp gate)

By now you may realize that Henry Cludd became something of a nemesis for me. I ended up spending years chasing him down, listening to recorded phone conversations, poring over files with his name in them. It almost became an obsession.

Along with others, I've gathered a vast amount of intelligence on the man, and I came to realize something obvious. His life experiences made him what he is—just like they do for any of us. In fact, his life and mine had certain parallels. For instance, we both developed our area of expertise around the same time, but in different parts of the world.

Though he is a villain and a killer, I can see him also as a tragic figure who was destined for a life of violence. And in certain moments I can admit to myself that I could have easily disappeared into the dark side, as he did.

In this chapter I will delve deep into the past to show you how a man like Henry Cludd could come to be. Nature or nurture? As far as the debate goes, I believe that both play an important role in child development—that seems undeniable. So it's fitting to begin the story with his mother. The research I did on her life crushed me—brought tears to my eyes, then anger, and even shame. Was she able to give him the love he needed, or did the death and destruction that surrounded her youth impair her ability to care, to connect?

Estzer was born in 1929 in Békéscsaba, one of the oldest towns in Hungary. The area has been inhabited since the ancient times. In the Iron Age, the area had been conquered by the Scythians, then the Celts, then then the Huns. After the Hungarian Conquest, there were many small villages in the area. They would routinely close ranks when threatened and spread throughout the valley when peace was upon them.

The village of Csaba was first mentioned in the 1330s. Besides Csaba, eight other villages stood where now the town stands. When the Turks conquered the southern and central parts of Hungary, and these territories became part of the Ottoman Empire, the town survived, but eventually the people rebelled against the hated Turks. They paid dearly and almost became extinct in the 17th century. The Turks didn't play well with others, simply killing as many people as they could.

By 1858, the railway line reached the town. This brought development: new houses and factories were built and the town began to prosper in a real way. Still, by the end of the 19th century, the unemployment was causing great tension, and in 1891 a revolt was suppressed with the help of Romanian soldiers. But after the revolt was put down, the Romanians stayed. The town was again obliged to go to bed with the enemy and wait—wait and survive like they had through the ages.

The area had been through much tumult throughout the ages, had survived invasions and revolts, with power changing hands and the Hungarian people surviving, enduring, persisting throughout. But Estzer was unconcerned with her town's dramatic past for the moment. She was busy planning her 15th birthday party—the first party her mother was allowing boys to attend. Her best friend, Doro (short for Doroty) was with her, helping her meticulously plan everything, from the decorations to the seating arrangements.

Doro's father was part Canadian and had spent six years there before the war. When he had returned, he brought some American dance records with him. Whenever Doro visited Estzer, she would bring a record over. They had no idea that the discs were considered serious contraband that could have got them in trouble. They had six albums in all—more than enough to impress their friends.

––––––––––

No battles were fought in their region of Hungary during World War II, and it was left mostly untouched for the majority of the war. Still, on the political front, things became fairly messy. Hungary made the mistake of aligning itself with the Axis powers, while simultaneously negotiating with the Americans and the British. When Hitler learned of Hungary's involvement with the Allies he was furious, and invaded the country on March 19, 1944. In fact, "invaded" might be too strong a term, since in fact they encountered little resistance.

The main victims of this occupation would be the Jews and Gypsies, who had remained relatively unpersecuted in the area for so long. Under the Nazis, however, the Nuremburg laws were quickly put in effect and Hungarian Jews like Doro and Estzer were no longer safe. In no time at all the German system was up and running slickly and seamlessly— an accomplishment quite different from the comparatively botched invasion when Germany conquered Poland.

By May, a number of local Jewish businesses and factories had been closed. Finally, Doro's father decided to act. Through underground contacts in Budapest, he acquired Canadian identification papers for himself and his family. But by the time he returned home, his family had already been taken, along with most other local Jews, and were being held at a tobacco drying plant. This included Estzer and her family. Doro's father wasn't a particularly brave man, but he had become a desperate one. Without hesitating, he went to the German authorities and demanded that his family be released. The officer in charge listened and carefully took notes, writing down the names of the family and all the pertinent information. Then he had Doro's father arrested and taken away. He was never heard from again.

———————

Doro and Estzer were among the strongest and healthiest prisoners in the camp at the former factory. They spent their time helping with smaller children and the elderly. At night they would sit and talk—amazingly, the same way every teenage girl in the world talks, if she has the chance. They gossiped about their parents, their neighbors—and, of course, boys.

They would leave their quarters every day, hand-in-hand, and go seek donations of food from people they knew in town. They had grown up together, and had been best friends all their lives; they would get through this together. On the surface, it didn't really seem that awful—the constant turnover of people even created some excitement, especially when friends and acquaintances turned up among the newcomers in the camp.

By the time the girls arrived, there were almost 4,000 people left in the improvised ghetto; 4,666 had already been deported. But eventually the girls' time ran out. Early in the morning of June 24, the Germans arrived with their clipboards and started calling out names. Doro's family was on the list. Doro clung to her friend; a guard had to grab her by the hair to pull her away. Just like that, she was gone from Estzer's life.

In fact, Doro's father had saved his family after all, but not in the way he had intended. Because of his intervention, the family ended up being among some 2,000 Jews sent to Strasshof, a concentration camp near Vienna. Almost 21,000 Jews from Hungary were brought to Strasshof as a result of an agreement made that June between SS officer Adolf Eichmann and the Relief and Rescue Committee of Budapest. The deal stipulated that Eichmann would spare the lives of one million Hungarian Jews in exchange for certain goods, including 10,000 trucks. He would start by interning 30,000 Hungarian Jews in Austria, as a gesture of goodwill that he hoped would move the agreement forward. Britain and the U.S., however, eventually refused the deal.

That fact is worth considering when you recall that both Britain and the U.S. claim that they didn't know about the genocide of the Jews until after the war. Aside from reluctance to equip the enemy with 10,000 trucks for its troops, Britain had several other reasons to refuse. The Allies were confident by that time that they would win the war. When they knew for sure, much of their focus immediately shifted to the possible advantages that could be secured in the post-war world. The most compelling question in their eyes was who would get what territory. But there was also the less appealing question of what to do with close to a million displaced people. Who would provide for them? Where would they be housed until the end of the war? The easiest option, it seemed, was to let the Germans hold on to the Jews and "deal with the problem." If there were any survivors, the Soviets could take care of them. A caring approach to humanity it was not.

The deal ultimately tanked. But while it was on the table, the SS was paid five million francs in exchange for the 21,000 Jews sent to Strasshof in Austria—including Doro and her family.

Amazingly, almost all of the Jews at Strasshof survived the war— even the elderly and children. That's not to say the conditions were good by any stretch of the imagination. But at least it wasn't a death camp; most were able to survive.

When they arrived in Strasshof, the new arrivals were disinfected, then registered and photographed and assigned to different slave labour camps. According to the camp records, there were 450 children under the age of two, 1,000 aged three to six, 1,800 aged seven to 12 and 750 aged 13 to 14. Doro was put in the children's daycare while her parents worked.

Living conditions were far from easy. Compared to what their lives were like before the war, it was like another universe, and just surviving from day to day was a struggle. But having her family there sustained Doro, gave her hope and strength, even in the hardest times. No matter how much she had to deal with, her last thoughts before going to sleep were always of home, her life before the war and, of course, her friend Estzer. She waited and waited for Estzer to arrive at the camp in a new shipment of prisoners, but she never appeared.

Meanwhile, back in Hungary, on June 26, 1944, the Germans returned to the tobacco factory. This time everyone left was moved, Ezster included. They assigned the prisoners different boxcar numbers, but there was only one destination: Auschwitz.

A transport list shows that Estzer was moved by train along with some 3,000 other prisoners. They travelled for three miserable days. There were nearly one hundred people to a boxcar, with no food or water. It was hell on earth. There was screaming and wailing, the prisoners calling out to God; but it seemed that God was not listening. There wasn't enough room for everyone to sit. The young people quickly organized a rotating seating plan. On the second day, several elderly people died, and with that every semblance of order disappeared. With no toilet facilities, the stench soon became intolerable.

At ten in the morning on the third day, the train slowed and eventually stopped. The passengers waited for over an hour before the door was opened. The sight that greeted them was a line of soldiers, some with machine guns and others with dogs. Men in striped clothing—prisoners of the concentration camp themselves—pulled people out and herded them down the ramp. There was general screaming. After three days of being unable to move, the frenzied prisoners spilled frantically out of the boxcar. Pressure from the rear of the car, from those desperate to get out and breathe the air, heightened the horror and chaos.

Estzer held her mother close and together they jumped out. Leaving everything they had on the ramp, they were pushed towards the front, where the new arrivals were being split into two groups. One of the camp prisoners in stripes said quietly, "Tell them you're a professional seamstress," and quickly moved away.

Estzer and her mother were moved through the first selection on the ramp without uttering a word. Along with the SS officers, two men in white medical coats assessed each prisoner and decided their fate. One of the men in medical garb directed them to the right with a small wave of his hand. With that single gesture, their lives had been spared. But they knew nothing of their good forture, so there was no joy at surviving; they had no idea that those directed to the left had been chosen for immediate "processing." Estzer's mother was sent to the BIII section, known as Mexico. Estzer, herself was sent to BIIe: the Gypsy camp.

Estzer became prisoner B-147821. Despite the selection that had been made, it became clear to most people that Estzer wasn't actually a Gypsy—a fact that may have saved her life. Being in the wrong camp seemed to offer her a kind of invisibility. She made herself small and kept out of the way.

In the meantime, things were going badly for the German armies. The Soviets were moving quickly from the East, and the Allies had landed in Normandy. Those outside the camps were beginning to see the writing on the wall. And the shift started to be reflected within the camps. People were still being killed daily by the thousands, but something had changed. The efficiency of the killing machine around Estzer seem to be breaking down bit by bit. Instinctively she knew she had to hold on just a little longer.

But then the barrack leader posted a list of prisoner numbers. Those on the list were to report for transport to Block 10 for "medical examination." Estzer's number was on the list. She lay awake most of the night thinking about her friends, her mother and her former life, sure that her fate was sealed.

Carl Clauberg is an example of the kind of depraved individual who determined the fate of people who ended up in Auschwitz—people like Estzer. Clauberg, a professor of gynaecology, had a kind face; the monster in him was well concealed. He came to the Auschwitz death camp as more than a willing participant; he initiated new atrocities daily, sick experiments that were products of his own twisted mind. He was given Block 10 for his pseudo-medical activities. Clauberg's primary interest was sterilization. During his experiments, he injected various chemical substances into the uteruses of thousands of women, Jewish and otherwise, without anaesthetics, causing excruciating pain.

Clauberg's example shows that even the most seemingly civilized and educated among us can contain a terrifying beast within. Usually we envision Nazis—the brown shirts, and then the SS—as brutes and thugs, certainly not as cultivated, intelligent people. But the Nazis made a very hospitable home for psychopaths of all kinds.

For years after the war, many horror stories involving scientists and doctors were uncovered. A few in this gallery of monsters—such as the notorious Doctor Mengele—still remain vivid in the collective memory, their macabre role in the camps often reported in books, documentaries and websites.

Carl Clauberg's unspeakable criminal performances are weirdly accessible to peruse, some 75 years later, via the internet:

> *In 1942 the good doctor approached Heinrich Himmler (who knew of him through his treatment of the wife of a senior SS officer) and asked him to give him an opportunity to sterilize women en masse for his experiments. Himmler agreed and Clauberg moved to Auschwitz concentration camp in December 1942. Part of the Block number 10 in the main camp became his laboratory. Clauberg looked for an easy and cheap way to sterilize women. He injected formaldehyde preparations into their uteruses—without anaesthetics. All of his test subjects were Jewish women who suffered permanent damage and serious infections. Some of the subjects died because of the tests. Estimates of those who survived but were sterilized are around 700.*
>
> *When the Red Army approached the camp, Clauberg moved to Ravensbrück, a women's concentration camp, to continue his experiments on Romani women. Soviet troops captured him there in 1945.*
>
> *After the war in 1948 Clauberg was put on trial in the Soviet Union and received 25 years. Seven years later he was released in the framework of a prisoners of war exchange between the Soviet Union and West Germany and returned to West Germany, where he was reinstated at his former clinic based on his prewar scientific output. Bizarre behavior, including openly boasting of his "achievements" in "developing a new sterilization technique at the Auschwitz concentration camp", destroyed any chance he might have had of staying unnoticed. After public outcry from groups of survivors, Clauberg was arrested in 1955 and was put on trial. He died of a heart attack in his cell before the trial could start. (From Wikipedia.)*

Additional experiments using sulphanilamide were also conducted against the prisoners.

For the benefit of the German Army, whose frontline soldiers suffered greatly from gas gangrene, a type of progressive gangrene, doctors at the Ravensbruck concentration camp performed studies to test the effectiveness of sulphanilamide and other drugs in curbing such infections. They inflicted battlefield-like wounds in victims, then, infected the wounds with bacteria such as streptococcus, tetanus, and gas gangrene. The doctors aggravated the resulting infection by rubbing ground glass and wood shavings into the wound, and they tied off blood vessels on either side of the injury to simulate what would happen to an actual war wound. Victims suffered intense agony and serious injury, and some of them died as a result. (From pbs.org.)

This is the kind of world Estzer lived in as a teenager.

The Germans abandoned Auschwitz on January 21, 1945; the Russians liberated it on January 27. The question that faced the Allies then was what to do with all the displaced people who had been freed. It was a problem that affected their approach during the war in disturbing ways: For instance, when it came to deciding whether to bomb crematoriums in the camps. In the last years of the war, they passed up many opportunities to demolish them. Some might say their reluctance was due to concern about having countless rescues on their hands. It is also widely held that things could have been brought to an end a lot more quickly—so why weren't they? Again and again, the Allies flew right over the camps to drop bombs on the German infrastructure, giving the inmates false hope that their day was coming. When freedom finally came, it was not at the hands of the Allies but the Soviets. For some, liberation brought the chance for retribution. Many prisoners finally struck back at the Germans and collaborators at whose hands they had suffered. How do you pay back such monstrous acts? In many cases, death seemed too small a price to pay.

Estzer—15 years old and weighing just 60 pounds—lay on the floor between two cots in the "recovery room," waiting for her turn to be taken to the gas chamber. Even in her weakened condition she could sense the change in the air. Then all at once the action reached her. The orderlies—other Jewish prisoners—were in a panic, grabbing whoever was within reach and dragging them outside. She found the strength to roll herself under the cot and lay still. That's where she was found by the Soviet soldier who carried her to the infirmary. Though battered and bruised, starved and mentally destroyed, she had survived.

As for Doro, she returned to Hungary on September 6, 1945, determined to go back to her former life—but that life no longer existed. The war had changed her world irrevocably. Along with all the loss, new dangers had emerged. The liberation of the Jews represented a grave threat to Hungarian collaborators and members of the secret police who had taken part in the deportations. Then there was the return of stolen possessions. When the Jews had been taken, their belongings had ended up in the eager hands of their former friends and neighbors, who were by no means looking forward to having to face the former owners of the property they now enjoyed.

Doro had filled her head with visions of a triumphant return, with friends and neighbors lining the streets and cheering. She remembered her family's little house at the edge of town and the rosebush-lined path leading to the front door. By train and truck, often walking, she had made the long journey home, and when she saw the ten-kilometer sign she felt a surge of excitement. But the sight that greeted her when she arrived was almost too much to bear. The memory of her home had sustained her throughout her ordeal. The modest, ordinary house had been transformed in her imagination, gaining the beauty and grandeur of a fairy tale.

When she stood in front of the building in 1945, she was devastated. The little house was a shell of what it had been. All the wood had been removed: windows, doors, everything. The wreck that stood before her was an awful embodiment of the ruin the war had wrought. She walked into what had been the family room and collapsed on the floor; she stayed there for a long time.

Sometime in the early evening, her neighbour, Mr. Rubin, stood above her and shook her lightly.

"You must not stay here," he said gently. "It's a dangerous place at night. Come with me."

She rose without question. Mr. Rubin took her suitcase and led her to his house. He fed her a thick soup and they ate in silence.

"They took everything," was all she could say.

"It doesn't matter now, child," Mr. Rubin said. "The life you remember is no longer here. This is a dangerous place for us Jews. Some people are saying it's all our fault; other are afraid that those who were taken away will return and demand their property back. Either way, it's over for us."

"Why do you stay?" she asked.

"At my age..." he smiled and shook his head. "I'm too old, where would I go? I can't leave, although they wish I would. I am a living reminder of their collaboration." He got up from the table. "You will sleep here tonight and we'll talk tomorrow."

He set her up on a straw mattress in the spare room and covered her with a heavy blanket. She spent the next few days resting and regaining her physical and mental strength. When she was strong enough, he sat her down to tell her what she'd been longing to hear: Before Doro had arrived, Estzer had visited looking for word of her. She had with her a one-year-old boy. She could not stay long, so she had left a parcel for Doro, knowing she would eventually return to her home.

Mr. Rubin placed the box in front of Doro and she opened it. Inside was a letter, some other documents and a roll of bills in the forint, the new Hungarian currency. It also contained a pendant with a small portrait of the two girls. Doro read the letter and tears filled her eyes. It was warm and full of news about Estzer's life since the two had been parted. It also told Doro that the documents in the box were for Estzer's son—Henry.

After Auschwitz had been liberated, Estzer had met a Canadian soldier. She also became a mother, from a rape she had suffered in the last days of the war. Even so, she and the soldier got married. Her husband was helping her immigrate to Canada, but she wouldn't—or couldn't—take her baby boy. She wanted to put her old life, with all its pain and horror behind her, and the child, who had been conceived in such violence, would be a constant reminder of that time. She left him with the local nuns, until Doro could come and take him. The money Estzer had left was to help Doro and baby Henry settle into a new life. And the pendant was to be a reminder of their happiest days together.

The next morning, Mr. Rubin took Doro to the convent. She was shocked at the condition of the orphanage. There were three children to a crib, with others on rags laid upon straw. Rendering assistance to religious institutions was not a priority for the communist government installed by the Soviets, so the nuns lived on donations and good will, both of which were in short supply.

Doro knew she and the child would be unable to stay in the town. Mr. Rubin took her to the train station. She would head for Budapest. She had decided on a new life and a second chance. She tried to give Mr. Rubin money for everything he'd done, but he wouldn't hear of it. As the train started moving toward the city, she visualized how her new life would be: It was scary, but it was exciting.

By that time, religion had changed its meaning for Doro: It had become linked with pain and survival. She took a long look in the mirror and realized that she could easily pass as Christian—no one would assume she was a Jew. With that choice, she put fear behind her. Her family would roll over in their grave if they knew of her decision. But she knew that sooner or later, Jews would end up as scapegoats again. That was how it went throughout history for Jews in the region. Their safety depended on the whim of this or that tyrant. They would face exile and aggression at every turn. Doro no longer wanted to be a part of it. She would raise a boy who would be more than a non-Jew; he would be an anti-Semite, someone whom no one would dare call a Jew. If her resolve ever wavered, she told herself, she would visit the Jewish cemetery in Budapest. Hundreds of thousands of Jews are buried in its expansive grounds. One section contains a large Holocaust memorial wall with the names of thousands of Jews from the city who lost their lives to the Nazis.

When Doro arrived in Budapest, she went to the commissar's office. There she registered as the widow of a Russian soldier who was killed in action. She was given a small apartment and told to report for factory work the following week.

The years began to flow one into another easily, as Doro had hoped. It seemed that the pain and violence she had experienced would remain in the past. She and her adopted child, Henry, lived reasonably well in the small flat provided for factory workers by the government. She did the best she could for him.

But Henry was different from other boys. As she watched him grow, Doro felt a growing sense of unease.

He was ten years old when his cat died. For most kids, this would be a traumatic event; but Henry calmly put the animal into a bag and buried it in the small garden out back. He showed no emotion and he never mentioned the incident again.

Doro would sometimes lose her temper when Henry misbehaved. When he was fourteen, she tried to give him a whack on the side of the head. Moving as fast as a cobra, he reached up and grabbed her by the wrist. He stared at her expressionlessly, and looking into his eyes she felt frightened. She had seen eyes like that a long time ago.

That's when Doro started to fear for her life.

Eventually Henry began hanging with a bad crowd, breaking into homes, stealing cars and shoplifting. He often disappeared for days at a time. Soon he was caught attempting to burglarize a store. He was the only one of his group of friends to get caught, but he refused to cooperate with the police, Ratting out his friends wasn't even a consideration. It was an explosive start to his lifelong relationship to crime —to a darkness that would always shadow him.

And then he lost the one source of good he seemed to have around him. Doro died from complications resulting from the treatment she had been subjected to in Auschwitz. She died while he was dealing with the legal fallout from the burglary, when he needed her the most. When he learned of her death, he didn't ask for details. All that mattered was that she was now unable to help him. He was alone and had to find his own way out of his predicament. He felt no sadness at losing her. In fact, he felt nothing at all.

Henry had no adult figure in his life to step in and guide him. He was alone in the world. But surprisingly, when he was sent to a youth prison he found himself in his element. His toughness and refusal to compromise was quickly noticed by recruiting agents. Criminal groups and secret police alike commonly used detention facilities as de facto training centers and as a source of new agents to perform particular assignments. Henry's potential soon came to the attention of a former KGB major by the name of Jivco. The boy clearly showed promise.

After twenty months in prison, Henry was surprised to learn that he had a visitor. Dressed in full uniform, Jivco didn't waste time on small talk.

"You will be released into my custody," he said to Henry.

Henry didn't ask who Jivco was or where he was taking him, and Jivco noted this with satisfaction. He had immediately accepted the man's authority: He had passed his first test. Jivco told him that a car would pick him up the next morning. He would then be taken to a military school where he would acquire the skills he would need for his future. Again, not a word of questioning or disagreement was uttered by the young man.

———————

Henry excelled in his new environment. He relished the discipline, structure and sense of security. Most of his education focused on firearms training and English. With his intelligence, he took to the program like a fish to water. Still, he was a brooding cadet who gave no impression of being happy. The administration noted this fact in his file. He kept to himself and worked hard at his studies. His life seemed bereft of joy.

A year to the day after he had started at the military school, he was called to the office and told to get his things together. He was being released the following day.

A car was waiting for him at the gate outside the school. They drove in silence; Henry watched the scenery go by. The car took him directly to the airport, where he boarded a two-hour flight to Moscow. By this time, Henry started to get concerned. He had never been to Moscow, and had heard some grim stories about what went on there.

Henry didn't know it, but his destination was the Hungarian embassy. That would be the base for his next level of training, where he would learn things that would make him an extremely dangerous person—he would learn how to be a spy.

By this time, Henry had matured. He was handsome in a roguish way, with a suave and distinguished air. In formal attire, he wouldn't have looked out of place on the cover of a magazine. His calm, confident demeanor might have concealed a stone-cold heart; but most people don't look that carefully. His steady gaze suggested he knew something you didn't—or was capable of acts that the rest of us could never imagine. His smile was never open but was somehow incomplete.

He had the ability to manipulate, using a charming smile or friendly manner when he needed to. But his surplus of confidence almost became a deficit. People below him saw him as arrogant; his superiors saw him as a potential rival. They didn't know that his ruthlessness and detachment was really rooted in fear. He trusted no one, and because of his isolation and his difficult past had a deep fear of abandonment, which he masked with false bravado.

Henry was given a small apartment near the embassy, and for a year he worked diligently, taking classes in English and electronics, firearms and photography. Where was it all leading? He was beginning to feel like a horse at the gate, waiting for the starting gun to go off.

Finally, Henry got a call from Jivco: He had a job for Henry. It would be a chance to prove himself and make some money to start a new life. Henry agreed without hesitation. He was ready for anything.

It must have looked like some TV drama: police vehicles racing toward Povarsky street in the center of Moscow, lights flashing and sirens wailing, responding to a report of shots fired. A crime boss, 75-year-old Aslan Usoyan, had been wounded in an attack. The news reported:

...he later died after being taken to Botkin Hospital. Over the years 'Grandpa Hassan' had managed to survive at least two previous assassination attempts: A would-be killer missed him in Sochi in 1998, and another one seriously injured Usoyan and his bodyguard in a Moscow shooting.

The reports said the assassin used a silenced 9 mm assault rifle designed for Soviet special operations forces. Of course, information doesn't flow especially freely in Russia; due to pressure from above, not everything is reported or reported accurately. There was a shallow interpretation of events and a biased explanation of possible motives and perpetrators. They were correct, however, about the weapon that was used: *"When disassembled, the rifle can fit into a briefcase. The weapon is fitted with a silencer and muzzle flash reducer, making it near impossible to detect the location of a shooter."*

The story continues:

One of Usoyan's bodyguards reportedly returned fire with several blind shots, but the fact that it took some time for police to find shooter's position showed that the bodyguard had failed completely at locating the sniper. The cops were slow to arrive and took care of the collateral damage first, which gave the killer plenty of time to leave the area. Also of note is that Val rifles can also easily shoot through body armour, and are capable of piercing a 6-millimeter-thick sheet of steel. The killer report-edly used armour-piercing bullets in the assassination.

After the sniper shot Usoyan in the head, a woman walking near the mob boss stepped into the assassin's firing line. According-ing to Life News daily's timeline, the hitman attempted to move her by shooting her in the thigh. When she remained upright, she was shot again in the chest and fell, allowing the sniper to hit Usoyan once more as his bodyguards grouped around their wounded boss.

The young woman, a waitress at the restaurant who was walking Usoyan to the exit, was rushed to a hospital for surgery and remained in critical condition due to heavy blood loss. The sniper's perch was discovered to be a stairwell between the fifth and sixth floor of a building facing the restaurant's yard. There, detectives found a folding chair, six used Val cartridges, three cigarette butts, sporting trousers and a piece of cloth.

Eventually, the waitress died—collateral damage. A finger-print of the hitman's hand was reportedly taken from an open windowpane. That should surprise no one. The police de-clared that a print was found in most major crime cases in Russia. It's very convenient if they decide they need to charge someone for the sake of expedience or politics. Shocking per-haps, but that's just the way things are done over there. Some believe it's a glimpse into the future of the West, that govern-ment and organized crime will become indistinguishable. However, in today's Russia you can use force to get your way with government agencies; you still need to be a little subtler on western shores. The difference can become glaring: There are a number of stories that show that Russian gangsters in North America haven't been able to adapt in a timely manner.

The assassin—none other than Henry—slipped away from the scene without being noticed and was soon in his car head-ing home. He performed breathing exercises to calm himself; his adrenalin was still pumping. He felt incredible.

In the days following the hit, he expected someone to visit him or at least contact him. But aside from the appearance of an envelope of cash, which he found on his bed, things went on exactly the same as before. He concluded that that in itself was supposed to be a lesson. Men like him need to be able to take extraordinary actions and then return to their lives, quietly waiting to be called upon again. There was no one he could share his achievement with, no one to help him celebrate. He had no one he could trust—and that was as it should be.

A few weeks later, an envelope appeared in his mailbox. Inside was a brief note, unsigned, instructing him to learn the rules on the other sheet—not just to memorize them, but to understand them. Then he was to burn the paper and wait for further instructions.

The list looked something like this.

CODE OF CONDUCT

1. Forsake all relatives—mother, father, brothers, sisters...
2. Not have a family of his own—no wife, no children; this does not however, preclude him from having a lover.
3. Never, under any circumstances, work, no matter how much difficulty this brings, but live only on means gleaned from member activities.
4. Help other members—both by moral and material support, utilizing the commune of members.
5. Keep secret all information about the whereabouts of accomplices.
6. In unavoidable situations, take the blame for someone else's crime; this buys the other person time of freedom.
7. Demand inquiry for the purpose of resolving disputes in the event of a conflict between oneself and other members.
8. If necessary, participate in such inquiries.

9. Carry out any punishment of offending member as decided by the group.
10. Not resist carrying out the decision of punishing an offending member who is found guilty, with punishment determined by the group.
11. Have a good command of the members' jargon.
12. Not gamble without being able to cover losses.
13. Teach the trade to young beginners. Have, if possible, informants from the rank and file.
15. Not lose your reasoning ability when using alcohol.
16. Have nothing to do with the authorities, nor participate in public activities, nor join any community organizations.
17. Not take weapons from the hands of authorities; not serve in the military.
18. Make good on promises given to other members.

The code appealed to Henry, to his taste for rigor and concision. The rules existed to keep soldiers in line, to give the higher-ups a legitimate way to take out an employee permanently if it suited their needs. That was no problem for him. He was no idealist and had no illusions.

On a snowy Monday morning at 7:30, Henry noticed a black car in front of his building. He knew instantly that it was for him. He didn't recognize the driver, but nonetheless he got in the back seat and looked out the window silently. He was driven across town, finally arriving at a small office building. The driver opened the garage door with a device in the car, and once he pulled in, the door closed behind them. Only then did the driver turn to him to speak.

"I am Sergio," he said with a smile. "Do not be alarmed. This is a great day for you."

That day he became a made man: a thief-in-law.

Soon after, he was transferred to the West Coast of North America. As a leader of Russian crime activities in the west, Jivco had interests from Vancouver to San Diego. Henry's job was to run several crews, each of which had their own region and specialty. Because of his English abilities, along with his knowledge of several Slavic languages, he could organize and supervise the gangs that worked independently of each other and help mediate and settle disagreements. Of course, having administrators costs money. The crews would have to pay tribute to the new chain of command in return for the protection and assistance it brought.

But Jivco had something for Henry to take care of before his transfer to the U.S. Jivco had been informed that a Pakistani warlord was arranging to send shipments of heroin to the U.S. via an Asian-Pakistani network. The Russians handled about eighty percent of the heroin from that area for their own network. So, they were very unhappy about this new development. The fist had to come down.

A short time later, the warlord in question was standing in a small post office in Chitril. Several men wearing ski masks burst in and opened fire with AK-47s. The five employees didn't stand a chance, nor did the three men in the back office – nor, most certainly, did the warlord. Then they were gone. The entire attack had lasted just five minutes.

Jivco was pleased his young protégé had done well. Henry had showed real leadership. Soon he could begin his work representing Jivco's interests on the West Coast. Jivco arranged for Henry's voyage to Vancouver to be another major lesson. He would travel by ship, as a crew member under the command of Jivco's brigadier. It would be a fast and direct way for him to learn the ropes.

Rule number one, he soon learned, was never do anything for free—unless the boss tells you to. More than any milieu Henry had witnessed before, everything revolved around money. And his new crew had their own special means of making it: the slave trade.

Henry had no qualms about playing a part in the sex trade, nor did he worry about its victims. That wasn't the way he saw the world: Human trafficking was just another industry to him. The women weren't victims, to his mind, whether he dealt with them personally or not. They were merely tools of the trade. Henry had had his share of sexual encounters, but never did they verge on developing into relationships. He just didn't feel the need. Jivco had sensed rightly when he'd decided to put Henry on a "skin run"—the horrible term used in that world. Henry was consistent, and wouldn't stray from seeing women as merchandise; emotional involvement wasn't an option. Dealing with slaves would also give Henry useful experience in leading with an iron fist and dominating a group of people. Working with Jivco's slave runners also helped him make many useful contacts. He met as many people as he could—his street sense told him that they could be useful down the road.

The voyage went smoothly. There were no major problems, except for one girl who refused to accept her new life. She had to be terminated, her body thrown overboard.

Their first stop was Amsterdam. There the girls were put to work for a few weeks. The choice of location wasn't random: The legality of prostitution in Amsterdam gave the girls the impression that all was lost—that the police wouldn't help even if they knew what was happening. In truth, the Dutch have a special squad to look after women in the trade; but the girls knew nothing about it.

Henry spent much of the week in Amsterdam making arrangements for their next destination: Tel Aviv. There supplies were brought on board and the girls were loaded into the hull of a small ship to make the trek across the Atlantic to the U.S. via Israel. Additional girls picked up in Tel Aviv brought the total to one hundred passengers, with a crew of just eight.

Human trafficking and forced prostitution are an enormous problem in Canada and one that is severely underreported. The nightmare of human slavery and its implications were also a part of the tangle of threads pulling Henry's world and mine together. It was as though a collision course had been set, and we were two cars speeding toward a single point. The crash to come would kill one or both of us. Throughout my career, Henry's world would become increasingly tied together, directly or indirectly. And, though in very different ways, Shannon's death loomed over both of us.

CHAPTER NINE

The Judas Files

Once entangled, the Church and the underworld may enter into doubtful undertakings that can lead to the highly lucrative business of blackmail, and thus in turn bring Henry and my worlds together.

It was years after the war before the truth about the involvement of top rankers within the Polish Catholic Church in Polish politics, was finally revealed. What happened during the transition from the Nazi to the Communist regimes represents one of the darkest aspects of my account. An article by Jonathan Luxmoore, published in *The Tablet*, does a better job of telling the story than I could.

Poland fears its Judas files
(Adapted with permission of author)

After the fall of the Communist empire, a number of countries in Eastern Europe released their secret police files. It was an attempt to overcome the past by exposing its sinister secrets. Now Poland is following suit. Inevitably, as the correspondent in Warsaw explains, some people—including some in the Catholic Church—are feeling nervous.

Last weekend Poland seemed to have taken a belated but important step towards reckoning with its Communist past when its Parliament named a team of lawyers and historians to open up the secret police archives. Victims of repression will have the right to inspect the files kept on them, and researchers will have access to material pre-

viously classified under Poland's 30-year rule. Yet the news has touched sensitive nerves, and not everyone has welcomed it.

A decade ago, the country's first post Communist premier, Tadeusz Mazowiecki, pledged to draw a "thick line" under the past. A judicial commission has so far investigated 1,120 Communist-era crimes—far fewer than the 12,000 scrutinized from the much shorter Nazi period. Only 400 suspects have been identified, and only 80 brought to court. A mere 25 have been convicted and sentenced. And although 2,450 death sentences are being re-examined, because of suspicion that they were passed for political reasons, no more than a dozen of Poland's 25,000 Communist-era judges have lost their privileged pension status, and no charges have been brought.

This could all begin to change once the files and folders come up for inspection. And among the institutions facing close scrutiny is Poland's majority Catholic Church, following new claims by a Catholic historian that it was more deeply infiltrated by Communist agents than previously supposed.

"The heroic resisters were probably more numerous, but there were also traitors in the Church," explains Andrzej Grajewski. "Since they're guilty of grave sins against society, they should apologies and accept the consequences. People who collaborated shouldn't be holding important church positions."

Grajewski's recent book, The Judas Complex, *compares the role of Catholic agents and informers in Eastern Europe under Communist rule. He estimates that around one in ten Polish priests acted as informers during the post-war Stalinist period, and that the secret police later ran as many as 200 church agents in each of the 22 counties of Poland.*

The Church would be wise to collect the facts itself, Grajewski argues, before they are brought to light through the new National Memorial Institute, where documents from the courts and prisons of the Communist era are housed. "Some church leaders seem ready to confront the issue, whereas others have tried to marginalize it by claiming that the one-time agents have all died out," says the his-

torian, who co-edits one of the two top-selling Catholic newspapers in Poland, the weekly Gosc Niedzielny (Sunday Visitor). "It would be better for the Church to establish the truth before it is revealed by sensation-seekers or people with an interest in causing harm."

Until now, Poland's 120 Catholic bishops have avoided discussing collaboration claims. Their Jesuit spokesman, Fr Adam Schulz, thinks Grajewski lacks a "sense of proportion."

"We aren't accustomed to commenting on books," Fr Schulz commented recently. "If particular lay people or priests feel guilty, there are certain courses of action they can take. But the Polish Church as a whole never collaborated. Instead, it was the engine of change, which led to the recovery of freedom throughout Eastern Europe. Let's deal with the facts, rather than just looking for holes in a seamless fabric."

From what is already known, the word "seamless" does not quite fit.

Communist rule was imposed in Soviet occupied Poland after the Second World War, and lasted till 1989. The Catholic Church, to which 95 percent of Poles belong, defended human rights through these long years, and won concessions for itself in the process as a reward for calming frustrations. In the 1980s, however, the picture became much more complex, when the Solidarity movement upset the long-nurtured Church-State system of checks and balances.

The minutes of a Church-State commission, published in 1993–6, show that negotiators from both sides, far from trading invective, co-operated quite amicably throughout the 1980s. Rumors of double-dealing by the Church have since surfaced periodically, including accusations that its leaders helped prepare the imposition of martial law in December 1981.

There was a sharp exchange this March in Poland's mass-circulation Gazeta Wyborcza daily between the last Communist Interior Minister, General Czeslaw Kiszczak, and the Church's former spokesman, Bishop Alojzy Orszulik. The bishop *denied maintaining discreet, respectful ties in his many meetings with top Communist Party officials. "This is an attempt to turn me into an agent," he protested. "I never treated my meetings as private, but rather for obtaining as much information as possible which I could also show to the opposition."*

But Andrzej Grajewski believes that onetime informers still hold senior posts in the Polish Church, and know their actions are being monitored by former Communist interlocutors. One example: He says a former colonel in the secret police, Adam Pietruszka, attended the Warsaw launch of The Judas Complex *in an apparent effort to intimidate Bishop Orszulik and other speakers. Pietruszka served a prison sentence for the murder in 1984 of the Solidarity priest, Jerzy Popieluszko. "I was shocked he had the nerve to come, particularly since several people could recognize him," Grajewski added. "I took it as a signal: Be careful, we're still here, and we're watching you."*

In neighboring Czechoslovakia, where a pro-regime clergy association, "Pacem in Terris," operated until 1989, around 10 percent of Catholic priests are believed to have worked with the secret police, or Statni Bezpecnosti. Many former collaborators were later suspended or transferred to distant parishes — although only one, Fr Alois Kansky, based in Prague, publicly admitted wrongdoing. In a 1992 pastoral letter, the Czech Catholic Bishops' Conference called for "forgiveness and reconciliation."

In another neighboring country, Hungary, the Catholic bishops admitted in 1989 that priests had come under pressure to inform. A parliamentary commission report on the role of church agents was left unpublished a year later. Though 6,000 judges, broadcasters and office-holders still face vetting under a 1994 law, the bishops have opposed calls for the Catholic Church to be included.

In the former East Germany, the Stasi secret police employed 86,000 full-timers in a population of 17 million, proportionately seven times as many as the secret police in Poland. The state institute handling Stasi archives, headed by Pastor Joachim Gauck, has reckoned regular informers in the Roman Catholic and Evangelical Churches together at just 156, with a further 300–500 acting as secret co-operators. A commission of the Catholic Church headed by Fr Dieter Grande reported in 1995 that 13 priests and lay church employees in the Dresden-Meissen diocese had had Stasi contacts; seven had consciously collaborated, but only one had signed a written undertaking.

A former director of Berlin's Evangelical Academy, Peter Hellmann, was given a suspended jail sentence in May after becoming the first church official to be convicted for secret police activities.

Fr Schulz insists, however, that the Catholic Church in Poland maintained a "healthy attitude to Communism." His bishops' conference has no plans, he says, to start issuing "apologies for other people." In his opinion, it is "a huge misunderstanding" to compare the record of the Polish Church to Czechoslovakia's or East Germany's. "The situation was totally different here," the Jesuit spokesman says. "Our Church isn't afraid of a good historical analysis covering the 1940s to 1960s, which would present the truth non-idealistically in both light and shadow. But since most archives have been erased, it's hard to find the right criteria or establish the credibility of what remains."

That does not quite fit either.

Documents identifying priest-collaborators were indeed destroyed after the return of democracy in 1989. But the Polish minister in charge of security services, Janusz Palubicki, warned last September that priests could still be blackmailed by former secret police agents who made their own private copies of shredded files.

The editor who published the minutes of the Church-State commission referred to earlier, Nina Smolar, says she got them from "private collections." Meanwhile, 80 meters of "lost" archives were discovered only this month in a cellar of the former HQ of the secret police at Mostowski Palace in Warsaw. Investigators said the dampened files included signed declarations of co-operation and payment receipts, mostly from the Interior Ministry's "Third Department," which covered opposition and trade union activities.

Andrzej Grajewski thinks the Church is being dangerously complacent and should use the opportunity created by the new Memorial Institute to appoint a team of experts similar to the commission headed by Fr Grande in the former East Germany.

Curiously, The Judas Complex says most Polish secret police agents were not personally anti-religious: Up to 80 percent married in church and had their children baptized. But it cites evidence that recruitment among priests intensified in the 1980s, when some acted as informers while denouncing Communism in their sermons. Though most collaborators were seeking benefits or acting under secret police blackmail, some informed to gain revenge on church superiors with the deliberate aim of inflicting damage.

The Church will be making a "serious mistake," Grajewski calculates, if it merely "waits for some heavenly tribunal" to absolve it. "The motives are less important—what matters is that these people consciously collaborated, and that among Christ's disciples there were also some Judases," the Catholic historian said. "Although our bishops' conference stated in a 1993 letter that collaboration was a sin against the nation, no one appears ever to have made a public admission of guilt."

But the immediate results could be messy too. Under a law passed last December, Polish officials must declare whether they informed during the Communist period. Meanwhile, even the naming of the institute committee was not without a touch of controversy. At least one of its 11 members, the historian Janusz Paczkowski, said he had decided to table a declaration detailing four separate attempts by the secret police to recruit him in the 1960s and 1970s.

Yet for now at least, the new institute looks set to put justice and truth-telling back on the map. If it does, the price of a few red faces will be a price well worth paying.

The publication of secrets from the past would not be painless for Poland or the Catholic Church. A list containing various names and incriminating information was stolen by the Russian mob for a highly lucrative purpose: blackmail.

With his former KGB status, none other than Jivco was selected by the Russian mafia as the perfect person to take charge of the blackmail operation. He put together a small group to put his plan into gear. Henry was one of those tapped for the job.

The list contained the names of those who collaborated with the Nazis and who subsequently supported the communists. The list also named the associates of the Vatican who helped major war criminals escape the Allies, and information on the routes that were used. We're not talking smaller figures who have been lost to history. The list had big players—the biggest. Does the name Karol Jozef Wojtyla ring any bells? Probably not: He was better known as Pope John Paul II.

Clearly the material contained enough information to devastate the Catholic Church, or at least give it a serious blow. The asking price for this information, which was stored on an insignificant-looking USB drive, was US$50 million. Anything with a price tag that big gets around the intelligence agencies. Soon that led to me getting involved. My old partner George, me and Guylaine, a female agent from the French gendarmerie, were called to Bonnie's office in early 2000. As usual, Bonnie didn't waste words. The information was as bare bones as it could get: An object had been stolen and was being sold by blackmailers.

"We want the item," she told us. "We want the enemy agents arrested and we want the merchandise seized and brought to us."

I watched her body language for clues as to the seriousness of the case, the level of danger that might be involved.

She was unreadable. I was used to it. At the level of law enforcement where I fit in, you're never given the full picture. You do your part and let others fit your piece into the greater puzzle. You never have enough information to form an opinion on the project. Everything operates on a need-to-know basis, and more often than not the agent just doesn't need to know.

"What is the package exactly?" I asked, hoping for an answer but not expecting one.

"Pack your bags," she said with a slight smile, ignoring my question. "You're going to France."

———————

You might be tempted to say that only in Germany would Catholics protect their Church so fiercely from the shame of past political missteps. Many stories about the role played by Roman Catholics during the war have been reported over the years in publications, documentaries as well as on the web. For instance, from Wikipedia:

> *Influential members of the German Resistance included Jesuits of the Kreisau Circle and laymen such as July plotters Klaus von Stauffenberg, Jakob Kaiser and Bernhard Letterhaus, whose faith inspired resistance. Elsewhere, vigorous resistance from bishops such as Johannes de Jong and Jules-Géraud Saliège, papal diplomats such as Angelo Rotta, and nuns such as Margit Slachta, can be contrasted with the apathy of others and the outright collaboration of Catholic politicians such as Slovakia's Msgr Jozef Tiso and fanatical Croat nationalists.*

Resistance for some, apathy for others. The Catholic Church is quick to bring up these names of these heroes but slow to acknowledge those with less appealing track records. *Geoffrey Blainey, quoted in Wikipedia, writes: "Christianity could not escape some indirect blame for Holocaust. The Jews and Christians were rivals, sometimes enemies, for a long period of history. Furthermore, it was traditional for Christians to blame Jewish leaders for the crucifixion of Christ..."*

And where do former Popes fit in? Outwardly they seemed to have opposed the Nazis on multiple occasions. But did they really do enough? John Paul II's involvement with the Nazis was covered up with the excuse that he was in Rome during that time and didn't return to Poland until 1948. But if that were true, the blackmail scheme wouldn't have raised so much concern. The full story, it seems, has yet to be told.

What isn't in doubt is that the information on that list showed clear ties between the Catholic Church—supposedly a model of morality and compassion—with one of the most evil political regimes in history. You can easily imagine the potential scandal the list would cause if it had only the names of a few cardinals and a handful of bishops. But there must be more to it. Hence the ruthlessness and duplicity that could come into play when it came to protecting the true extent of the damning information.

The story goes deep and is very involved, but the bottom line for me personally was simple: It wasn't my problem. You have to be practical. We were brought in to get the USB drive, not to make judgments about the contents one way or the other. If you want to find out more, there's no shortage of information out there for anyone who wants to dig: Scandal and controversy abound.

When your boss tells you you're going to France, your first thought is of Paris, the *Folies Bergères*, fine restaurants and strolls along the Left Bank—that's what I imagined, at least. But I wasn't even close. Our destination was the city of Nantes. If you've never heard of it, you're as ignorant as I was then.

As it turns out, Nantes is well worth a visit. It's a beautiful little city in the west of France, on the banks of the Loire River, with a population of about a quarter million people. It's a sophisticated place, a home for intellectuals and liberal thinkers who can get to Paris in just a few hours using the fast rail service. But the bad guys may have had other reasons to pick that spot. With the Bay of Biscayne at its back, just a few nautical miles from the English Channel, it offered a nice escape route.

George, Guylaine and I flew to Amsterdam. We were met by French police agents and a representative of Europol whose role was to act as an observer. The next morning we had a breakfast meeting with a Vatican rep. As he spoke I had a hard time listening, distracted by the fascinating gathering of people around me. It was quite an international assortment of characters. It seemed to heighten the value of the item we were seeking—that secret list that could draw such disparate people to a foreign land.

Soon our discussion turned to the plan for the exchange. The man from the Vatican spoke up quickly. We would not be invoved in making payment to the Russians, he said firmly. As he addressed us with authority, he reminded me strangely of Gandalf, the wizard from Tolkien's *The Hobbit*. Unlike Gandalf, however, I sensed his motivations weren't entirely altruistic. He informed us that he would take possession of the drive as soon as we had it. I was surprised to hear that. We had been told quite clearly to bring the drive home. Unless that order was revoked, I knew what we would do, regardless of Gandalf's opinion on the matter. I had first seen the priest as excess baggage—now I wondered if he could be a bigger problem than that.

Then the Europol representative took over. His organization had been in contact with the blackmailers and had already arranged to transfer funds to an offshore account upon receipt of the drive. Not having to worry about money took several problems off the table. We still had to go through the show and tell, but then we would just make the arrests once we were sure they had the goods.

But I started to wonder why we had been asked to get involved in the first place. It was shaping up to be a simple, straightforward deal. We get the drive, they punch in the bank account numbers for the transfer. Then the arrests are made and everyone goes home. Why did they need us? Something wasn't adding up. Maybe they weren't really going to make the payment and we were meant to be the fall guy: The blackmailers could blame the rip-off on us. I decided to watch carefully as things went down and not to take anything for granted.

On the way to Nantes we got more specific with our plan. We would get adjoining rooms. Guylaine would wait in one room with a laptop. George and I would get the drive and bring it next door to Guylaine, who would check that it was legit. Then we would give the blackmailers the account numbers, and then the cops would swoop in to make the arrests. The priest, if he really was such, would wait out in the hallway with the cops. It would basically go down like a drug deal. There should be no problem, as long as the gendarmes were in the hall ready to bust in at the right moment. Then the suspects would be worked over at the police station until one of them opted to make a deal and spill his guts. I suggested that they arrest us at the same time; there was no reason to blow our cover at that point. But apparently they use different methods for undercover work in France, and my suggestion was soundly rejected. It was worth a shot.

We checked in to connecting rooms at Nantes' Hotel de la Gare. Then a phone call came in from the front desk saying that our meeting would be in one hour. The game was on. I've always hated the downtime when you're waiting to make a deal. It could be the last hour of your life—you never know what could go wrong in the event, and you're usually dealing with very dangerous people—and you end up just sitting around pointlessly killing time. It seems so absurd. There are different ways to handle the tension. Some agents talk—some talk endlessly, in fact, seemingly unable to stop. Others just sit and stare, doing nothing. As for me, I don't have a set pattern. It depends on my mood.

Finally we got the signal from the cop downstairs. Two men were on their way up. The wait was forgotten, and suddenly things seemed to happen so fast. There were two knocks at the door. George opened it, and there stood two of the most nervous-looking men I'd ever seen. George welcomed them in using the friendliest voice he could muster. They entered and sat side by side on the settee—a bad move on their part, strategically speaking. They seemed to be making mistake after mistake. Were they rookies?

One of them reached in his pocket and took out the small USB drive. He handed it to George. The other guy sat still and kept one hand inside his coat. It didn't take a brilliant detective to see that he was armed. I considered him carefully. The fear and tension in his eyes made me worry that he was ready to jump up and start shooting. And then I noticed something else: They had no electronic devices with them. That meant there was no way they could check the account numbers.

Suddenly, I saw the situation as clear as day. The whole thing was a setup. The drive had to be a dud.

Either way, the game plan remained the same: The cops in the hallway would make the arrests once we left. George had passed the USB key next door to Guylaine, and a few minutes had passed—it had to have been enough time. I knocked on the adjoining door. There was no answer. I opened the door: the room was empty.

I was stunned. We had no plan for a development like this. I could only think that we had to get out of the room safely, and we could assess what had happened later. I went back in and gave George a look.

"Everything is cool," I said. "Give them the numbers and let's get this over with."

George gave one of them a sheet of paper with the account numbers. I asked the guy to give us ten minutes before they followed us downstairs. He nodded and put the sheet of paper in his pocket without even glancing at it. I was right: They couldn't check the numbers even if they wanted to. As we left, the cops in the hallway poured in to arrest them.

One of the cops gave us a ride back to the police office. When we got there, I spoke to the superintendent and tried to piece things together. It turned out that Guylaine wasn't the only person who had disappeared: The Vatican rep had vanished, too. I sensed that he was holding something back and knew much more than what he was telling me. He put on a show of gratitude, saying how sorry he was that we had come all that way for nothing. I could tell that underneath he wanted us gone as soon as possible. No, we couldn't talk to the suspects. That wasn't an option. Thank you again for all your help, and goodbye.

We went back to the hotel, unsure of what to do next. I called Bonnie for advice. I should have expected it: She knew everything before I even had a chance to explain. She told me we were to return home and speak to no one till she had a chance to debrief us. Pretty odd that we needed debriefing, I thought. We really hadn't done anything, and with Guylaine and the USB drive having vanished, it seemed to be a complete washout. All I knew was that I didn't seem to have a handle on this case.

We got back to Canada late at night. I said goodnight to George and went home. The next day we met up again to see Bonnie. We knew better than to just walk into her office—you never knew who might be in there with her. But the secretary told us to go right in.

Care to guess who was sitting in there, comfortable as can be? If you guessed Guylaine, you'd be half right. The priest—

Gandalf himself—was there too, in regular clothes with no clerical collar—nothing to show he was with the Church. When we came in, Bonnie asked the two of them to leave. As she left, Guylaine turned to George and I and said she was sorry for what happened—she didn't elaborate, but she seemed sincere. The priest, on the other hand, didn't even glance at us.

I was in no mood to wait patiently for answers. I asked Bonnie flat out for an explanation. She turned to stone. It was the toughest side of her I'd seen yet—not a friendly face by any means.

"You'll get your answer once," she told me, in a voice like ice. "And then you'll never challenge or question my methods again."

I stayed silent, and hoped that was enough to show my consent.

"I always double up my teams in case of problems," she continued. "In case someone gets shot—by the bad guys, or by me, for pissing me off." She glared at me.

"What about the drive?" I asked her. "Was it the right one? Where is it now?"

"I have it, and it's going where it belongs," she said. "In the garbage."

Bonnie is usually straight with me, but I didn't buy that last bit. I don't think the drive was trashed. It represented too much potential, too much leverage that could be wielded. The people who run these organizations are not the type to dispose of something with that value. They would at least make a copy and then hand the original back to the Church. You learn to see signs of that kind of approach when you work for them for long enough. It's not a system that builds trust, loyalty and cohesiveness among agents. What it does accomplish very effectively, though, is to keep all the control in the hands of a select few.

After my European getaway, I returned to the slavery case. It was a massive project whose scope extended far beyond my understanding. But I was beginning to carve out a small part that made sense. It was like a huge steak, too big to consume whole: You had to cut it into smaller pieces to manage it. As for why they had put me on the case, I had a hunch. Bonnie and her people knew that if I chose to go after Henry, Jivco was very likely to get hit in the crossfire. He was in fact their real target. But I kept that suspicion to myself.

———————

As the case progressed, I delved deeper into the horrors of human slavery and sex trafficking carried out by the Russian mob, my thoughts of revenge started to shift out of focus. The enormity of this kind of crime, which destroys so many lives, seemed to cloud over everything else.

Tel Aviv may be part of the promised land for Jews, but for sex slaves it's hell on earth. There are three hundred brothels operating in the city. Let's do a conservative estimate and say there are five girls in each one. That makes fifteen hundred girls working at any given time. They aren't in Tel Aviv permanently, though. Sooner or later their number comes up, and they're taken in the middle of the night and sent to ports unknown. To me it seems to heighten the tragedy that this could happen in a city whose people went through so much trauma and personal loss themselves. No matter who is involved, though, the suffering is tragic beyond measure.

The Law of Return provides that all Jews have the right to become citizens of Israel. For a time, the Russians (formerly the Soviets) took advantage of that law by sending in a steady stream of criminals and spies. From there, a common trajectory involves moving to Montreal, then finally into the U.S. and the West Coast. It's a pathway the Russian mob in North America uses to replenish its numbers.

The network is expansive and crosses many borders. The tangled web connects Eastern European girls with Jewish gangsters, criminal organizations from Montreal to Vancouver, and innumerable strip clubs, escort services and massage parlors. At each stop, money is accumulated to pad the wallets of the Russian mob. The routes could never be maintained without the cooperation of various cops and border guards, lawyers, real estate agents and countless others who are all too happy to close their eyes and take a cut. It's a vast industry based on the sale, slavery and exploitation of victims.

These victims are no different from you or me. Their circumstances have forced them into misery and eliminated personal freedom completely. And at some point it ends up happening in our midst. That's where we need to focus our energies: making it hard to run the businesses that profit off victims. Making the consequences severe. Laws can make a real difference—think of the seatbelt law, or prohibitions on smoking in bars. Our very culture has changed as a result of them.

We also need to put real investigative work into stopping criminals who use the internet to promote and support their exploitative businesses. Spend an hour or two online and you can get to some very dark places. Why do we tolerate it? It's more widespread today, but it's not really anything new. People's appetites for sex and satisfaction via exploitation existed before the worldwide web. Take the following example: Many years ago I heard rumors of a "snuff film" being shown at a doctor's house in the wealthy North Vancouver area. My memory might be off, but I think the price for a viewing was $200. High class people watching death and torture for entertainment. At the time I didn't believe it. Now I'm not so sure.

As the plane to Moscow started to descend, Henry lifted his tray into the upright position as the voice over the intercom instructed. He reached over and gently woke Guylaine, who was sleeping next to him. That's right: the same Guylaine mentioned earlier, whom I'd encountered in working the case of the missing list. "We're landing," Henry told her. He was anxious to get home. Guylaine was too. That feeling would have vanished had she known what was in store for her.

A few days before she and Henry had boarded that flight, Guylaine had made an international call to a girlfriend from her hotel room. She told her friend she was dissatisfied with her relationship with Henry. She went so far as to complain that he should treat her better—after all, she said, she knew enough to cause him real harm. She was a smart woman; but that was a very dumb mistake. As per standard policy by the Russian mob, all calls made from her room were being recorded.

Contrary to her expectations, Guylaine's fling with the mysterious Russian had become something more real for her than she could have imagined. Love makes each of us vulnerable—but in this case, Guylaine's vulnerability had put her life on the line. She had made the tragic mistake of thinking she really meant something to Henry. To him, women were mere tools to use and discard. Attachment was out of the question.

We know through sources at the airport that Henry was met at the gate by his own people and walked through customs. Guylaine was escorted to a separate car and driven away. Several weeks were spent trying to find out what happened to her using different sources and informants. It wasn't just out of concern for her well-being. If she could be found, if she was still alive, she might be persuaded to inform, to give up Henry and provide the information needed to put him away. But she had simply disappeared.

Henry was brought back to his apartment. The driver told him he would be picked up the next morning and that he should have enough packed for a week away. The driver didn't tell Henry where he was going and, as usual Henry didn't ask.

But you never know who you can trust. The driver was actually an informant for MI6, Britain's intelligence service.

I imagine that at that moment he felt good, secure. The trip to Russia would give him a nice break from potential threats— threats like me. Because he had been told to pack for a week, he suspected that he would end up getting some nice relaxation time. He believed he was headed for the Black Sea resort owned by Jivco, his mentor.

The car picked him up the next morning as scheduled. Before leaving town, they made one stop. To any passersby the building they arrived at would probably seem like just another government office building. It was actually the Moscow headquarters of GRU, or Main Intelligence Directorate. A separate being from the KGB, GRU is Russia's biggest intelligence agency. The organization has been around for a long time and had a major role during WWII as an expert in sabotage and covert operations. Stalin, paranoid and frightened for his own safety, had had the head of the organization executed and its units disbanded. Despite that blow, GRU was the best of the best in the world of intelligence.

Henry got out at the building's front gate. He showed his papers to a guard and was taken inside. At this point the facts get a little blurry. It's more than likely that he met with Sulim Yamadayev, a former Chechen rebel leader who ended up switching sides and aligning himself with Russia. Regardless, whoever spoke with Henry that day told him it was time for the ultimate test.

His mission: to assassinate his former mentor, Jivco. After the killing, Henry would replace his former mentor as the head of the Russian criminal network in the U.S.

That the topic of the conversation was Jivco is something we know for a fact. The information was provided by a GRU double agent. This agent also told us that a purge of former KGB agents was taking place at the time. The more experience an agent had and the higher up he was in the organization, the more of a threat he posed. If he knew too much and had too many contacts in the West, he could no longer be trusted. The threat had to be removed.

The meeting lasted less than an hour, and then he was off to the Black Sea as he had thought— but with a purpose he had not expected.

You may not be aware of it, but there exists a place that was once known as the Russian Riviera. Gagra is a gorgeous scenic area on the Black Sea coast in Georgia. Communist fat cats took their mistresses there to celebrate the good life in opulent resorts while their people back home starved. After a brutal war and the massacre of thousands of Georgians, the beautiful beachside buildings lay in ruins for decades. Gagra became a ghost town. Today, there are finally signs of a regrowth.

When Henry showed up, Gagra was still in its glory days. But he had no plans to linger on the sunny beach. Just after he arrived, he was ready to take action. He told his driver to be ready to leave within the hour. That would be enough time to take care of Jivco—his mentor, his father figure, maybe even the closest thing he had to a friend.

Jivco was later found on his couch, with a single bullet wound that had entered the back of his head. The weapon, a survival knife with a built-in mechanism capable of firing a 7.62x42 mm cartridge—the same one used in a PSS silent pistol. He sat bent forward, as though looking at his own brains, which lay splattered across the coffee table.

Henry's car was almost back in Moscow when the news came over the car radio. It said that a man had been found dead in his villa. The victim was thought to be a gangster, believed to have been shot by one of his own men. The police were actively looking for a suspect named Henry Cludd. He was considered armed and dangerous.

Henry immediately realized he had been set up. He couldn't go home—they would be waiting for him there. He told the driver to pull over. He had to think. He was afraid that they would shoot him on sight. It would make things simpler for them. And, after all, that's what he would do.

Then the driver spoke up. He told Henry to trust him, said he had a solution. In a little while the car pulled up in front of the U.S. embassy. The driver got out and spoke to the marine posted at the gate. Then the gate swung open.

That's the dramatic story of how Henry became a defector. The double agent I mentioned above, who gave us information about what happened at GRU headquarters? It was Henry himself. He was interrogated at length and arrangements were made to get him to the U.S. There he was interrogated further. He must have had a lot to say—they held on to him for almost five weeks.

When he was finally released, it wasn't as a free man. Henry presented the feds with a unique opportunity for them to go after the U.S. arm of the Red Mafia. He was given money and a green card and sent out to enter the mafia game in Los Angeles. From that point on, the feds owned him. Or so they hoped.

These events are interesting in themselves: the strange tale of a dangerous man and the twists and turns of his life outside morality and the law. For me personally, however, they were important for one simple reason. They brought Henry back into my world, which meant my best chance for vengeance.

There was irony in the way things were playing out. Henry had fled his life, his country and everything that made him who he was, to save himself—but it took him right into my hands. Would a religious man think it was God or the devil behind it all? And for someone like me, who doesn't believe in any of that: Whom should I thank?

I learned of Henry's return to these shores through Bonnie, when she warned me that I should take no steps to find him now that he was in California. Perhaps she thought I already knew. With a straight face, I told her I was over all of that—life goes on. But I might have answered too quickly. She looked up at me with her penetrating eyes. It was a look I'd seen before, one that bores right through you, looking for traces of deceit. I maintained my best poker face for as long as I thought necessary and left without another word.

Inside, though, I was like a live wire. I had to know more. I still had many friends in low places, and I knew that by flexing my muscles a little I could find out where he was and what his circumstances were. One thing was certain: Guys like Henry don't go straight. They may change their passports, but they don't change their stripes.

But the bigger question was what to do with the information once I got it. It wasn't like I could walk up to Henry and shoot him in the head. That had a certain appeal, I admit. But it wasn't safe and would take a lot more planning than you might think. No, I had to be more inventive.

———

It took less than a month before I got a knock on the door. I opened it to two men standing in suits—never a good sign. They flashed DEA credentials; but they seemed strangely uncomfortable. People in my line of work develop a sixth sense about stuff like that—we can sense when we're being lied to. Maybe they were cops, but DEA? I highly doubted it.

Not one for polite gestures, I didn't invite them in. They stood at the entrance to my apartment, which I hoped would keep the balance of power in my favor. While one of them spoke, the other remained completely silent. I pegged him as a hunter, a dangerous predator—someone to steer clear of.

"You're tracking Henry," he said flatly. Not asking a question but stating a fact.

"What's it to you?" I shot back.

"Henry is ours," he said. "Lay off him, and I mean it. Stay the fuck away."

At that point I shifted gears and gave them exactly what they wanted. "Not a problem," I said. "I didn't mean to step on anyone's toes." I added a small closed-mouth smile for good measure.

He seemed relieved. He nodded his head to confirm that we understood each other, and they left.

I would have to be careful. I thought about what I knew thus far. Henry was in or near San Diego. He had hooked up with a Caucasian woman named Gabriela who was in the country on an extended visa and had a two-year-old-girl with brain damage. I didn't know precisely where he hung his hat, but I didn't need to. It was almost certain that the baby needed frequent care. I staked out the children's hospital, figuring sooner or later he'd show up.

I was right. On the fifth day, I saw him pull into the parking lot. And he wasn't alone: The Feds were right behind him. That changed everything. There was no way I could get him. One car tailing right behind him meant there would probably be another one patrolling the perimeter. I had to back off—I didn't stand a chance.

It was back to the drawing board. I returned to my contacts to find out more about Henry's activities. True to form, he was working with a group of Eastern European drug traffickers and gunrunners. A nasty crew to be sure. I pondered the situation for a few days. No matter what I considered, I kept coming back to a single, inevitable solution. But it was far less than what I'd hoped for. All I had to do was make a single phone call: Contact the Russians and give him up. They would make short work of the problem, guaranteed. It answered the problem, but it didn't seem like enough. Maybe revenge is a dish best served cold, but this was a long way below zero.

But I wasn't ready to call it off. I advanced, step by step. A little undercover work produced the phone number I needed. Eventually I ended up sitting in a motel room holding a throwaway phone, staring at the number written on a piece of paper. What was I waiting for? A one-minute call and it would all be over.

But there were other things to consider. What if his girlfriend and her little girl were around when the hit took place? I knew enough about the Russian mob to know they would just clean house, sparing no one. Besides, there was no honor in this victory. It would be like going on a hunting trip and settling for road kill. I just couldn't do it. I knew that if he were in my shoes, he wouldn't hesitate—but I felt I was better than him.

I lit the paper on fire and let it burn to nothing in the ashtray. Then I packed up my stuff and left town. I felt anything but satisfied, and I can't even say I felt proud for doing the right thing. We all have limits, values that we can't or won't push aside. I tried to convince myself that I'd find another way, but deep inside I knew it was over. I had had him and I chose to let him slip away. My fifteen-year quest had reached an unsatisfying but undeniable end. There would be no rematch.

When I have a story I want to tell, it's because I'm passionate about the subject. I have to have information I want to share and credible sources for facts that might not be widely known to the public.

Human trafficking and sex slavery combines all of the above for me. While it's not the focus of this book, I'm hoping to provide some context, little by little—to create a backdrop so people can start to make sense of this vast and overwhelming problem.

Just telling a story can make a difference in the world. I often think of the words of Georges Danton, a leader of the French revolution: *Il nous faut de l'audace, et encore de l'audace, et toujours de l'audace.* Translation, in a nutshell: You have to live with guts. It starts with research, figuring out what we really know and what we can find out next. Then the information has to be shared and discussed.

That's where you come in, Dear Reader. My hope is that some of you sit around the table and talk about the problems we face. One thing I've learned from thirty years of criminal investigations is always to pay attention to what somebody might contribute to a case—even someone who seems totally unconnected. Like they say, you can always use a fresh pair of eyes.

I've mainly worked alone, and Lord knows I'm tired. Dealing in such a dirty business really takes its toll. You plug one hole and another takes its place. I helped bust Phillip Yu for drug smuggling in the 1980s when he was importing heroin from Hong Kong. Ten years later I was asked to bust his son for the same thing. I passed on the second job, both for my own safety and on general principle. Things like that just make you shake your head and consider doing something else with your life.

My goal is to break one link of the chain. Anger can be power. I want to use my anger against those who engage in and profit from slavery, to make them pay, even it only means saving one victim at a time. Meanwhile, others are pushing forward with the same goals but using different means, in spheres in which I have neither the power nor the patience to operate. But no matter how you're attacking the problem, you're going to spend a lot of time feeling like you're spinning your wheels. The problem is so vast and entrenched that you can get lost in the maze. I've met people who have spent years even their whole careers working on this stuff, and except for a few arrests have never really changed anything. Still they patiently keep pushing ahead, doing what they can. They might not be dodging bullets, but that type of bravery and resolve might be the most admirable of all.

Human trafficking ring dismantled in Portugal

On 14 July 2014, Portuguese law enforcement authorities, with the support of Europol, dismantled an organized criminal group of West African and Portuguese nationals suspected of trafficking young mostly Nigerian women to Portugal and other EU countries in order to exploit them through forced prostitution.

Seven suspects were arrested in Portugal and seven house searches carried out. Mobile phones, computers and tablets and other significant evidentiary material relevant to the investigation were seized including a false passport.

These results are part of the long-running 'Operation NAIRA', an investigation into human trafficking for the purpose of sexual exploitation, led by the Portuguese Immigration Service (SEF). The investigation has been focusing on an organized crime network that trafficked young African females, from West Africa, to Portugal, France and Spain where they were forced into prostitution.

The victims of this particular criminal group are generally young Nigerian women from Benin City (Edo State) who are recruited in their places of origin, from where their trips are organized. Members of the criminal network in Portugal take care of logistics such as contacting the victims, providing accommodation and ID documents. The women often travel with forged travel documents or sometimes no documents at all. On arrival at their destinations, most of the women identify themselves verbally as minors originating in Nigeria, Guinea and

Mali and claim asylum (as allegedly instructed by their traffickers). They are then placed in shelters from where they later abscond and disappear. Victims are subsequently moved to other EU countries. The trafficking process often includes debt bondage, the use of threats against the victims and/or their relatives, physical and sexual violence, and the use of "voodoo" rituals.

Europol actively supported this investigation into human trafficking operations and provided operational analytical support throughout the investigation to the countries involved. This included facilitating information exchange and analysis, organizing an operational meeting at Europol and delivering real-time crosschecks of all data gathered in the course of the field action through the deployment of a Europol mobile office and Europol analyst in Portugal.

— Europol, July 16, 2014

A major hit on a human trafficking ring is always good news. But unfortunately, headlines like this require some perspective. It represents a single battle and should not be mistaken for the war—it is not the end but the beginning. A relatively minor success story like this one can even work against the larger cause. The top brass takes their bows and receives their accolades. But the news cycle is fickle and the attention of the public is quick to move on. A moment of back-patting, and then it's, "Great, what else have you got?"

That's exactly what happened in Montreal with the big takedown of the biker gangs in 2001. With all the ingredients to make a Hollywood movie, the story made a huge splash. Special courtrooms were built for the accused. It was a massive case. But there have been other major biker busts since then, and they barely made a ripple. It sometimes seemed that the main focus was the difficulties we have when prosecuting large numbers of people. The cases moved so slowly through the courts that any new busts created a backlog. Dozens of bikers were released simply because the court acknowledged that it was unable to try them within a reasonable amount of time. It was a mess.

Over time, the police squads targeting bikers lost some of their prestige. The new priority, with all the ensuing media attention, is terrorism. But that's nothing new; after all, the biker cops became king of the hill by stealing the limelight from Mafia investigators.

Many of the top expert biker investigators are retiring, with thirty years of detective work behind them. It's the end of an era; many of these people could name each biker in a gang, one by one, and explain the relationships between all of them, past and present. All that accumulated experience and knowledge is being put out to pasture. However, other countries are also suffering from the blight of biker gangs, and they are starting to call on our venerable experts for consultation. This I consider a good thing. No one wants to feel that his or her life was wasted chasing ghosts.

My own role was a little more specialized and definitely more extreme, and that leaves me feeling kind of untethered. Unlike real bikers who turned on their cohorts, I got no big payouts. I did my job, as messy and risky as it could sometimes be, and got a paycheck every two weeks like any other employee. Another big difference, though, is that you don't get a pension in my profession. When you think about it, it would be next to impossible: How can you supply a pension to someone who doesn't exist, for doing work that never took place?

But I've made my choices. I may lack a retirement fund and other comforts, but I've gained unbelievable stories and life-changing experiences. The job has left me with an active and curious mind. When I hear something interesting on the radio or read it in a newspaper, I get a strong urge to go out and do something about it.

That's why I keep coming back to the issue of human slavery. Sometimes I feel I've made progress with research and understanding, with finding a way to fight it; at other times the enormity of it all crashes down on me and I'm left feeling there's nothing I can do.

The problems are too enormous. And in the long run, do people really care enough to stop it? There's something easy about worrying abstractly about issues like world poverty, deadly viruses on another continent or global warming. Why can't we also empathize when it comes to a terrible situation in our own backyard? I'm referring now to the issue that I ended up facing when I followed the chain of violence and horror: the disappearances and murder of aboriginal women. It's happening right here in Canada, year after year, and there's no problem that's demands our attention more.

It's been said before but I'll say it again: If these were blond, blue-eyed girls from the suburbs, things would be different. Our country would be screaming for a stop to the violence. I'm trying to make that scream happen. There are few things that move politicians like an irate public. Our usual response when we read an article or watch a report is to shake our heads in disgust; then we move on to other things. I guess it's a way to deal with it without driving ourselves crazy. But it's time to turn our disgust into real change.

Let's start by identifying exactly what we're talking about. The UN defines human trafficking as follows:

a) "Trafficking in persons" shall mean the recruitment, transportation, transfer, harbouring or receipt of persons, by means of the threat or use of force or other forms of coercion, of abduction, of fraud, of deception, of the abuse of power or of a position of vulnerability or of the giving or receiving of payments or benefits to achieve the consent of a person having control over another person, for the purpose of exploitation.

b) Exploitation shall include, at a minimum, the exploitation of the prostitution of others or other forms of sexual exploitation, forced labour or services, slavery or practices similar to slavery, servitude or the removal of organs.

c) The recruitment, transportation, transfer, harbouring or receipt of a child for the purpose of exploitation shall be considered "trafficking in persons" even if this does not involve any of the means set forth in subparagraph (a) of this article.

d) "Child" shall mean any person under eighteen years of age.

It sounds neat and tidy, a formal definition of a criminal act. But the reality of it, and its size and scope, the horror of it, can crush you—get too close to the truth and you have to push it aside to stay sane. But even if you avoid it, it comes back at you again and again. An article in the newspaper or on the radio, just the tip of the iceberg, but it sends your mind spinning, and in no time at all you're overwhelmed again. You know that each arrest, each criminal charge, each dollar figure cited is a drop in the bucket.

Still, each little step forward serves a valuable purpose. One fact connects to another and another. Each story is the start of a trail, if you only have the drive to follow it.

The trails can lead in unexpected directions. Ever heard of the black market for organs? It's not something from a horror movie: It's very real and operates closer to home than you might think. It's a hard one to infiltrate, and ghastly to contemplate. But sometimes a solid, clear-cut case comes around and it's a little harder to ignore.

Right in the cultured, sophisticated city of New York, a disgusting crime was being funded, so barbaric that it seems out of place with the modern world. Here's the overview:

A New York City man was sentenced to 2 1/2 years in prison Wednesday in what experts said was the first federal conviction for profiting from the illegal sale of human organs.

Levy Izhak Rosenbaum, an Israeli native who resides in Brooklyn, pleaded guilty in October to brokering three illegal kidney transplants for New Jersey-based customers in exchange for payments of $120,000 or more.

Rosenbaum [was] arrested in July 2009 in a sweeping federal case that became the largest corruption sting in New Jersey history.

Prosecutors allege Rosenbaum would buy organs from vulnerable people in Israel for as little as $10,000 and sell them to desperate patients for more than $100,000.

The transplants took place at top U.S. hospitals, including the Albert Einstein Medical Center in Philadelphia.

Assistant U.S. Attorney Mark McCarren said Rosenbaum engaged in the practice for up to a decade and made millions by exploiting desperate recipients and paying donors paltry sums.

"The defendant has attempted to portray himself as the `Robin Hood' of kidneys," McCarren said. "There is only one thing that his story has in common with Robin Hood, and that is, it is fiction."

(Excerpted from an article by Samantha Henry for
Associated Press, 2012)

This is one case of a heinous crime being exposed, and thankfully so. It's not a movie—it's real life, and it's as ugly as it gets. Justice doesn't even come into the picture. Connect the dots from there and you're caught in an endless web. It's too big for one person, and much too big for me. The most I can be is a small cog in a machine chugging away at the juggernaut of global crime. How can one person affect what's happening in, say, Mauritania, or even in a European country?

Problems like this only become a concern for the government when the facts seep out, when sweeping them under the rug stops working—that's when public outrage becomes a powerful lever.

Let's look at what might seem like a successful case. Twenty Russian mobsters are arrested, resulting in the breakup of a human trafficking ring operating out of Russia and extending to Europe and Israel based on the exploitation of women from Eastern Europe. The icing on the cake: One hundred women and children are rescued. It all makes for great front-page stuff. Everyone (except the agents on the ground, of course) has their photo taken at a packed news conference.

What about the aftermath? The Russian mob has literally thousands of criminals waiting to pick up the slack. The "rescued" women will soon be sent back to their home country. Say they go back to the village they grew up in: Everyone knows what they've been through, and they may end up being shunned, their families disgraced. The women's dreams of going to America and sending back money, maybe even moving their families there, are gone. Now the families are worse off than before, with more mouths to feed. And they now owe the criminal group thousands of dollars for the women's transportation and "upkeep" up until they were arrested—easily somewhere in the range of US $30,000 per woman. How can a family living in poverty possibly repay such a sum? You guessed it: The woman enters the cycle again. With any luck she doesn't have a sister who can be dragged away along with her. Testifying against the gangsters in court would be out of the question—it would put her entire family in grave danger. So: A victory in the headlines; in the life of one family, a questionable outcome at best.

Of course, this scenario doesn't even touch more contemporary approaches to human trafficking; methods that achieve the same results with less wear and tear on the merchandise. The internet has opened a whole new chapter in human trafficking. It may be under the guise of wedding sites, student visas, sporting competitions. It may be portrayed as lonely hearts clubs, or offers for temporary visas abroad. The London Olympics in 2012 created a perfect opportunity for this kind of trade. Thousands of people flooded in and never returned home; they either stayed in Britain or used it as a springboard to get to another country. Passport numbers, credit card numbers, birth certificates—the Russian mob can get whatever it needs to create a legal person.

Then there's the proliferation of online porn sites. Criminals can make even more money with far fewer risks. All they need is video equipment, a little privacy and some actors. You can keep the women on the premises, use them and get rid of them without worrying about dealing with the public or the authorities. Maybe that means that the numbers seem to go down for sex slavery. But just because things have moved online doesn't mean it's time to pat ourselves on the back.

I've done my share of cases, but I'm not getting any younger. These crimes affect me deeply and they're hard to shake off. When you're young, you bounce back and move on. It's harder to do that now. With age and experience comes realism and painful awareness. And the fact is that it's not getting better—it ebbs and flows, changes forms, but somehow remains the same.

But we'll leave all this aside for now. The water's too muddy and the action too far-reaching. To be continued.

CHAPTER TEN

To Catch a Mole

Whether you consider it to be caused by poor judgment or high-level political protection, the Robert Philip Hanssen case was explosive and rattled the intelligence community. Since I was involved in a minor way, I'll share it with you here. Does it demonstrate the sheer stupidity that can be demonstrated by the FBI? I'll let you be the judge of that.

In 2000, I was called in to be part of an investigation team whose mission was to bring down Robert Philip Hanssen. Aside from his name, I knew very little about the FBI agent who was under suspicion. What I could gather at the time was that he had access to classified databases with information on current investigations, their plans and targets. Hanssen could look through any agent's file in the country and see what he was working on. Agents from friendly governments—agents like me—weren't part of that network, so he couldn't get access to our information. But that's just what I gathered from talking to my handler, who was short on details in that regard.

Our job was simply to keep track of him. There were six of us, usually working in teams of two on eight-hour shifts. On the surface it seemed a pretty dull affair. This was a guy that went to work everyday, and to Church on Sundays. He was a member of the fundamentalist Catholic group Opus Dei and attended mass in Latin.

Only once our part of the case of over did I learn that Hanssen had been the most harmful mole in his organization, a dangerous spy against his own—and mine. For years he had been selling classified information to a foreign government. On one level he had been very cautious and skilful; paradoxically, he also maintained a secret life consisting of strippers, gambling and the like. He was a man of two personae.

To nail him, the feds needed to catch him on a dead drop. That's when you drop something in a certain location—say, under a certain rock in a park—and pick up payment at another location. The item and the payment are never in the same place at the same time. Typically you need to indicate to other parties that the pickup took place. Hanssen's method was to locate a tree on which a strip of reflective tape had been placed. As he walked by, he placed another piece of tape over it in the form of a cross. Opus Dei, crosses—I didn't make the connection at the time. From what I've read about the case since then, it doesn't appear that anyone else has made the connection either.

Selling top secret information to foreign governments is an extreme act. But like anything else, after a certain number of times the extraordinary becomes trivial. This was certainly true for Hanssen, who went about his business without a great deal of caution as we tagged along behind him.

After one of his drops, a swat team came out of the bushes and arrested him. Surprisingly, he seemed relieved that it was all over.

The next morning the other agents and I showed up to finish our notes, get our walking papers and prepare to head home. That was a little premature. But I'm getting ahead of myself. Let's start at the beginning.

For a period of 22 years, Robert Philip Hanssen spied within the FBI for the KGB. Born and raised in Chicago, his mother was of German origin and his father Danish. The latter was a police officer, an authoritarian man, emotionally abusive to his son. Hanssen Senior constantly denigrated him, arguing that he would never succeed at anything in his life.

Hanssen graduated from William Howard Taft High School in 1962 and went on to attend Knox College in Galesburg, Illinois, where he earned a bachelor's degree in chemistry in 1966. While at Knox, he took an interest in Russian through elective courses.

Many amongst his first attempts for work turned into false starts and disappointments. For instance, he applied for a cryptographer position in the NSA, the National Security Agency, but was turned down due to budgetary restraints. Since he once contemplated medical science, Hanssen took the opportunity to attend dental school at Northwestern University. He did well academically, but said that he "didn't like spit all that much." After three years, he aimed at business and received an MBA in accounting and information systems in 1971. His first employment was with an accounting firm, but he left early to join the Department of Internal Affairs of the Chicago Police. He specialized in forensic accounting. Hanssen left the department after four years and joined the FBI as a special agent, in January 1976.

During his years at university, Hanssen met Bernadette (nicknamed Bonnie) Wauck. She was one of eight children from a staunchly Roman Catholic family. The couple married in 1968, and shortly after, he converted from Lutheranism to his wife's Catholicism. He became a fervent believer, and got extensively involved in Opus Dei.

He learned the ropes with the Bureau at the field office of Gary, Indiana. In 1978, Hanssen was transferred to New York City, and assigned to counterintelligence with the task of compiling a database on Soviet espionage for the FBI. Within three years he had begun his treason as a Russian spy.

Over his first espionage cycle, he informed GRU (Soviet military intelligence agency) of FBI surveillance activities and passed on the Bureau's lists of suspected Soviet agents in the U.S. His most important revelation to the Soviets was the identity of Dmitri Polyakov, code name Tophat, a CIA inform-ant in the Soviet Army. For unknown reasons, Moscow did not act on their intelligence about Polyakov until he was betrayed a second time by CIA mole Aldrich Ames in 1985. Polyakov was arrested in 1986 and executed in 1988. Ames was official-ly blamed for giving Polyakov's name to the Soviets, while Hanssen's attempt was not revealed until after his 2001 cap-ture.

Hanssen was nearly exposed in 1981, when his wife Bon-nie caught him in their basement writing a note to his con-tacts. Hanssen admitted to her that he had been giving information to Russia for monetary gain, and that he had received US$30,000 as payment. However, he claimed to his wife that he was only passing along false intelligence.

Several weeks later, he was transferred to the Washington, D.C. office and settled in the suburb of Vienna, Virginia. His new job in the FBI's budget office gave him access to informa-tion related to FBI operations. This included all the Bureau activities related to wiretapping and electronic surveillance, which were Hanssen's responsibility. He became known in the Bureau as an expert on computers.

Hanssen's career put him in positions that were perfectly suited for his purpose. For instance, in 1984, he was trans-ferred to the Soviet analytical unit, which was directly respon-sible for studying, identifying, and capturing Soviet spies and intelligence operatives in the U.S. Hanssen's section was in charge of evaluating Soviet agents who volunteered to give intelligence betray and determining whether they were genu-ine or double agents. In 1985, Hanssen moved back to the FBI's field office in New York City, where he continued to work in counterintelligence against the Soviets. This began his second cycle in espionage; this time, he became an operative for the KGB.

On October 1, 1985, Hanssen sent an anonymous letter to the KGB offering his services and asking for US$100,000 in cash. In the letter, Hanssen gave the names of three KGB agents in the U.S. secretly working for the FBI: Boris Yuzhin, Valery Martynov and Sergei Motorin. Unbeknownst to Hanssen, all three had already been exposed earlier that year by another mole: CIA employee Aldrich Ames. Martynov and Motorin were executed. Yuzhin was imprisoned for six years, and eventually immigrated to the U.S. Since the FBI blamed Ames for the leak, Hanssen was not suspected nor investigated. The October 1 letter initiated a long, active espionage period for Hanssen. He remained busy with KGB correspondence over the next several years.

In 1987, Hanssen was recalled yet again to Washington. He was given the task of making a study of all known and alleged infiltrations of the FBI in order to find the man who had betrayed Martynov and Motorin. This meant that he was looking for himself. Hanssen ensured that he did not unmask himself with his study, but in addition, he turned over to the KGB the results of his entire work, including a list of all Soviets who had contacted the FBI about moles. Also, according to a Bureau report, Hanssen "committed a serious security breach" by revealing secret information to a Soviet defector during a debriefing. The agents working underneath him reported this breach to a supervisor, but, incredibly, no action was taken.

In 1989, Hanssen handed over extensive information about American planning for Measurement and Signature Intelligence (MASINT), an umbrella term for intelligence collected by a wide array of electronic means, such as radar, underwater hydrophones for naval intelligence, spy satellites and signal intercepts. When the Soviets began construction on a new embassy, the FBI dug a tunnel beneath the building, right under a decoding room. The FBI planned to use it for eavesdropping, but never did for fear of being caught. Hanssen disclosed this detailed information to the Soviets in September 1989 and received a US$55,000 payment the next month. On two occasions, Hanssen gave the Soviets complete lists of American double agents.

Also in 1989, Hanssen compromised the FBI investigation of Felix Bloch. Bloch was a State Department official who had served all over the world for more than 30 years before falling under suspicion. French agents had spotted him meeting a known KGB operative with whom he exchanged a black bag. Bloch was a stamp collector and claimed that the bag contained stamp albums. Hanssen warned the KGB that Bloch was under investigation. The following month, he called Bloch and said that he could not see him any more, saying that "a contagious disease was suspected"—probably a coded warning.

An investigation was launched into Bloch that dragged on for months. Bloch maintained his innocence. The FBI was unable to produce any hard evidence, and as a result, the suspect was never charged with a crime, although the State Department later terminated his employment and denied his pension. The collapse of the Bloch investigation, and the FBI's inquiry on how the KGB knew that the FBI knew about Bloch, triggered the mole hunt that eventually led to Hanssen's arrest—but that comes later.

In 1990, Hanssen's brother-in-law, Mark Wauck, who was also an FBI employee, recommended to the bureau that Hanssen be investigated for espionage; this was because Mark and Bonnie Hanssen's sister Jeanne Beglis had found a pile of cash sitting on a dresser in the Hanssens' house in 1990 and then told Mark. Five years earlier in 1985, Bonnie had told her brother that her husband once talked about retiring to Poland, then part of the USSR's Eastern Bloc. Mark Wauck knew that the FBI was hunting for a mole and so, after some hesitation, he spoke with his supervisor, who, astonishingly, took no action.

When the Soviet Union collapsed in December 1991, Hanssen, possibly worried that he would be exposed during the ensuing political upheaval, broke off communications with his handlers and was out of contact for a time. He resumed his spying activities in 1992, this time for the newly formed Russian Federation, As they say, the new boss looks the same as the old boss.

Hanssen made a very risky approach to GRU, with which he had not been in contact since his initial foray into espionage in 1979. While he had previously kept his face and name hidden from the Russians, he went this time in person to their embassy, and approached a GRU officer in the parking garage. Hanssen had with him a parcel of documents; he identified himself by his Soviet code name, "Ramon Garcia" adding that he was "a disaffected FBI agent" and offered his services as a spy. The Russian officer, who evidently did not recognize Hanssen's code name, simply drove off. The Russians then filed an official protest with the State Department, believing Hanssen to be a double agent. Despite having shown his face, disclosing his code name, and revealing his FBI affiliation, Hanssen again escaped arrest when the Bureau's investigation into the incident came to a standstill.

In 1993, he continued his activities as an unrepentant risk taker. He hacked into the computer of fellow FBI agent Ray Mislock, printed out a classified document from Mislock's computer, and took the copy to Mislock, saying, "You didn't believe me that the system was insecure." His superiors were not amused and launched an investigation. In the end, FBI officials believed Hanssen's cover story; Hanssen told them that he was merely demonstrating flaws in the FBI's security system. Mislock has since theorized that Hanssen probably went onto his computer to see if his superiors were investigating him for espionage, and invented the document story to cover his tracks.

In 1994, Hanssen expressed interest in a transfer to the new National Counterintelligence Center, which coordinated counterintelligence activities. When a superior told him that he would have to take a lie detector test to join, he changed his mind. Three years later, convicted FBI mole Earl Edwin Pitts told the Bureau that he suspected Hanssen was dirty due to the Mislock incident. Pitts was the second FBI agent to mention Hanssen by name as a possible mole, but the FBI's hierarchy was still unconvinced. As before, no action was taken.

Hanssen was sent in 1995 to the Office of Foreign Missions at the State Department as the senior FBI liaison, with the task of co-ordinating travel by foreign diplomats in the United States. On his weekly visits back to FBI headquarters he frequently visited Johnnie Sullivan, Chief of the National Security Division's (NSD) Intelligence Information Services (IIS) Unit. Hanssen's interest was mostly to chat about his interest in computer security technology and the new Intelink-FBI network that Sullivan's unit was building and installing throughout the Bureau's major field offices.

In 1997, IT personnel from the IIS Unit were sent to investigate Hanssen's FBI desktop computer following a reported failure. Sullivan ordered the computer impounded after it appeared to have been tampered with. A digital investigation by Sullivan and his IT staff found that an attempted hacking had taken place using a password cracking program installed by Hanssen, causing a security alert and lockup. Following confirmation by the FBI CART Unit, Sullivan filed a report with the Office of Professional Responsibility requesting further investigation of Hanssen's attempted penetration of the Bureau's high-security network operated by the National Security Division. Hanssen claimed all he wanted to do was connect a color printer to his computer, but needed the password cracker to bypass the administrative password. The FBI believed his story and Hanssen was let off with a warning never to do it again. However, Sullivan felt that Hanssen's story was grossly inconsistent with the evidence and refused to withdraw the security violation report. The report was first ridiculed and later ignored by the NSD Security Countermeasures Unit.

During the same time period, Hanssen would go into the FBI's internal computer case record and search to see if he was under investigation. He was indiscreet enough to type his own name into FBI search engines (which were logged, leaving a trail that could be followed). Finding nothing, he decided to resume his spying career. He established contact with the SVR (successor to the Soviet-era KGB) in the fall of 1999. He continued to perform highly incriminating searches of FBI files for his own name and address. In November 2000, he sent his last letter to the Russians.

The existence of two moles working simultaneously—Aldrich Ames at CIA and Hanssen at the FBI—complicated counterintelligence efforts in the 1990s. Ames was arrested in 1994; his capture explained many asset losses. However, two cases stuck out and remained unsolved. For one, the Felix Bloch case remained a mystery. Ames had been stationed in Rome at the time of the Bloch investigation, and as such could not have been responsible for that breach. Additionally, there was no explanation for the mysterious telephone warning. Authorities were satisfied that Ames had no knowledge of the case, as he did not work for the FBI and is not thought to have had access to the case files. In addition, the exposure of the tunnel under the Russian embassy in Washington was a second intelligence failure that could not be blamed on Ames (for the same reason, that it was an FBI initiative).

In 1994, after the arrest of Ames, the FBI and CIA formed a joint mole-hunting team to find the suspected second intelligence leak. They formed a list of all agents known to have access to cases that were compromised. The FBI's codename for the suspected spy was "Graysuit." Some promising suspects were cleared, and the mole hunt found other infiltrators such as CIA officer Harold James Nicholson. But Hanssen escaped being noticed.

By 1998, using FBI criminal profiling techniques, the hunters had zeroed in on an innocent man: Brian Kelley, a CIA operative. Kelley was the agent who identified the very KGB agent who met with and took the bag from Felix Bloch, but now he found himself suspected of being the leak who had blown the case to the Soviets. The CIA and FBI searched his house, tapped his phone, and put him under round-the-clock surveillance, following him and his family everywhere. In November 1998, they had a man with a foreign accent come to Kelley's door, warn him that the FBI knew he was a spy, and tell him to show up at a metro station the next day in order to escape. Kelley instead reported the incident to the FBI. In 1999, the FBI even called Kelley in for questioning and directly accused him of being a Russian spy. Over the next two days the Bureau interrogated his ex-wife, his two sisters, and three children. Kelley and his family denied everything, and his CIA career suffered permanent damage. He was eventually placed on administrative leave, where he remained, falsely accused, for nearly two years, until after Hanssen was arrested.

Out of frustration of interrogating Kelley for a year, and having failed to either bring a case against him or find another suspect, the FBI decided on a new tactic—buying the mole's identity. They searched for possible candidates to buy off and found one—a Russian businessman and former KGB agent whose identity remains classified to this day. An American company cooperated by inviting him to the U.S. for a business meeting. After his arrival in New York City, the FBI offered him a large sum of money if he would give up the name of the mole. The Russian responded that he did not know the name, but that he could get the actual KGB/SVR file regarding the mole. He managed to steal the file from SVR headquarters. The file covered the mole's correspondence with the KGB from 1985 to 1991. The FBI agreed to pay US$7 million for the file, and set up the KGB officer and his family with new identities in the U.S. In November 2000, the FBI finally obtained the file, consisting of a package, "a medium-sized suit-case." Among the host of documents and computer disks was an audiotape of a July 21, 1986, conversation between the mole and a KGB agent.

When the FBI listened to the tape, they expected to hear the voice of Kelley, still the prime suspect. However, the voice on the recording was definitely not Kelley. FBI agent Michael Waguespack, listening to the tape, recognized the voice as familiar but could not remember who it was. Rif-ling through the rest of the file, they found notes of the mole using a quote from General George S. Patton about "the purple-pissing Japanese." FBI analyst Bob King re-membered Robert Hanssen using that same quote. Waguespack listened to the tape again and recognized it as the voice of Robert Hanssen.

The FBI finally had its man. Once the name was known, everything else fell into place—locations, cases, dates, refer-ences to Chicago, etc. All these factors were a perfect match with Hanssen's activities during the time period. Also in the file was one of Hanssen's original packages for the KGB, com-plete with a trash bag with two fingerprints on it, which were analyzed and proven to be Hanssen's. The weight of evidence against Hanssen was overwhelming and conclusive.

The FBI placed Hanssen under round-the-clock surveil-lance and soon discovered that he was again in contact with the Russians. In order to bring him back to FBI headquarters, where he could be monitored and kept from sensitive data, they promoted him in December and gave him a new job supervising FBI computer security. In January, Hanssen got an office and an assistant, Eric O'Neill, who was actually a young FBI employee assigned to watch Hanssen. O'Neill ascertained that Hanssen was using a Palm III PDA to store his informa-tion. When O'Neill was able to briefly obtain Hanssen's PDA and have agents download and decode its encrypted contents, the FBI had its "smoking gun."

Hanssen realized during his final days with the FBI that something was wrong. In early February, he asked a friend of his at a computer technology company for a job. Hanssen also believed he was hearing noises on his car radio that indicated his car was bugged, although the FBI was later unable to reproduce the noises Hanssen claimed to have heard. In the last letter he ever wrote to the Russians, which was picked up by the FBI when he was arrested, Hanssen said that he had been promoted to a "do-nothing job ... outside of regular access to information," and that, "something has aroused the sleeping tiger."

However, his suspicions did not stop him from making another drop. After dropping off a friend at the airport on February 18, 2001, Hanssen drove to Virginia's Foxstone Park. He placed a white piece of tape on a park sign—a signal to his Russian contacts that there was information at the dead drop. He then followed his usual routine, taking a package that consisted of a sealed garbage bag full of classified material and taping it to the bottom side of a wooden footbridge over a creek. The FBI, having caught him in the act, swooped in and arrested him on the spot. Subsequently, he was charged with selling US secrets to the USSR and Russia for more than US$1.4 million in cash and diamonds over a 22-year period. On July 6, 2001, he pleaded guilty to 15 counts of espionage in the U.S. District Court for the Eastern District of Virginia. He was then sentenced to 15 life terms without the possibility of parole. His crime was later described by the U.S. Department of Justice, Commission for the Review of FBI Security Programs, as "...possibly the worst intelligence disaster in U.S. history."

Upon his arrest, Hanssen realized his espionage days against the FBI were over, and said, "What took you so long?" The FBI waited two days for any of Hanssen's SVR handlers to show up at the Foxstone Park site. When they failed to do so, the Justice Department announced the arrest on February 20.

With the representation of Washington lawyer Plato Cacheris, Hanssen negotiated a plea bargain that enabled him to escape the death penalty in exchange for cooperating with authorities.

"I apologize for my behavior. I am shamed by it," Hanssen told U.S. District Judge Claude Hilton. "I have opened the door for calumny against my totally innocent wife and children. I have hurt so many deeply." His wife Bonnie, along with their six children, received the survivor's part of Hanssen's pension, $38,000 per year.

Hanssen is Federal Bureau of Prisons prisoner #48551-083. He is serving his sentence at a federal super maximum penitentiary in Florence, Colorado in solitary confinement 23 hours a day.

Hanssen never told the KGB or GRU his identity and refused to meet them personally, with the exception of the abortive 1993 contact in the Russian embassy garage. The FBI believes the Russians never knew the name of their source. He went by the alias "Ramon" or "Ramon Garcia" when corresponding with the Soviets. He passed intelligence and received payments through an old-fashioned dead drop system with no trace.

In the words of David Major, one of his superiors at the FBI, Hanssen was "diabolically brilliant." He refused to use the dead drop sites that his Russian handler, Victor Cherkashin, suggested and instead picked his own. He also designated a code to be used when dates were exchanged. Six was to be added to the month, day and time of a designated drop time, so that, for example, a drop scheduled for January 6 at 1 pm would be written as July 12 at 7 pm.

Despite these efforts at caution and security, he could at times be reckless. He once said in a letter to the KGB that it should emulate the management style of Mayor of Chicago Richard J. Daley—a comment that easily could have led an investigator to look at people from Chicago. He took the risk of recommending to his handlers that they try to recruit his closest friend, a colonel in the army. In an early letter to Cherkashin, he claims, "As far as the funds are concerned, I have little need or utility for more than the $100,000." But during long hours of interrogations, Hanssen maintained that money had been his only incentive. Still, even though he was asked on several times, he always declined having any political or ideological motivation. So why did he do it?

According to *USA Today*, those who knew the Hanssens described them as a close family. As mentioned earlier, they attended Mass weekly and were very active in Opus Dei. Robert Hanssen's three sons attended The Heights School in Potomac, Maryland, an all-boys preparatory school. His daughters attended Oakcrest School for Girls, an independent Roman Catholic school. Both schools are associated with Opus Dei. Bonnie Hanssen taught religion at Oakcrest.

The priest at Oakcrest said that Hanssen himself had regularly attended a 6:30 a.m. daily mass for more than a decade. Opus Dei member Father C. John McCloskey III said Hanssen also occasionally attended the daily noontime Mass at the Catholic Information Center in downtown Washington, D.C. After going to prison, Hanssen claimed he periodically admitted his espionage to priests in confession. He urged fellow Catholics in the Bureau to attend Mass more often and denounced the Russians as "godless," even though he was spying for them.

However, there was a another side to Hanssen's private life much as there was another side to his professional life. At Hanssen's suggestion, and without the knowledge of his wife, a friend named Jack Horschauer, a retired army officer, would sometimes watch the Hanssens having sex through a bedroom window. Hanssen then began to secretly videotape his sexual encounters and shared the videotapes with his friend. Later, he hid a video camera in the bedroom that was connected via closed-circuit television line so that his friend could observe the Hanssens from his guest bedroom. He also explicitly described the sexual details of his marriage on internet chat rooms, giving information sufficient for those who knew them to recognize the couple.

Hanssen also frequently visited D.C. strip clubs, and spent a great deal of time with a Washington, D.C., stripper named Priscilla Sue Galey. She went to Hong Kong with Hanssen on a trip and on a visit to the FBI training facility in Quantico, Virginia. He gave her money, jewels and a used Mercedes, but cut off contact with her before his arrest, when she fell into drug abuse and prostitution. Galey claims that although she offered to sleep with him, Hanssen declined, saying that he was trying to convert her to Catholicism. What a bunch of crap.

CHAPTER ELEVEN

Messing Up With a Badge

It's nothing new that people in charge, leaders of organizations, the top brass can mess things up beyond belief—plenty of cases have become legendary.

Well, incompetence and the inability to take action is well and truly alive today, right here in Canada within our trusted RCMP. Now, before you go writing me an email saying, "How dare you!" please understand that I know that there are problems everywhere, on different scales, that no organization is perfect. My point is still worth making. I've been dealing with the RCMP for many years now and their unreliability has gotten me into some serious jams.

Bunglings and betrayals go all the way back to my Hong Kong days, in 1978. I had made the first deal with my suppliers, Rocky and his accomplices, but the arrest had not happened yet. I told you the story already in this book—but here's the part you don't know. The Mounties saw our job as a one-shot deal, and they decided to use it as leverage to establish credibility for an agent they were trying to insert into a gang that was closely linked with Rocky's. The agent's cover was that he was a hoodlum of some sort who had valuable inside police information, via his personal connections—a valuable asset to any gang.

So far so good. But after a certain amount of time, the bad guys demanded to see the goods; they wanted proof that Bobby Johnson (the name the Mounty's agent used) could get them accurate and useful intelligence. How did the Mounties establish their agent's credibility? Simple: by giving up me and my partner Pineault and informing them that we were infiltrators. Even more crazy was that no one ever informed *us* of this decision.

Thus the agent handed over the information to the gang leader, Joey Howden—oblivious to the fact that Howden was connected to Hobo, with whom I had carefully built a sense of trust—and Hobo was connected to Rocky, with whom I was trying to make a very dangerous deal. The poorly thought out decision led directly to consequences that could have been disastrous for me: Hobo immediately sent word to Rocky in Hong Kong.

Unaware that our cover had pretty much been blown, we arrived in Hong Kong and waited a few days before contacting the triads to arrange the deal. We had committed to making a down payment of a half a million dollars for a supply of heroin with a street value of fourteen million. It was a big enough deal that we were confident we could take down a number of Rocky's partners.

After we made contact, Rocky and Davy Mah picked us up with the plan of heading to some public place to work out the specifics of the deal. As the car wound furiously through the streets of Hong Kong, Davy turned back from the front seat and asked us for our passports. A very odd request, I thought; but making an issue of it could cost us the deal. Who knew what his motives were? For all I knew, he may have wanted to show Rocky what a Canadian passport looked like. I decided to play along and we gave him the passports. After taking a quick look, he said, "You arrived yesterday. Why did you wait till today to call us?"

Immediately I knew that something had gone wrong. My mind raced. Finally I answered him. "Yeah, we didn't call you right away. We're sitting on half a million, and we needed to secure it before announcing that we'd arrived. It's not that we don't trust you. We don't trust anyone when it comes to that amount of cash."

Davy listened in silence, and then turned to Rocky to translate what I'd said into Chinese. Rocky just nodded; it seemed that he bought my explanation. But we weren't out of the danger zone yet—not by a long shot.

The drive ended at the water. We followed Rocky and Davy onto the wharf and got into a small boat, which took us toward a maze of boats all moored to each other. It was rush hour in the bay for traders, fishermen and smugglers of all sorts—Chinese, Vietnamese and others. Our ride took us into the center of the flotilla, where we moved onto a bigger boat, which was unoccupied, except for a guy in the corner holding an AK-47. My suspicion reached new heights; I was sure we were being tricked.

Rocky handed a piece of paper to Davy, who laid it on the table. "This is a note from Joe Howden," he said. "It says you guys are cops."

My main thought on hearing this was that, without fighting, we would never get off that boat alive.

I said a few quick words to Pineault, in French—we had maintained a ruse that his English was weak. If worse came to worst, I told him, we should do everything we could to keep Rocky in the scrum, to use him as a screen against the machine gun. Running was out of the question: There was nowhere to hide.

Then I turned to Rocky and Davy and exploded with indignation. I told him that from that moment on Howden was an enemy to me. I vowed that I would take care of him as soon as I got back. I also demanded to know whether they had heard the information from Hobo directly. The tension was palpable. Davy was obviously thrown off balance by my tirade. No, he said, he hadn't got the information straight from Hobo. Perfect: I had found a lifeline—a point to shift the balance back. But I had to keep up the pressure.

"If you guys can't produce, just fucking say so," I said furiously. "Don't give me this song and dance. We came all this way with all this money and now we get this? You can go fuck yourself."

I told him we wanted out of the deal. Davy Mah translated it to Rocky, whose expression turned to horror. My gamble was right: Rocky had people to answer to and he couldn't afford to lose this deal. Then it was like someone had changed the channel, and the tension vanished. Davy asked me to sit down. Then they apologized earnestly, telling me they were just being careful but that they had been reassured. The deal could proceed.

I could barely stand to think of how close we had come. We had lost our backup long ago in the maze-like back streets of Hong Kong; no one had any idea where we were. From my standpoint, we were totally on our own, lost in a void. I was livid. Later it turned out that our handler, Scott Paterson, had known about the Bobby Johnson ploy, but had assured his boss that we could handle the new development. When I asked Johnson for an explanation, all he said was he figured we could get out of any trouble. And look, he had been right, he added—and hey, good job.

"And, what if we hadn't got out of trouble?" I asked him. "What then?"

"Well, you win some, you lose some," he answered .

I never trusted him again.

The whole ugly story is well documented in the first book of *Befriend and Betray*. Mistakes like that can get somebody killed. It's just one of the many bumblings I've seen over my thirty years of covert operations. Although it would take too long to describe all of the debacles, I will tell you about one of them that, despite all my experience, I didn't see coming. And it cost me dearly.

You've probably heard of a "probe"—a tactic commonly used in the field. This is how it is supposed to happen. Say a street unit is seeing a rise in crime and violence in their area. They come up with a battle plan against the criminal or gang they think is responsible. They draft a plan for a three-month probe to ascertain the extent of the crimes and how to stop them, to take down the perpetrators. The plan has to be comprehensive, including every contingency and all costs like vehicles, overtime, agent fees, and buy money should it be needed during the probe. An example from my past: Southern Ontario's "Project Winner" called for three million dollars. The submission was approved and we were off to the races.

After three months, the project is either extended for an additional six months or terminated. It's a good system for all, and nobody wastes their time beating a dead horse. But one of the key elements had changed, and no one informed me.

The new procedure consisted in getting evidence to validate a project *before* it can be approved or rejected. So my work as an agent would be essentially on spec. I had never done that before and was totally confused by the way things were developing.

After I signed up things took off quickly. I figured out my "in" and went about getting my infiltration work done. Same as usual, at first.

While previously working in San Diego, I had met a Hells friend named Bobby Perez and taken several photos of him as part of my cover as a photographer. Now, in 2005, Perez was dead, killed by a shotgun blast to the face and I was once again working undercover, assigned by the Mounties to infiltrate the Hells Angels in Mission, B.C. For my "in," I had decided to use "Ears," a friend of Perez's and a member of the Mission chapter.

I developed all my photos of Perez and was off to the Mission club bunker. I left a note with my name and number and addressed it to Ears, asking him to call me and saying it was about Perez.

Ears called a day later. I made arrangements to meet him in a Vancouver restaurant the next day at one o'clock. It all happened so fast the cops just weren't ready for it. Still, I went on with it and gave Ears the photos, saying that Bobby Perez had sent them to me and that I had been carrying them around till I could get to Vancouver.

It worked like a charm. My handlers got busy writing notes. But my intelligence would get halfway up the chain, to someone who might have a question, and down it would come. Answer the question, get it sent back up again. Get past that person to the next level, hit another snag and down it would come again. Like a yoyo. The chain was completely tangled; it was ridiculous. Then there were the holidays when the necessary people weren't there at the right moment; I would have to wait weeks for things to move one way or the other. In the meantime I was piling up evidence and opportunity. Gunrunners, drug dealers and others were there for the taking. With no money to make buys, maintaining my cover become more and more difficult.

My reputation was starting to verge on that of a bullshitter. Not a good thing. It got extremely uncomfortable when some Surrey gunrunners thought I was a ripoff artist who was after their stash of weapons. They came after me—luckily I was tipped off beforehand by one of my new friends.

I called my handler and it was decided I should leave town for now. Well, I had an apartment with all my stuff. No time to pack. The cops promised to come in, clear everything out and put it in storage for me. I left and, you guessed it, they never bothered with my apartment. Possibly that's because there was a hitman parked in front of my place for days on end. Either way, I don't know if the landlord took everything after the rent came due or whether the bad guys emptied it out. The bottom line is that I lost everything. I mean everything. All my personal belongings: photo albums, a computer, a printer, all gone. I went into hiding in a safe location in northern Saskatchewan. From then, it took another three long months before the project was approved. But of course I was unavailable.

Among other blunders, let's not forget a news conference held in 1995 by the Sûreté du Québec, the provincial police. I had been contracted to look into the Hells Angels chapter in Sherbrooke, Quebec—also referred to as the money chapter. Leaders in the community had been frustrated and vocal about the bikers' presence in the region. They were calling for results. So I was called in to get to work.

Two days after I had gotten in town, the cops held a news conference to announce the steps they were taking to put an end to the gang activities and to shut down their bunker in the nearby town of Lennoxville. In its statement to the media, the SQ hinted quite clearly that they had brought in professional infiltrators.

I was the only new guy on the block. There wasn't a lot of ambiguity. I soon got a call from an Angel associate telling me that I should leave town. They didn't accuse me per se, but under the circumstances, how could they not have suspected me?

I immediately called the whole thing off. There was no way the bikers would cut me any slack after the message they'd heard. I'd be wasting tax dollars and, furthermore, risking my life.

The officer responsible for this brilliant move eventually stepped down from the police and was later elected as a provincial MP. Hopefully that means that guys like me will end up a little safer.

Canada is currently fighting a war—a new kind of war, one with no finish line— and it's a war we can't afford to lose. That means we need to be sure that we have the best available elements invested. There is no margin for error in this conflict, and this is not a time to lose confidence in those assigned to protect us.

Yet I have real concerns. The RCMP is an institution that wants and needs to shine. It's time for them to rehabilitate their image and regain their prestige, despite repeated blunders as well as the constant shade cast by certain CSIS activities. Let's face it: Some of the shit they've pulled over the last few years doesn't inspire confidence.

Those who have read my work or witnessed my appearances in the media will notice that I always stand up for the cops and acknowledge the effort they put into their work. But I must admit that it's getting harder and harder to maintain that position. Respecting the police has always been important to me, since I was acting as a partner with them throughout my career. Respecting police work is on some level the same as respecting the work I was doing.

It's not easy to befriend somebody knowing full well that your intent is to betray them and put them behind bars. One needs a strong moral compass to keep doing that again and again, to not be affected by it. That's why I've noticed that, in our personal lives, we infiltrating agents go out of our way to be totally honest, to live the best lives we can, almost as a way to counterbalance the deception required by our professional lives.

With questions of ethics and justice being such a force in our lives, you can see how the moral code of the people we work with is very important to us. You try to give people the benefit of the doubt, and I've struggled to explain away some of the terrible actions and non-actions that have happened in recent years—there's always the "few bad apples" excuse. But it becomes hard—really hard—when new problems keep hitting the news. And so, at the end of this book, I present a few of the worst stories among the most embarrassing, in order to show that my business is more than just dangerous: Like any other, it can be fraught with weaknesses and failures. I was not personally involved in the following incidents, but their importance is such that I will depict them to you.

The Robert Dziekanski affair

The events that took place on that day in October 2007 at the Vancouver airport are revolting enough. But the sequence of lies and cover-ups that followed was even more sickening. They were not the actions of those on the wrong side of the law, of criminals and gangsters: They were deliberate initiatives of the RCMP itself. Endless arguments on police ethics, multiple roadblocks to the inquiry, endless legal procedures: They used all the digressive tools at their disposal. As a result, it took the Crown seven years before the RCMP officer who stunned Robert Dziekanski with a Taser gun, which caused his death, faced charges of perjury in Court. But that wasn't the first mistruth. The prosecutor alleged that the four Mounties involved in the victim's death lied to a public inquiry that released its report five years earlier.

The official report stated that an individual in the international transit area of Vancouver Airport had suddenly demonstrated troubled behavior. Although unarmed, he became violent, throwing furniture in the terminal. The man was a Polish immigrant who spoke no English. He ignored warnings from RCMP agents.

Swiftly, officer Kwesi Millington deployed his Taser gun five times, despite Dziekanski's screams. He fell to the ground and was handcuffed. He died soon after.

Following public criticism and uproars from human rights organizations, the B.C. government ultimately called a public inquiry to examine the procedures and policies surrounding Taser use, and the circumstances of Dziekanski's death.

Seven years later, the Crown said that the explanations from the four Mounties didn't match the reality. He went further, accusing them of a calculated attempt to square their lies with an amateur video of the incident.

Kwesi Millington's case was addressed separately because he was the one who pulled the trigger. He was in fact the third officer to face trial. Constable Bill Bentley had previously been acquitted; Corporal Benjamin Robinson's trial began simultaneously in another courtroom.

There was extensive and thorough press coverage of each court case, with expert features, analysts in police procedures and comparison of training and practices within other North American police corps. The Crown repeatedly insisted that all officers involved lied on two occasions: once to investigators and then again at the public inquiry into the event. Prosecutors stated that the three police officers made identical lies in their accounts of the incident, and that their acccount had been contradicted by an amateur video. Crown counsel Eric Gottardi: "We argue that Constable Millington, along with his partners, gave under oath false testimony with intent to mislead the inquiry".

Crown counsel Gottardi argued that the officers must have colluded before being interrogated. It was confirmed by an eyewitness that they had indeed had a meeting beforehand.

Rulings, disciplinary measures and convictions are one thing—but that's not really my priority here. I'm mainly concerned with the behavior and mindset that are at the root of these incidents. These are dealings that one would expect only from criminals and mobsters. That's what I want to look at here.

In the stormy mountains

A visitor would expect the city of Kamloops to be always in harmony with its mountainous setting, its community living peacefully amidst the splendid scenery of the Rockies. But over the years the RCMP detachment there became an extremely toxic workplace. In the summer of 2010, it was under the command of Inspector Yves Lacasse who would be later described in court as an "extreme bully."

Gary Kerr, a retired staff sergeant, was in charge of the detachment's major-crimes unit at the time of the event. He was later summoned as a witness at the trial. Kerr reported that as a commanding officer Lacasse had allowed highly dysfunctional behavior to prevail among the personnel. As Kerr put it: "Simply stated, the officer in charge, Inspector Lacasse, was extremely, extremely difficult to work for, maintaining an atmosphere where officers felt bullied."

The story, widely reported in the media, was that police and wardens allegedly watched, via closed circuit video, two intoxicated women engaging in explicit sex acts in a detachment jail cell. In the early morning hours of August 18, 2010, Corporal Rick Brown was assigned for the day to the post of watching officer. He was later to be charged with one account of breach of trust by a public officer. At the trial, Brown was accused of allegedly watching the sex acts with other Mounties, and some jail guards—nobody intervened. The court heard earlier that one of the two women came forward later and claimed to be HIV-positive.

Kerr testified that he considered Brown a friend and colleague. He said: "Brown became very emotional when I told him on Aug. 23, 2010 what had happened in the cells five days earlier." He added that "Brown was sobbing and was too intimidated and scared to talk to Lacasse about the incident."

According to Kerr, relations were so bad among the detachment that nobody would dare talk openly about the incident. In fact, because he was the first investigator assigned to the event, he had to cope with "extreme pressure" from Lacasse, who was very concerned abouth any possibility of a deposition that could create embarrassment for the RCMP, such as a statement to the press. Kerr admitted that he insisted on putting out a press release: "I was very adamant something had to get out, but Lacasse basically quashed on that idea in no uncertain terms."

News of the investigation was eventually leaked to the media, and the RCMP was obliged to issue a news release mentioning "an incident" in a jail cell. Later, in 2013, Lacasse left the organization. At the time, Brown had been on administrative leave for three years. Paid leave, essentially a holiday: probably not too shabby an outcome for such a transgression.

For observers with little connection to the law or knowledge of its tortuous workings, it can seem like the facts are all that matters. For insiders like me, the compromises that take place within the system are sometimes almost too much to bear.

The Starlight Tour

In other Canadian cities, it's known as the "Midnight Ride." In Saskatoon, it's called the "Starlight Tour." A local police constable named Brian Trainor once described the practice in a newspaper column that was apparently a thinly veiled account of life on the beat. Two officers on patrol, dubbed Hawk and Gumby, are depicted picking up a drunk outside the Salvation Army. They decide to take him for a drive. "An uneasy silence had overcome the man in the back," Trainor wrote. "A few quick turns and the car came to an abrupt stop in front of the Queen Elizabeth Power Station. Climbing out and opening the rear door, Hawk yelled for the man to get out. . . Quickly gathering his wits, the drunk scrambled out of the car and into the thickets along the riverbank, disappearing from view. One less guest for breakfast." During this freezy winter night, temperature stayed well below zero.

Too often "the tour" has turned out to be deadly. On November 1990, this following story appeared amongst The Star Phoenix fillers. *While walking alongside a field near Saskatoon's northeast boundary, two workers came across the corpse of a young man. Police have launched an investigation upon the circumstances of his death. An autopsy was performed.*

The pathologist observed: "the entire body was frozen. We were unable to straighten the flexed arm. The knees were slightly flexed." Coroner B.J. Fern concluded that "Neil Stonechild had died about two days earlier, likely of exposure to intense cold, possibly while inebriated."

Most media stories on the incident meshed with each other. One journalist followed up the story in such a way that a full investigation could not be avoided. *The National Post's* Brian Hutchinson in Vancouver, was then with The Star Phoenix in Saskatoon. Many of his articles on the matter were reproduced in other publications, such as *Saturday Night Magazine*, creating national awareness. They forced police authorities to comment, and later, replenished the files of prosecutors in Courts. The following text is made of highlights and excerpts from Hutchinson's coverage.

The victim was Neil Stonechild, an aboriginal young offender, a fugitive at the time of his death. Following a brief investigation, the Saskatoon Police Service speculated that the seventeen-year-old boy had been heading to a provincial correctional centre on the edge of the city to turn himself in. He wandered into a neighbouring field, fell to the ground, and never got up. His death was an "accident."

But for Stonechild's mother, Stella Bignell, the story is totally different. She is convinced that her son was the victim of a cruel, cold-blooded murder. She believes in allegations that Saskatoon police officers abandoned intoxicated aboriginals to their death, out in the cold

In fact, the victim wasn't the first native to die out there in the dark in freezing weather. It was common for police to drive them out there and throw them out of the car, supposedly to walk back to town.

When talking to the press, Stella Bignell has reiterated every time she could that the police department's account was undermined by several facts. Her son had been AWOL for two weeks from a private group home in Saskatoon and had no reason to make his way to an isolated adult prison. Moreover, during that time he had been staying at his mother's home and had never shown any compulsion to turn himself in, nor had she advised him to do so. He was found with only one shoe, which would have made walking to the edge of the city difficult. He was without his favourite baseball cap, which his mother says he always wore. Blood drawn by the pathologist showed there was alcohol in Stonechild's system, but not enough to produce "marked incapacitation or coma. No other explanation for an altered mental state was found." The pathologist also noted a number of "recent abrasions" on his face, his chest, and lower body.

Bignell expressed her concerns to an acquaintance, a veteran Saskatoon cop whose son used to play with Stonechild. He says he looked at the Stonechild file early in 1991, adding "I didn't like it, but it wasn't my case."

Most troubling, however, was an account by Stonechild's friend Jason Roy, the last person who admits to having seen him alive. He had also been on the lam and was wanted by police. Roy, who has told the same story to a number of people over the years, said that he had been partying with Stonechild on the evening of November 24. Together, they ended up at an apartment building in west Saskatoon, where a young woman whom Stonechild had been seeing was baby-sitting. The young woman refused to let them in and they began buzzing other apartments in the building, prompting a neighbour to call the police. Stonechild made off into the night, alone. Roy sought refuge from the bitter cold inside a convenience store. After warming up for a few minutes he returned to the street and started walking to where he had last seen his friend. A police cruiser pulled out of an alleyway and came up beside him. There were two police officers sitting up front. Stonechild, Roy said, was sitting in the back, his face cut and bleeding. He was screaming and begging for help, Roy alleged. The police asked Roy his identity; frightened, he gave them a false name and they drove away. No one has admitted to having seen Stonechild after that.

As quickly as possible, the Saskatoon police destroyed most of the Neil Stonechild file in December 1999, in a disposal of old documents. By then, Stella Bignell had resigned herself to the notion that the circumstances surrounding her son's death would remain shrouded in mystery. As far as the police were concerned, the matter was long closed. But within six weeks of the file being destroyed, two more aboriginal men were found dead and frozen in another remote industrial area of Saskatoon. The gruesome discoveries bore striking similarities to the Stonechild case. Still, these deaths would probably have been written off as accidental as well, had not yet another aboriginal man given a chilling account of abuse at the hands of the Saskatoon city police.

These latest incidents soon set in motion the largest criminal investigation in the history of Saskatchewan. Led by the RCMP's major-crimes unit, a task force has reviewed concerns that Saskatoon police officers may have mistreated seven aboriginal men, five of whom died. In acknowledgment of the distrust natives have always had of the RCMP, the task force hired private sleuths to conduct a shadow investigation. Authorities in Regina and Winnipeg also announced their own investigations into potential "dumping" by police officers, leading some to suggest that the Saskatoon revelations merely represent the tip of an iceberg. And yet, despite a disturbing pattern of anecdotal evidence, there are persistent fears in the aboriginal community that justice will again be delayed—or denied.

A man lurches through a city's streets at night. He's drunk or stoned. Perhaps he's causing a disturbance. The police pick him up. Instead of taking him to the station, tossing him into the tank, and filing a report, they drive him to an empty lot on the edge of town, push him out of their car, and tell him to walk it off. No muss, no fuss, no paperwork.

Some people might figure that dumping drunks at the city limits is a practical way of dealing with what's become a chronic problem, especially among Saskatoon's large aboriginal population. In the middle of winter, when the temperature drops below twenty degrees Celsius, it can be deadly. The former Saskatoon police officer whose son played with Stonechild says he'd heard about dumping *"for years, but not in the winter, when someone might die. Sometimes people are manhandled a little rougher than they should be . . . I can't say that no one has ever been hospitalized because of police treatment."*

"I'm hoping such things never did happen," says Sergeant Rick Wychreschuk, spokesman for the RCMP task force that's investigating the complaints. "Maybe I'm just being naive."

As the reader may suspect, I prefer to insist that we must not be blind!

When "dumping tours" turned into a deadly spiral

It was a cloudless, miserably cold winter of a January morning. In line with his routine, Pat Lorie, a New Democrat member of Saskatchewan's legislative assembly, went for a run. She followed her usual route through a semi-developed industrial park, within sight of the power station. Lorie had paused briefly at the top of a slope when she spotted a man standing at the side of the road, peering down at something. He turned to her and started yelling. "Come here, come here," he shouted. Lorie ran over and saw what looked like a rolled-up carpet lying on the ground. She realized it was an aboriginal male in his mid-twenties, naked from the waist up. His eyes were partially open. A frozen strand of saliva hung from his lip.

As Lorie stood waiting for the police to arrive, three possible scenarios crossed her mind. Perhaps the young man had been involved in a break-and-enter gone wrong. But that didn't seem to fit the scene. Maybe he had been drinking with his buddies and had got into a fight. But there was no sign of a struggle. "I didn't see how someone so scantily dressed could have been there on purpose," she said. Her last thought was that someone, perhaps the police according to recent allegations in the media, might have dumped him there. She couldn't explain why.

A patrol car arrived within minutes.

"You know, I think he was dumped here," Lorie told the officers. "They said, 'No, you can see his tracks in the snow.'"

But the tracks indicated that he had circled, fallen down, gotten up, and fallen down again.

The corpse was covered with tattoos, which helped police identify the body. Rodney (Steven) Naistus, a twenty-five-year-old member of the Onion Lake Reserve near Lloydminster, Saskatchewan, had been released from a Saskatoon detention facility three days earlier. In a celebratory mood, he had gone out drinking with his brother and met up with people in a west-end bar. He was last seen heading downtown with a stranger, apparently on his way to a nightclub.

A few days later, on February 3, another body was discovered. The evening before, Lawrence Wegner, a thirty-year-old college student, had been injecting a mixture of morphine and synthetic cocaine in a west-end apartment before staggering outside and causing a disturbance. He was, according to eyewitnesses, wearing only a T-shirt, jeans, and wool socks. A woman called the police shortly after midnight. Another eyewitness saw a man matching Wegner's description arguing with police a few blocks away, outside St. Paul's Hospital. The eyewitness stated the man was shoved into the back of a squad car. The next day, railway workers found his frozen corpse lying in a shallow depression 200 metres south of the power station.

RCMP investigators later told Wegner's parents that Saskatoon police had indeed been called to a disturbance near the hospital that evening. Apparently, no report was filed and there's no record that Lawrence Wegner was ever apprehended. Saskatoon police told the Wegners that their son had probably walked from the hospital to the power station, a distance of six kilometres, in his stocking feet. Curiously, there were no holes in the socks he'd been wearing that night. Mary Wegner later saw her son's body in the city morgue. There were scratches on the back of his hand, she recalls, an ugly bruise on his forehead, and a "purple mark all around his face. [The police] said it was from exposure to cold . . ."

I think he was killed with freezing winter cold as a murder weapon.

Darrell Night was driving around Saskatoon with his uncle and nephew the day Wegner's corpse was found; they had heard about the discovery on the car radio. Because Night's nephew was not wearing a seat belt, a police constable named Bruce Ehalt stopped their vehicle. Night's uncle asked if the police had identified the body.

Ehalt paused. "Why do you ask?" Night responded, "I can't help but think that what happened to that man is the same thing that happened to me."

Night recounted his story. He had been drinking the night of January 28. A big man, thirty-four years old, with a lengthy record of alcohol-related convictions, he had been ambling towards his sister's house on Saskatoon's west side when he was stopped by two police officers. The 15-year veterans of the Saskatoon Police Service handcuffed Night and drove him to the southwest edge of the city, next to the power station. They yanked him from the car, removed the cuffs, and left him standing in an empty field.

"I'm going to freeze out here," Night complained. "It's twenty-five below." The officers drove off.

A light was on inside the power station. Night walked towards the main entrance and started banging on a door. A night watchman answered and Night told him what had happened. The guard said he didn't believe the story, but did call Night a taxi. He finally arrived at his sister's apartment, shaken and scared, but feeling fortunate to be alive.

After listening to Night's story, Ehalt asked why he hadn't filed a complaint. "Who would believe him?" Night's uncle replied. The officer wrote out a seventy-five-dollar ticket for the seat-belt infraction and drove away. But he did not let the matter pass; after all, two men had just been found dead in the same area where Night claimed to have been dumped. "I could either choose to believe what Night told me, or brush it off," says Ehalt, a twenty-two-year police veteran. "I chose to believe him."

Ehalt went straight to Police Chief Dave Scott, who told him to bring Night into the station for an interview. The following day, Ehalt took Night's statement and turned him over to Internal Affairs. "Only when I followed up did I realize the potential of what I was dealing with," says Ehalt. "You never want it to be like this, but when the worst happens, you have to deal with it honestly."

Fifteen members of the Saskatoon police force were called to a meeting chaired by senior police supervisors and told of Night's complaint. No one came forward at that time, but within forty-eight hours Dan Hatchen and Ken Munson, two constables who were at the meeting, acknowledged that they had dropped Night off at the power station. They were subsequently suspended without pay.

"Hatchen and Munson have always thought they made an error in judgment, but they thought at the same time that there was a reason for what they did," explained Al Stickney, president of the Saskatoon police union. "I'm not going to say that it was a good reason."

Within two weeks, at Chief Scott's request, Saskatchewan's Ministry of Justice asked the RCMP to launch a criminal investigation into Night's allegations and the deaths of Wegner and Naistus. The Mounties assembled their task force of fifteen investigators plus support staff; weeks later, its mandate expanded to encompass the case of Neil Stonechild, after reports of his death appeared in local media. The investigation also grew to include the cases of two other aboriginal men who had died earlier in the year, after being released from the custody of Saskatoon police.

And that deadly winter continued. Lloyd Joseph Dustyhorn was found frozen outside a Saskatoon apartment building. He had been drinking heavily before being arrested and then discharged. Darcy Dean Ironchild died in his apartment, hours after his release from a Saskatoon drunk tank. While their deaths differed from the others, they added to concerns that Saskatoon police treat aboriginal men with reckless disregard.

Finally, with April came Spring. Police officers Hatchen and Munson were charged with unlawfully confining and assaulting Darrell Night. In June, after receiving "numerous calls" about police abuse, the task force added a seventh case to its list. Rodney Wailing claims that in 1995, he was sniffing lacquer thinner in Saskatoon's west-end when he was apprehended by two officers and put in the back of their patrol car. Wailing claimed the officers grabbed his container of lacquer thinner and doused him with the chemical. He said he was taken to a field near the Queen Elizabeth Power Station, dragged to the South Saskatchewan River which runs nearby, and dunked several times. He didn't bother filing a complaint until the RCMP launched its probe. He argued that he simply forgot about the incident and went on with his life.

In June, I flew to Saskatoon, rented a car, and drove to the Queen Elizabeth Power Station. It's on the very southern edge of the city, next to a large landfill site. I sat down and stared at the depression where Lawrence Wegner had been found. It was a warm day, sunny and utterly peaceful, save for the relentless hum emanating from the plant's electrical transformers.

Saskatoon's population is 212,000, but the city feels like a small town. No traffic jams, no shrieking road warriors. Drive in any direction and you find open countryside and sprawling fields in minutes; agriculture still dominates the local economy. The city seems stuck in an earlier era. For many aboriginals, however, this means hardship, unhappiness.

Indians make up 15 percent of Saskatoon's population. In the city's west end, they predominate. I took a walk down 20th Street West, which, lined with bars, bingo halls, and greasy diners, is the area's main commercial strip. Young aboriginal prostitutes stood on a corner. A drunken man threatened to sic the cops on me after I photographed a church mission. A rough-looking pair of panhandlers approached me. One, who appeared to be in his twenties, had a hole in his throat the size of a two-dollar coin, the result of a tracheotomy. Abuse, addiction, unemployment, crime, illness—to say that a large segment of Saskatchewan's aboriginal population is plagued by these circumstances is not an ugly stereotype; it's a fact. Tragedy seems to dog them all.

On the Injustice Busters website, Brian Hutchinson, again, has given an account of his investigation into the case.

> The next day I drove two hours to the Saulteaux Reserve near North Battleford, where Lawrence Wegner's parents live. Looking for their house, I stopped at the band office. It was a Saturday, and the place was deserted. "Zero tolerance to verbal and/ or physical abuse," read a notice taped to the building. "Please be advised that any dogs running at large will be shot," warned another.
>
> The Wegners live in a blue house at the far end of the reserve. I found Mary, Lawrence's mother, standing outside, next to a bed of flowers. "I was just thinking, it's summer break and Lawrence would be home right now, helping with the yard or out at the lake swimming. That's what we'd usually do on Saturdays." She started to cry. "There's always a void, always a missing piece."

Seated under a tarp, Gary, her husband, was eating Kentucky Fried Chicken. He told me that their son had been a survivor. "A lot of times we almost lost him. He was involved in a car accident when he was two weeks old. Hit by a truck once, knocked fifty feet. When he was four, he got into some rat poison. I drove him into North Battleford and he started vomiting blood." Lawrence was a bright kid, Gary added, but he "had a dark side." He would drink and get high. He landed in a group home and trashed his room. In 1997, he'd stolen eleven dollars from a gas station and received three months' probation. The cops were always hassling him, Gary said. "But he didn't deserve to die."

West from Saulteaux near the Alberta border is the Onion Lake Reserve, where I met Rodney Naistus's brother, Darrell, and their grandfather Alphonse. We sat at a battered table in Alphonse's house, where he lives with his second wife and a cluster of children, some of whom are their own, some of whom they were looking after. Darrell and Rodney's parents separated when the boys were infants and they were raised in foster homes and group homes, on and off the reserve. "There was one place in Edmonton where we used to get whipped all the time," Darrell recalled. "We were seven or eight. A little old white lady used to whip us with willow branches and lock us up because we were late coming home from school."

The boys got into trouble. Someone offered them money to commit a break-and-enter in Edmonton. They were caught and received a sentence of four months' probation. They wound up back on the reserve, this time in a group home run by aboriginals. When that closed, Darrell and Rodney lived by themselves in an abandoned house, across the road from their grandfather's place.

Neither boy finished high school and they couldn't find jobs. Rodney was a quiet individual who would often draw tattoo patterns: dragons, eagles, and skulls. Last year, he broke into a store in Lloydminster, an oil town on the Alberta border. The police found him walking back to the reserve. Sentenced to do

*time at an urban work camp in Saskatoon, he was released in
late January, the coldest time of the year. Then, he went out
drinking with his brother, for the last time.*

*Alphonse was working in his garage when an RCMP cruis-
er pulled into his driveway. "He said that Rodney had passed
away. The cop just told me that and then he drove off."*

The curtain ringers

A code of silence has descended over most of Saskatoon's
embattled police force. Constables Hatchen and Munson, suspended and facing trial, refused obstinately to discuss their
role in the Night incident. Munson, a Scottish immigrant and
a member of a church choir, was away painting houses when
I and a showed up at his door; his home was for sale. Like
Hatchen, he was keeping a low profile although his lawyer
was much more in the public eye. Morris Bodnar had been
counsel to Jack Ramsay, a former Reform Party MP, who was
convicted of attempting to rape a young aboriginal girl at the
time when he was an RCMP officer. To many, this choice of
lawyer tinged the case from the start.

Bruce Ehalt, the officer who had taken Darrell Night's
statement, suggested that Saskatoon should have a short-term
detoxification facility, where severely incapacitated people can
spend a night under medical supervision. That was his way to
ease the blame on the force.

"When police are faced with no alternative, he said, some
will opt for dumping drunks at the edge of town or at a rela-
tive's house, when they should be treated instead. Police get
frustrated. You don't want to keep locking someone up.
There's no help. We're glorified babysitters."

Saskatoon's police chief, Dave Scott, whom I met, quali-
fied the recent allegations of police brutality as "every chief's
nightmare." But he refused to point at his officers and suggested that if there was a problem, it might be with the aboriginal community itself.

"There's nothing worse than an unemployed person," he told me. "We've got to make sure that there are menial jobs where these people with low skills can get some kind of life . . . The root issue is alcoholism. Over eighty percent of the people coming to our detention facilities are sniffed up, drunk, or on drugs. I'm fed up with it."

This didn't reassure the aboriginal community. Fearing that the RCMP's investigation might amount to little more than a public-relations exercise, Saskatchewan's main aboriginal body, the Federation of Saskatchewan Indian Nations, hired two private investigators to shadow the task force, at a budgeted cost of $300,000.

According to Oliver Williams, one of the private eyes, the whole inquiry was a mess. "There were too many people involved, scrambling," he commented. Williams said he had heard that the Saskatoon police were not interested in helping the RCMP with their investigation. "Only the case involving Neil Stonechild might lead to more charges. As for the others, I don't know if there will be enough to ever go on," Williams said.

In the end, Hatchen and Munson were found guilty of unlawful confinement. They did some time and were acknowledged by the Saskatoon Police Service for having served 17 years with the force. The Police Association stood by them and paid for their defence until they were convicted. Only then were they fired.

These cases were indefensible; and yet there seemed to be little outrage. Through the weeks and years following those terrible events, nothing happened that could have appeased my sadness and anger. In fact, for the most part, all the headlines, statements, news scrums appeared to me as just so many efforts to conceal the unbearable truth.

The story becomes shockingly obvious just following the trail of news headlines. They show a concerted effort to block the search for justice:

"Justice Minister promises the Native leaders a referral to the Feds for ways to keep Natives out of jail" (March 3)

"RCMP task force wraps-up Night investigation" (March 21)

"Hatchen and Munson to get paid" (March 23)

"New probe of Natives deaths: Private eyes to investigate Saskatoon police" (April 11)

" City still owes explanations for recent police practice" (May 11)

"Police Chief rules no discipline needed" (May 12)

"Stonechild case closed: RCMP refuses to add decade old cases to its investigation on suspicious deaths in Saskatoon" (February 23, 2000)

"Jail alternatives key to justice system overhaul" (Min. of Justice, February 26, 2000)

"Justice Minister Axworthy refuses to call a public inquiry on Natives deaths" (March 2000)

The importance of these cases today stretches beyond the bounds of Saskatoon. What about all the missing and murdered Aboriginal women—more than twelve hundred victims? The police forces of yesterday generate the police forces of today. Not enough changes. It makes me wonder about our real commitment to protecting the marginalized, the less fortunate, and the refusal to create an inquiry is just mind blowing. As I learn more, my apprehension only grows.

The predators

As of May 2015, 362 women across Canada had made similar claims of sexual harassment and assault. They sought legal action against their police corps, the RCMP. From nine provinces and three territories they all had come forward to denounce their experiences.

The lawyer bringing the class action said in the two years since the lawsuit was filed, hundreds of women, one-third of them still with the force, have come forward.

"When we hit 100 I was surprised," said lawyer David Klein of Klein Lyons, the firm handling the class action. "As we hit 200, I was less surprised, and then 300 even less, because we were beginning to have a sense of the magnitude of the internal problem at the RCMP with women in the force."

The suit accounted for 336 complainants. It alleged widespread systemic discrimination by the RCMP against female members. Janet Merlo, a former RCMP officer based in Nanaimo who filed the lawsuit on behalf of the others, said she suffered bullying and harassment throughout her career of nearly 20 years.

Corporal Catherine Galliford, a former RCMP spokeswoman whose claims of sexual harassment in 2011 have been credited with opening the door for others, said she is encouraged to see women coming forward, but saddened they did not before.

Corporal Galliford, who said she still suffered from post-traumatic stress disorder from years of harassment, has been on sick leave since 2006. An internal RCMP report released in 2012 suggested gender-based harassment happened frequently to the female officers who participated in a study of their experiences of being bullied by colleagues and superiors. In response to the report, Deputy Commissioner Craig Callens announced the creation of a 100-member team to investigate harassment complaints.

Anitra Singh alleged in a notice of civil claim filed in B.C. Supreme Court that Inspector Tim Shields sexually harassed and assaulted her from 2009 to 2011. Ms. Singh, a civilian RCMP member, was a senior communications adviser from February, 2008, until taking sick leave in September 2012. She reported to Inspector Shields, who was then in charge of B.C.'s RCMP "E" Division.

Among the allegations, Ms. Singh claims Inspector Shields made lewd comments to her both verbally and through text messages, exposed himself to her and confined her in a bathroom, forcing her to touch him in an inappropriate manner, according to court documents.

Ms. Singh accuses Inspector Shields of abusing his position of trust and authority, and his rank. As a result of his actions, Ms. Singh says she has post-traumatic stress disorder, depression, anxiety and other ailments, according to the court documents.

Another woman also filed a civil suit against Inspector Shields alleging similar misconduct. Atoya Montague, who held several communications positions as a civilian employee with the RCMP from 2002 until 2011, claimed Inspector Shields exposed himself to her, made dirty comments and sent sexually explicit text messages.

RCMP spokesman Sgt. Rob Vermeulen noted the force's formal response to the allegations will be filed in a statement of defence. "These unproven allegations now form part of a recently filed civil suit, and as such, we are not able to comment further," he said.

A University of Toronto professor is bolstering a proposed class-action lawsuit against the RCMP, saying women who experience gender-based discrimination and harassment can witness their personal and professional well-being spiral downwards. Jennifer Berdahl, an associate professor of organizational behavior at the University of Toronto's Rotman School of Management, filed an affidavit in B.C. Supreme Court as part of a larger court action launched in March 2012 by a former member of the RCMP, named Janet Merlo.

Merlo alleges that during her 19-year career with the force, she was subjected to name calling, sexist pranks, and demands for sexual favors. Her case has yet to be certified and the allegations have yet to be proven in court.

"The impact on women who have been the subject of gender-based discrimination and/or harassment in the workplace is typically a downward spiral of impaired professional and personal well-being, especially if the discrimination and/or harassment is not stopped," states Prof. Berdahl in her affidavit.

As a result, women can experience diminished professional reputation, impaired concentration, decreased motivation and job satisfaction, increased work withdrawal, social rejection and isolation, the deterioration of personal relationships, depression, post-traumatic stress and even alcohol and substance abuse.

Berdahl states employers can take steps to protect female employees by providing workers with written guidelines and training and by following provincial health and safety rules, and federal human-rights legislation.

––––––––––––

There are several more incidents of surprisingly bad deeds from what is supposed to be Canada's best. How could this have no impact on our faith in this institution?

As I said, we're in a war against people who want to kill us. We need our RCMP now more then ever. Among other things, the mounties are a key player in INSET (Integrated National Security Enforcement Team). I've worked with many of these men and women, and, for many of them, I did so with great pleasure. I have faith, and there is still hope. The problem areas must be understood and not allowed to spread or continue: The police force as a whole must focus their efforts and join the fight. And I should mention a particular bright spot: the OPP (Ontario Provincial Police), truly a force to reckon with. Toronto, the largest city in the Canada, and the country's most populated area, southern Ontario, are under the OPP umbrella, and for that we should be grateful.

The old adage tells us that one bad apple can ruin the bunch. The analogy doesn't quite fit: The ratio of bad to good is much less reassuring than that. But there are good apples, and therein lies our hope.

CHAPTER TWELVE

Dumb and Dumber

I've often wondered where I got my wanderlust. Ever since I was a child, I was never satisfied where I was—I've always been moving on, even when I knew the road ahead was the same road I travelled a month or two earlier, going in the other direction. I guess I wasn't the only one. In the late sixties, the youth of Canada were hitting the road in large numbers, hitchhiking across the country. Like Jim Morrison said in the iconic Doors song, The End: "The West is the best / Get here, we'll do the rest." Following the call, thousands hit the road. Kids from broken homes, or no homes, young girls running from abuse or the drudgery of isolated farm life—all types headed out for adventure and a new beginning. And the road fulfilled its promises. You might meet someone one night in a traveller's hostel and journey with them for a day or two, then go your separate ways.

Our Prime Minister at the time, Pierre Trudeau, encouraged young people to travel. He even had shelters set up all the way across the country so that they could safely get a good night's sleep, wash their clothes and so on. Amazingly, there were school buses travelling the desolate northern route through Ontario—a sprawling, rugged part of the country—to bring travellers to the next shelter. Kindred spirits would compare notes on the road ahead. Information was shared: which church was good for a meal, which small town should be avoided at all costs. It wasn't just chatter. For those with limited means, the information could be crucial. A lot of them were travelling with a sense of desperation, running from something back home or something within themselves. But no matter the destination, you always bring your ghosts with you. No amount of running can shake them.

In the evening we'd sit around and someone always had a guitar. We'd sing songs by Peter, Paul and Mary and other popular folk heroes. At some point, the conversation would inevitably turn to the question, "So, why are you on the road?" A few glib answers at first, and then the morsels of truth would start coming out. Someone would pick up on one admission and add their own to it. Before you knew it, stories started piling up. Stories about so-called good, regular people: priests, church ministers, gym teachers, even fathers, uncles and brothers, doing the unthinkable, the unforgivable. You'd hear some of the most tragic stories, ones that would tear your heart out.

We grouped everyone over thirty into the same category. There were clinical names for most of these criminals, but that didn't change anything—it didn't stop the pain or mend a shattered life. The older generation shook their heads and wondered why my own was so rebellious and hard to control. The seeds of mistrust grow in the dark, where no sunshine reaches. It takes root in the cracks and holes, and it can be covered up, but it's very hard to remove. So many of us felt that way about the adults who were supposed to guide and protect us. But then we found each other. Sharing pain with one another helped lighten the burden and strengthen our bonds. No one who had that of kind of encounter on the road walked away from it untouched, unmoved, unaffected.

As you can see, it stays with you. Some fifty years later and I'm sitting here feeling totally pissed off, exactly as I was then. It's like there's a compartment in your head where the heavy stuff sits unchanged. Will it ever go away?

A sidenote, of sorts: The next time some asshole tells you Aboriginal people should just get over the residential school issue, get over it and move on—and there are plenty of people like that out there—remember my story, the tales of pain I heard, and multiply it by a thousand. The Métis in me is still enraged. I have to calm down, so I'm going outside for a smoke. Back in a jiffy.

Anyway. Most people who lived the vagabond life during those years eventually got to Vancouver and stayed put. Unless you decided to go home, that was the end of the road. The years of bohemian living softened into adulthood and the desire to settle down and make a home. That history is a reason Vancouver is one of the best places to live in Canada and maybe the world. The wisdom those young people picked up on their travels, the openness and nonjudgmental attitude and the desire for peace and community never really left them, but took deep roots in this city at the edge of the world.

———————

It was 1962. I was 14, and my brother Pete was 16. Pete had met a girl who was visiting Hull with her family to spend time with relatives—or so I assumed. Why else would a family from Montreal come to Hull? I don't know how he met her, but he was smitten. When it came time for her to return to Montreal, we both heard the same thing as clear as a bell: the call of adventure. We weren't worried. We were used to finding our way around Hull—a small city, with a population of sixty-five thousand. How different could Montreal be? With twelve bucks in our pockets and the boldness of youth in our hearts, we were confident that we had it covered

And so, bright and early one Monday morning, we hit the road. We opted for the Quebec side of the Ottawa River. There were small towns all along the route, so if there were any problems on the way we wouldn't be stranded in the middle of nowhere. The obvious route on the Ontario side was the

401, a fast highway with exits into towns: a faster route if you're driving, but offering less flexibility for hitchhiking, with its cars going way too fast to stop. Thus we town-hopped our way to Montreal at a leisurely pace. It took us five or six hours to cover the two hundred kilometers. It was a fun, pleasant trip.

By mid-afternoon, we were in bustling downtown Montreal. The leisurely journey was over, and I was definitely starting to feel overwhelmed. I couldn't believe the flood of people rushing up and down Saint-Catherine Street. Deciding to stop and assess our next move, we bought hot dogs and pop and headed to a small park.

We felt totally lost. Then a question occurred to me that seemed relevant. Did her parents know we were coming? No—, Pete said, they had no idea that we even existed. I followed up with a related question. Did she know we were coming? Again, no.

I started to see flaws in the plan. Even if we did find her, then what? I kept that question to myself—no need to rain further on the parade. With that, however, I went from adventure to survival mood—a state of mind that I would get pretty used to in the years to come. I considered the fact that we had to get home again. Maybe we should phone her, I suggested. But he didn't have the number—just the address.

I told him I'd be right back and went off to find a phone book. I soon found one, and her phone number was in it. I gave it to Pete and he went to make the call. While I waited for him to return, I asked a stranger where the address was. Bad news: it was way out on the south shore of Montreal, of the island and across the Jacques Cartier Bridge, much too far to walk. There was no subway in Montreal back then and the buses were too complicated for us.

As it turned out, the distance didn't matter. Peter came back and said he had spoken with her and she didn't want to meet. She was busy doing other things and had no interest in seeing him again. Saint-Catherine is a very long street, like Yonge Street in Toronto, and we didn't even know which direction to walk. We needed help, and with Pete feeling wounded from the rejection I figured it was up to me.

I saw two cops standing in a doorway near Saint-Laurent Street — the start of the famous (or maybe at that time infamous) district known as the Main, a dangerous place to wander around back then. I told Pete to follow my lead. I walked right up to the cops and told that our mother was supposed to be in Montreal, but the phone number we had was wrong. We were from Hull, I said, and she had left us years ago. Now we were lost and just wanted to go home. They called a patrol car, which came and took us to a youth shelter for the night where we got a meal and a good sleep. Today I wonder if I had needed to come up with a story at all; they probably would have helped us either way. The next morning they gave us a bus ticket to Hull and a ride to the bus station—they even packed a lunch for us. We were safe and on our way.

It worked out well, but maybe it would have been better if we had suffered more and learned a different lesson from the experience. We had travelled on a whim, with no money to speak of, and had survived using wit and deception. It definitely gave our confidence a boost. It's funny how my career since then has involved almost exactly the same thing as that early misadventure. I travel to cities I don't know, attach myself to strangers, and use whatever cunning I have to get the job done. You never know how early you might inadvertently carve out a niche for yourself in the world.

The travel itch may be the reason why I didn't stop when I reached Vancouver in those wandering years, I wasn't ready to settle down and maybe I never would be. From coast to coast, from north to south—the role of drifter, free of responsibility, living out of a bag, was a perfect fit for me. If things get dicey, you just leave. And that's where the downsides come in, the other side of the coin. When you don't put down roots, you're never forced to deal with the harder parts of relation-ships. You can always just run away. And that downside has affected me in no small measure. As good as I was at my job, I was sometimes terrible in my private life. That lack of com-mitment, having one foot out the door—even today it hasn't totally left me. But while my mind might be ready to race toward the next highway, my body, with louder and louder protests, is starting to tell me otherwise.

Another part of my adult life can be traced straight back to my rough and tumble youth in Hull: my association with criminals, tough guys and gangsters. From the earliest age, my group of friends was always pitted against another group—more than pals, we Hull locals were a gang. As I got older, though, our tight little unit began to change. Our close bond, almost like a brotherhood, seemed to be falling apart.

It started when drugs were brought into the mix. Then came the girls: "working girls," to various degrees. There were no pimps, per se, but we protected them, and in return they helped us out when they were flush. Meanwhile the drugs really started to flow in from Montreal: hash, ecstasy, acid, all of it. When meth finally hit the street, things completely fell apart. The ad-diction, paranoia and everything that goes with it, was devastat-ing for our community. Up to that point we had thought we were tough and cool—and maybe we were, in our little world. But the real world made our own seem like a very small and innocent place.

When Montreal's ambitious criminal Adrien Dubois decided to expand his drug distribution network, Hull and Gatineau were high on his list. Adrien and his cronies were powerful and lethal figures on the organized crime scene—we local hoods didn't stand a chance. Their reach was long and their interests were many—their tactics ranged from brutal fistfights to straight-out murder. We were punks in comparison. Dubois' name was known by all, but I'd never met anyone who actually knew him. I at least had been to Montreal, although my view of its dark side was just a glimpse of the surface—the neon signs and window displays hawking strippers and other kinds of vice. In that respect, it felt like I knew more than most of my friends from Hull—but really I knew nothing at all.

Now, decades later, I've put together the sordid history of the menace known as Adrien Dubois, who was just one year older than me but light years ahead in terms of criminal experience.

If Montreal's crime and sin reached out like the darkness from Mordor (yes, another reference to *The Lord of the Rings*.) and engulfed Hull, Gatineau and all the towns in-between, Sauron (Google it!) took the form of Adrien Dubois.

The youngest of the infamous Dubois brothers, Adrien was born in 1946. He grew up in Saint-Henri, a rough lower class district of Montreal. His existence then wasn't so different from ours. That helped make his entry into the world of crime smooth and effortless.

He would follow his brothers into crime and quickly outdo them to become one of the city's most powerful drug traffickers and loan sharks.

In Montreal in the 1960s, the Harlem Paradise was a nightclub frequented by the wrong kind of people: mobsters and criminals of all kinds. Adrien took control of the place, located on Saint-Antoine Street downtown, and made it his headquarters for prostitution. Local pimps who had long controlled this sector of the city threatened Dubois, but they were dealt with brutally.

Later, Bryce Richardson, a gang leader from the west-end, planned to take over the nightclub. Adrien was informed about it and turned to a hitman, Yvon Belzile, to deal with the situation. Belzile fired three times at Richardson, who survived but was left paralysed.

The 70s were years of plenty for the Dubois brothers. Adrien was the most prosperous of them all, mainly because of his successful loansharking operation and a large-scale drug network that stretched as far as Hull across from Ottawa. He supplied much of the local market with marijuana, hashish, amphetamines and cocaine.

However, problems emerged from time to time. Adrien became a prime suspect in the case of the abduction and disappearance of Yvon Bertin, a well-known criminal who was seen for the last time being forced into an automobile on November 26, 1971. Police investigation showed that Bertin had began dealing drugs on Adrien's territory without permission. His body was never found.

Another battle for drug turf took place in 1974. Newspapers referred to it as the "War of the West." Dubois led his organization in this brutal war with the McSween gang. Nine people were murdered and more than a dozen were wounded before the Dubois gang emerged victorious.

In the late 1970s, Adrien needed a legitimate business that would make it possible to launder money for his organization. To this end, he opened a clothing business on Saint-Augustin Street in the heart of Saint-Henri.

Adrien's work involved increasing levels of violence. When his brother Claude was on trial for first-degree murder, he devised a plan to prevent a hitman, Donald Lavoie, from testifying. The plan involved killing Lavoie's brother-in-law. Police were informed of the plot and took action to protect the intended victim from the members of the Hells Angels Montreal Chapter hired for the job.

Adrien's battles against legal authorities made headlines on several occasions. The press reported every aspect with fascination—their coverage almost resembled a crime drama. As for examples, these are excerpts from published articles and websites.

> Police arrested Adrien on June 29, 1982 and charged him with the murder of Jacques McSween, shot to death in Longueuil on October 5, 1974. Adrien's brother Jean-Guy, who was already behind bars on a murder conviction, and Claude Dubeau, who was also jailed awaiting trial for the murder of Richard Désormiers, were also charged with the murder.
>
> The trial began on February 1, 1983 and featured testimony from several underworld informants. Donald Lavoie claimed to have been present when the three defendants murdered Jacques McSween, and described the event in vivid detail. Paul Pomerleau, a small-time extortionist, and Claude Jodoin, a former Dubois Gang member, also provided damaging testimony. But not all of the jury believed what the rats spewed, and the trial, which lasted two-and-a-half months, ended in a deadlock. A new trial was agreed upon.
>
> Adrien's lawyer, the most famous criminalist Léo-René Maranda, managed to have his client freed on bail until the second trial was scheduled. On June 1, 1983, while liberated, Adrien was arrested downtown in a hotel on Sherbrooke Street and charged with importing 480 kilograms of hashish.
>
> The second McSween murder trial began soon after and consisted of the same three government witnesses. The jury gave little credibility to the informants and took little time reaching their decision. Adrien, his brother Jean-Guy, and Claude Dubeau were acquitted of murder on June 14, 1985. Friends and family of the defendants applauded loudly as the Superior Court jury brought down its verdict.

Eventually Adrien moved to Saint-Adele, a small town in the Laurentians, just north of Montreal. According to newspaper articles, he remained on good terms with the West End Gang, the Italian Mafia and the Hells Angels. During his final years, Adrien Dubois lived discreetly, presiding over a company he registered as a real-estate management firm. A public notice for his death made no mention of his past or his criminal brothers. After a life of tumult, Adrien passed away peacefully. It seems extraordinary, if not downright unjust.

When he died, they said he would be sorely missed. I guess that depends on whom you ask.

CHAPTER THIRTEEN

Nominees for a Deadfall

Retirement is a wonderful thing for most people. The highlights of your day are afternoon naps and walks to and from the store. The redness of the tomatoes in the garden starts to seem important. Curling on TV perfectly suits your energy level. Life becomes quiet and sedate—and that's not a bad thing. Especially after a career like mine, filled with too many close calls—your dues have been paid and it's time to relax.

You may have convinced those around you of all this. But have you convinced yourself? After all, there's the other side of the coin, too. Getting on in years definitely has its downside—especially if you're single. The dating scene certainly doesn't feel quite as fiery as it once did. On top of that, other men stop seeing you as a threat. Somehow that feels important to you. It's hard to explain, but there it is.

———————

October 2014. The phone rang in the middle of the night. I hurried to answer it before it woke up the whole house. An unknown number—probably a wrong number, I thought. But it turned out there was no mistake.

The caller wanted to talk to someone who had vanished a long time ago. Maybe I should have just told them it was a wrong number. Instead I slipped right into my old skin, and the years seemed to wash away.

And so I've got one more story for you. But in telling it, I have to exercise some caution. This case isn't long buried—it's very much ongoing as I write. In a way, that makes it simpler for me: All too often, the powers that be impose silence on anyone involved in a case once it's over. This is my chance to put something on the record before it's too late. And besides, how often does a reader get the chance to get right inside an ongoing case? Not just to read about it years later, but to be right there in the thick of it? So, reader, come along for one last ride.

We live in the midst of a secret war. A war against those who would kill for ideological purposes, in cold blood and without a second thought. Extremists—what kind doesn't matter, because really, they're all the same: equally obsessed and equally lethal. This is the story of a handful of old timers who got recruited because of their years of experience in this war, and their willingness to put themselves on the line for the cause one more time. As important as it is, I can't honestly say we took the job just for the sake of protecting the public. Partly we took it because we're the type who can't resist feeling important. It beats watering the garden or taking yet another afternoon nap.

But maybe there was another reason they chose us: because we're all expendable. It may sound melodramatic, but I think there's a kernel of truth in it. Who would miss us? A gaggle of aging agents with a lot of valuable knowledge and too much time on our hands—I guess you could say that we were all on their least wanted list.

When our first meeting came around, I encountered agents I hadn't seen in years. I was shocked—everybody seemed so old. I guess I probably did too. But one thing hadn't changed: the light in their eyes, as intense as it ever was, shining with excitement and determination.

We were given a list of eighteen names: all Canadian citizens, fourteen immigrants from overseas and four who were born here, all of them with families in Canada. All were Muslims since birth, except for three who were converts. All of them were suspected of being a threat. Our job was to find them, get information on them and determine whether they represented a real danger.

We eliminated four right off the bat—they were clearly all bark and no bite, big talkers who represented no threat except maybe to themselves. Two others were apparently off fighting for their cause in another country, so they weren't an immediate problem. That left twelve unaccounted for.

A CSIS informant gave our guys a tip: a man living in Toronto knew the location of two of our targets. The address he gave was in the Glebe neighbourhood of Ottawa, Ontario. Tensions were still high in the nation's capital following the murder of a soldier at the National War Memorial in November. We decided to send two of our guys to Toronto to talk to the informant for any details that could give a sense of his character and motivation.

We went back to our rooms to get some sleep, planning to meet in the morning to form a plan. One member of our team—an ex-Ontario Provincial policeman and a real go-getter—stayed behind at the office to do some web searching on this guy. While he was there, he got a call from Toronto with some surprising news: The informant had vanished without a trace. Our intel told us that our target was still at the address in Ottawa, but no one knew for how long he would stay there. The situation had become urgent.

Then the ex-cop—I'll call him Gerry—decided that the best thing for him to do was make a solo move. He didn't call us until he was a couple of hours away from Ottawa. There was no way we could catch up with him—all we could do was tell him to be careful. We wanted him to take the Toronto police with him, but he didn't think it was necessary. Who knows what was driving him: a worldview, an emotional attitude or just single-mindedness. The very things that make us good at what we do can be our worst enemy. We headed back to our rooms and waited to hear whatever news came next. There wasn't anything else to do for the moment—besides, Gerry had turned his phone off. He was on his own.

Gerry arrived at the address in no time. According to a witness, he ran up the three storeys to the apartment. He found the door slightly ajar—perfect, he thought, no warrant needed. Fuelled by adrenalin, he ignored the basic principles you're supposed to follow in that kind of situation, the ones that should kick in automatically. He pushed the door open and rushed in, gun in hand. It all happened much too fast to see the fishing line that was tied from the door to a single chair. A shotgun was taped to the back of the chair; the fishing line was wrapped around it and tied to the trigger. Gerry never had a chance. The gunshot blew him out of the apartment and his blood splattered against the hallway wall. His body lay crumpled on the floor. As I write this, the death was yesterday: December 13, 2014.

No one said very much when we got the news. We dealt with it privately. This morning, everyone's attitude seems to have undergone a change. It doesn't show so much in our words, but I can sense it. The air is charged. The assignment has taken on a new meaning—it has become personal. That, along with our skills and our determination, makes the six of us who remain a very serious weapon.

As for Gerry, his death was probably reported as being caused by car accident somewhere in Nowheresville, Ontario. That kind of practice isn't just to protect the agencies. The subterfuge is also a way to ensure the victim's family can still receive life insurance. You don't want them to suffer because of his occupation and the risks he had to take—or in this case, chose to take.

Meanwhile, we were faced with an urgent question. How did they know we were after them? Was there a leak on our side? The game had changed—and so would the venue. We were all booked on flights to Saint Lucia and from there to Dominica, a small island country in the Caribbean. As tiny as it is, it has only a small, uninspiring airstrip that can't take large planes and a port where one cruise ship docks for a day once a week. It has volcanoes and rainforests, and the world's second-largest thermal lake, but not many beaches. Roseau, the capital, is a jumble of people, shanty town houses and shops. Still, capitalism reaches into surprising places: In the middle of it all, I spotted a Royal Bank branch.

As for getting good undercover work done, it's less than ideal: In a setting like this, it's impossible not to look like a foreigner. As a white guy, I was part of a very tiny minority on the island. No matter how nonchalant you try to seem, you stick out like a sore thumb. To be less conspicuous, we stayed in pairs at different hotels, meeting all together only when we had to.

Soon we got news from Canada. We were given an address in the town of Mahaut, about three miles from the Rouseau, on the coastal road—if you could call it a road. One of our crew went off to rent a vehicle while we studied the map. We had acquired a solid dose of caution since Gerry's death. We decided to hit our target early the next morning, around 5:30 am. We would all sleep in the same room tonight, two to a bed and the rest of us wherever we could get comfortable. I knew it didn't really matter, that sleep would be elusive. No one mentioned Gerry—it would seem like bad luck—but I'm sure he was on everybody's mind. He was certainly on mine.

The hour finally came. As we approached the house, we found that circumstances would be different from the average bust back home. The house had two sides. The front faced the mountain, and the back had a patio that ended at a cliff over-looking the ocean. The back was clearly out of the question;

we had no ropes or pulleys, and it would have been too risky either way. That left the front, and a side entrance via the driveway. One man stayed in the van and we positioned two in front. Then we kicked in the side door and swarmed through the place.

There was only one occupant. A handgun lay on the small table next to him. I saw him glance at it, but he wisely decided against the "hail of bullets" option. It turned out he was alone in the house; his partner was away arranging a drug deal. Clearly he thought we were DEA or some other drug-law enforcement agency. We sat him down at a small table and he started talking. In no time he was burying his friend, giving him up as the main drug-runner and downplaying his own involvement —not an impressive case of standing one's ground. He seemed to know nothing about the hit on Gerry.

We talked for a full hour, and gradually brought the conversation around to terrorist activity. He seemed truly perplexed at that. We were getting nowhere on that topic, and I believe that he really didn't know anything. We got all the information we could about his friend, where he was at the moment and information on their drug contact: some member of the Brothers, a motorcycle club that was a puppet gang for the Hells Angels. We pried him for phone numbers and nicknames. That was going to be the end of it.

Why the guy suddenly decided to throw himself off his patio, falling 100 feet to the rocks below, is a mystery. Who knows what was running through his brain—but it was certainly a shock to us. Regardless, it signalled an abrupt end to our work there, and in five minutes we were loaded up and gone. We called in the intelligence we'd gathered and headed back to the hotel. As for the remaining guy, the missing drug partner, I hoped he enjoyed spending time on the island. There was no way he could go back to Canada, and with the DEA on his case he was cooked for good.

And so our list was down to ten. Then an event occurred that made our mission more urgent: a terrorist attack in Australia involving a hostage-taking in a café in December 2014. There was reason to believe the incident would be seen by our targets as a reason to act—they may have hoped to emulate the gesture. That meant we had to move on faster.

The group was definitely unsatisfied with how things were going. We couldn't just keep tracking down our targets one by one—the list would be obsolete before we reached the bottom. Of course, we didn't know all the details; other parties may have been working different angles simultaneously. The scary thing was that if we missed just one suspect, it could still spell a major disaster: He could strap himself to plastic explosives and wreak havoc at any time.

The further the case went on, the more apparent it was to me that our society just doesn't know how to fight these threats. You can't clamp down on everybody wearing a beard or belonging to the Islamic faith. We can't shut down our borders. These tactics would go against the very essence of what we are as a people. So how do you prevent attacks? As it stands now, we are mostly limited to reacting—being proactive is where it gets tricky. Until someone comes up with something better, that's just the way it is. The dramatic events at the Charlie Hebdo satirical magazine in Paris in January 2015, and others since, are a horrible case in point.

Aside from these broader concerns, things took a turn in our little group as well. One member, Barney, had gone to return the rental van and he never came back. To say we were concerned would be an understatement. We stayed close to each other and waited for some kind of word. It came via a staff member from the Canadian consulate in Barbados, who visited us accompanied by someone from the local military. He told us that Barney would not be coming back, that he had been reassigned in accordance with new plans from Ottawa. We were to stand down and wait for instructions. While the guests were in the room no one among us said anything, which seemed to make them understandably uncomfortable. They promptly left.

By morning, we had each received new orders. Mine were simple and straightforward. My boss and I were to report to a yet-to-be disclosed location in Vancouver for further instruction. I don't know what the others were told; they didn't volunteer the information and I didn't ask. The upside was that we were given several days to relax at a beach hotel on Saint Lucia. Finally we would get a taste of the perks of the business.

For once in my life, I agreed with the powers that be. We would be a lot more effective separate than as a single unit. Wherever I ended up, I hoped it would be out of the firing line. The last month had reinforced what was already obvious. Like the rest of the crew, I was too old and didn't have that reckless drive I had as a young agent. Life had a little more meaning. It's hard to explain. It was not about being a coward or anything like that—I just didn't have it anymore. It's inevitable maybe, but it's still a hard thing to come to grips with.

I reserved a place on the ferry for Saint Lucia the next morning, looking forward to doing absolutely nothing in the sun for a bit. But by the end of the day, things had changed again. The DEA had asked our bosses to keep us down there for a few more days. We were to stay at the location and wait for the missing partner, the drug smuggler, and hold him till the DEA could arrive and take custody. We were stuck with another stakeout. We didn't take the news particularly well, especially since it cut right in to our break time. But there was nothing to be done.

It was my turn to stay up on the night shift when we got a call from one of the Americans directing us: Special Agent-in-Charge Stillwell. He told me they were covering the address we gave them for the smuggler and he needed to double-check it. That sent off warning bells for me. I checked my notebook and gave him confirmation for the address: 187

Caracasbaaiweg on the island of Curacao in the Caribbean. The place was a biker clubhouse for the Brothers. The smuggler was supposed to do a pick-up on Wednesday at nine o'clock. Stillwell asked if there was anything else he should know; I said no, and he hung up.

All the information I gave him he could have gotten straight from the file or from our handler, but instead he had called me. Why? Nothing was ever what it seemed when dealing with Americans. I supposed I would find out in good time.

The man we were waiting for showed up on Christmas Eve. I wasn't on duty at the time, but I read the report. Our guys were right behind him when he walked into the house. They arrested him and tied him to a chair. They called the DEA, and within hours they came to take him into custody. And that was that—our job was done.

———————

That meant it was time for us to head to the island of Saint Lucia—this time for real. We had to take the ferry there, to catch our flights home, and we would spend a few days relaxing before leaving. The ferry dumps you in Castries, the capital city—just forty miles from the airport, but it's an hour and a half drive, which shows you the condition of the roads. Driving in the region is an experience. Once you leave the city there are no speed limits or traffic lights, no direction signs or passing lanes—nothing. Just a narrow strip of pavement twisting and turning every which way, filled with potholes that could swallow a Volkswagen. The locals zip around the corners without slowing, resulting in constant near-misses with oncoming vehicles. It's a harrowing experience to be sure.

But because of the ferry schedule, we had another day of sitting around before getting to our tropical vacation spot. We were advised not to wander around but to stick close to the hotel. I spent most of the day bored out of my skull. I couldn't wait to get out of there. It seemed strange: People save all their money just to be able to come to the Caribbean during that time of year, when home is buried in snow. The thought of what everyone back home was doing for Christmas just dampened the already heavy mood for me.

My thoughts turned to the Christmases of my youth. The whole community would show up at midnight mass, individual family members waiting at the front steps of the church till the whole family had arrived. Everyone went in as a unit and would sit together, except for a few of the women who stayed at home preparing the feast called the *réveillon*. Some years, if we were lucky, it would snow in big flakes as we came out of the church. After church we would walk to my Grandma's house. What a meal! Ragoût de pattes, tourtière, a big turkey with mashed potatoes, cranberries—an incredible spread. Of course there was a kid's table, always full of cousins we hardly knew. In the living room, after eating, my uncle Fred would take out his fiddle, someone would play the spoons and the *chansons à répondre* would start. Us kids would soon be sent to bed so Santa could do his thing, and the grownups would party on into the night. We'd be asleep as soon as our heads touched the pillow.

It might all sound a bit corny now, but back then it was a magical experience. All the pieces fit together to make Christmas a very special time, and none of us ever forgot that feeling, even many years later. Just a few months ago I wrote down the names of all the relatives in the house on Christmas Eve: almost forty people. It's hard to believe that they've all passed away now. I was one of six kids: three brothers and three sisters. I'm the only one left; they're gone, along with my parents and aunts and uncles.

That life only exists in my heart now. Maybe the traditions involved in French-Canadian Christmas have survived in small communities. In bigger cities like Montreal, families tend to be small, sometimes with no kids, so it's different; they have their own kind of celebrations.

But this time I was having one of the strangest Christmases you could imagine: in a tropical place, with a group of friends who were grizzled agents. A ninety-day mission, with a third of it completed. But I was there for good reason: We were involved in an important action in the fight against terror. I never doubted that we were doing the right thing. If we succeeded in preventing only one attack then it would be well worth it. I was determined to do whatever was required of me during my commitment. We had already reduced the list nearly by half, and we could sense that another plan had already been devised —maybe one that would be even more effective.

The ferry to Saint Lucia was pleasant and comfortable, a two-hour trip for a US$100. There were two cars waiting for us in Castries. I assumed one was for me and the other was for the two other team members going back to Canada. I certainly hadn't expected that the DEA agent who had called me for the drug bust would be the driver of my car. You think you've seen it all, but some things still end up surprising you. Obviously, this wasn't about giving me a guided tour. He was there for a chit-chat session that would last about an hour and a half.

In case you haven't read the first *Befriend and Betray*, I'll recap the technique the DEA uses with guys like me. To give you an illustration, let's go way back to the early 80s, when I had just finished the last Hong Kong deal. It was downtime for me, and I was waiting for Gary Kilgore to organize my next assignment in Thailand. During that time, Scott Paterson called me to say that the DEA in Blaine, Washington, wanted to talk to me. I travelled down from Vancouver and paid them a visit to see what was up. That's when they threw the Bandidos biker case at me. They were well aware that I was in waiting mode, with another new mission that was already taking shape. All they wanted, they said, was a thirty-day commitment to get general information on the Bandidos in the U.S.

I had never even been on a motorcycle—so, reasonably, I refused. Or at least, I tried to refuse. But the money was good, and my job would be limited to collecting intelligence—nothing too risky. That was supposed to be enough for them—it was what they needed to submit a plan to their head office. So I went for it. The thirty days flew by, and I was making a lot of headway into the Bandidos organization. Meanwhile, the Thailand job had hit a snag. So I stayed on for another thirty. Well, you can guess how things went from there. I ended up doing a two-year case, becoming a full club member—and, maybe most surprisingly, at some level a "real" biker.

Now, in the midst of the case in the Caribbean, things were starting to feel very similar. This time they asked me for two weeks—the max, they assured me—to wrap up the Brothers biker gang case on Curaçao. The guy we had caught had talked and talked and given up information on a Canadian bagman—or maybe moneyman is more accurate—with whom he worked. The plan they proposed was actually pretty sound, but I could smell another agenda in the background. Because the Brothers were a puppet club for the Angels, after infiltrating the first gang it would be a simple proposal to cross over and start working on the bigger group.

But I was a lot wiser than I had been back in the 80s. Back then, I had quickly ended up stereotyped as a biker infiltrator—it was a niche that was hard to shake off. What's more, I hated the field. It was highly dangerous and never-ending. You could lose your life with a wrong word. An adversary within the group could shoot you dead right on the street.

Plus, the bigwigs in all the major clubs didn't deal on the street anymore; you could arrest the street soldiers again and again and it wouldn't really slow the flow of drugs. You might have to go through four or five dealers before reaching anyone important. Also, all the puppet clubs seeking favors were ready to do anything to show loyalty. I would say conservatively it takes a five-year project to get anywhere in a biker gang. Who has that kind of time? Not me, that's for sure.

The job at hand had clearly taught me that I was too old for fieldwork. To head back into the work I did in my earlier years—my mind was ready to do what I could and my experience gave me the skills, but my body just couldn't keep up. The roughness and hardship of the biker life was just too taxing. As we pulled into the hotel entrance, the agent told me to at least think it over. I promised I would, took his card and went inside to check in. In the lobby I left a message for my friends and then I went up for a nap. I was impressed: it was a really nice resort, certainly more than I could have afforded if I was paying the tab. I took a quick shower, crawled into bed and was out like a light.

I woke up in the dark and saw a blinking red light on the phone. I turned the light on and sat up to pull myself together before calling downstairs. There was a message for me from a woman named Sarah, who had left a local number. I called it and she picked up immediately. She said she wasn't far away and would meet me at a nearby bar in half an hour. I agreed. I have to admit that I've come to hate meeting female agents for the first time—even though I understand their position. They tend to feel they have to be tough as nails and strictly business to keep the alpha males from making inappropriate moves on them. I wasn't that type of guy, but she wouldn't know that.

She turned up at the bar wearing a business suit and a business attitude. She explained that she had been assigned to do two things: keep me out of trouble and answer any questions I might have as the week went on. She also told me that she had no information on where my friends were. I didn't believe that for a second, but it wasn't a big deal. Either way, I was on my own for the next week.

I was surprised to find out that my new assignment had nothing to do with the terrorist list: I was being asked to spend my time putting a course together on infiltration: not the general stuff, but the nitty gritty, the little things that make all the difference. I would fly to Vancouver and be picked up at the airport and brought to a compound. I would stay there for six weeks, coaching rookies on how to do undercover work. It all sounded great to me: I would be out of harm's way but still helping the cause. I knew that what I could teach them could save their lives. Still, it wasn't all perfect. As experienced as I am about going after gang members, traffickers and mobsters, my line of work has dramatically changed over the last ten years, and not necessarily for the better.

Today, there is less room for new initiatives in the midst of an investigation. Everything takes forever; you have to go up the ladder and get everyone's stamp of approval. There's no independence, and those calling the shots are too far removed from the game. Let's say you're in the middle of an investigation and you have a question: By the time the answer comes down, you have to send it back up for a second round of approval from other higher-ups. It makes it impossible to do the concrete work at hand.

Say you meet a bad guy in a bar and he offers you some contraband: drugs or guns, whatever. No can do; there's no money available on the spot. It could take days, and the window on the deal is usually long closed by then. That's just one example, but it can happen over and over. This kind of criminal doesn't use banks like regular people—they operate in a cash-based world. If I were a bad guy, I would insist that the buyer get the money within the hour. If the guy responded that he will call tomorrow, I wouldn't deal with him any further. I would even go further: If I made a deal for ten in the morning, I might surprise him and show up at nine with the stuff. After all, to a hoodlum there's no difference between nine and ten. Let's say he then insisted on ten: I would leave it with him and tell him I'd be back at eleven for the money. At eleven I would send someone else, who would wait at the door for the money, not even entering the apartment.

Every step of the infiltration process is geared to have maximum effect in the courts: chain of custody, searching the agent before the buy, searching the agent's car, following the car to the location then back to the safe house, then searching him and his car again. Moving forward becomes a precarious balancing act. But one fact remains true: Criminals are greedy. A good agent will keep things happening so fast that the bad guy has no time to think and get worried. The odds are that if he sees the money, the deal will go through.

Another major change I've seen in the business has to do with entrapment, an issue I mentioned at the very beginning of this book. It's always been something I'm concerned with. But over time, the meaning has shifted. It revolves around this question: Would a crime still happen if we weren't around to make it so? Imagine a target is sitting in a bar. You approach and ask him if he can get some drugs for you. He says yes; you work out a price and make the deal. Wham—he gets arrested for trafficking drugs. To the cops, it's a great bust, and perfectly legitimate. In their eyes, the man is a dealer and sells drugs regardless of whether the agent is involved.

But to me it's not that simple. I don't think his past actions should have an impact on the present. Maybe he was trying to change his ways; it's unlikely, maybe, but it's possible. He certainly wouldn't have made *that* deal without me instigating it. I would feel better about the whole thing if it went like this: I sit down with him and complain about not finding drugs at a reasonable price. If at that point he offers me some, then he should go down. Maybe it seems like I'm splitting hairs, but

I really believe it's a different situation. As time went on, I was having more and more problems with that difference: the gray area between catching the bad guys and setting people up for a fall.

For an agent like me, the road ahead is unknown. The hunt for terrorists has become a top priority and it's vastly different from the operations we used to do. Many of my experiences involved planning to infiltrate a criminal organization with one overriding priority: not getting caught. With the new focus, there is no clear territory to move into. The threat may come from anywhere—within your own country or outside it. The playing field is undefined. Everything becomes suspect, all tangled together: means of transportation, stores and public malls, government buildings, video propaganda showing slaughters and beheadings—the symbolic nature of terror seeps into every crack in our world. Targets vary constantly. Potential attacks originate from well-organized and well-funded cells and from solitary lunatics inspired by propaganda on the internet.

While governments are increasingly joining efforts on cyber surveillance, especially after the violence and killings in Paris, this can't be seen as a replacement for fieldwork and infiltration. There are definitely new skills and tactics to be developed against fundamentalist terrorists. Western governments are being forced to adapt, and fail to do so at their peril.

It all made teaching the next generation of agents a real challenge. Sarah, my guide in the process, would help me to stay focused and decide what the best objectives would be for my six weeks of coaching. It was a highly controlled situation: I would stay at the compound with no access to phones and limited internet. She said she knew I was writing a book—the one you're now holding—and that my writing partner had been given security clearance. Still, emails between us would be subject to scrutiny. The understanding was that older cases were okay to write about, but not current information about the training—and certainly none of the specific techniques I would teach, or any information that could indicate the whereabouts of the compound. It all made sense to me. Thus that brings my tale of this case to an end, at least for now. Perhaps I can pick it up again after the course is done, but I'll need permission, and if the training activities result in new agents being sent out into the field, that's definitely not a sure thing.

EPILOGUE

Turning down the U.S.'s offer to investigate the Brothers biker club felt good; I suspected I'd saved myself a lot of grief. Besides, I knew by now that if push comes to shove the Americans will leave you high and dry. It's well known in the business—it's a miracle they get anyone to sign up.

Aside from that, it was about me accepting my new circumstances. I could see I was too old for the game—or maybe just for the frontline positions. But it's like when sports players become coaches or commentators: There's more than one way to be useful. I was ready to find a new role. Maybe I had found it without even realizing it: writing books and describing my experiences. The process gave me back a new power of insight into the choices that I had made over the years. Looking at them in this way gave me a totally different perspective. Would I change anything if I could do it all over? I absolutely would.

One purpose of writing about my experiences is to warn people about the pitfalls of this kind of life—that of an infiltrator or anyone in a related line of work. Yes, I've had excitement and travel, but that's not how it turns out for everybody. All too often, an agent ends up relegated to a single case, mainly for the simple reason that you've already been accepted in one area and bringing in another outsider to replace you would be like taking a bunch of steps backwards. That can be the hardest and most thankless outcome for an agent. There's no way they or their families can know the price they will end up having to pay. It's like buying an item with no payments for a year: The year will pass, but the debt remains.

It might be worthwhile to stop and compare the post-career life of agents to that of informants. The most vulnerable people who end up in witness protection programs tend to be women—very often, at least in my field, women who work in strip clubs. They may already have low self-esteem, reinforced by a biker or gangster boyfriend, usually through fear or the enabling of a drug addiction. Many of the women take "private clients" after work to make extra money. They don't get to keep much of the profits, of course, because that kind of service usually involves a pimp who takes a major cut. Women in this situation may end up making porn, as well. In short, it's one story of exploitation after another, with the pain and suffering that come along with it. They usually have an end goal, however. They'll say something like, "I'll do it for a while and save some money, and then get out." But they aren't as free to exit as they might like to think. They make friends with other women they work with and at a certain moment they share their intentions. Time and again, the information is then relayed to the pimp—often the very same night—and that means there's hell to pay.

But in the cycle in which these women are caught, a window of possibility opens up right at that moment. Disciplined violently by their pimp and feeling depressed and powerless, they may try something very desperate. At worst, suicide; at best, a distress call. If it ends up being cops at the other end of the line, they are usually quick to act. They will make sure to meet her within a day, to begin the process of turning her into a source. These particular cops are trained in "resource development," and they know how to play the role to the hilt. The first interview is to create a profile analysis; that helps them figure out the best way to handle the victim. Their strategy is to try to seem like potential friends, the only people she can trust, and to make her feel that through them she has a degree of protection. But it's a thin line to walk. They don't want to overdo it—they can't have her decide to suddenly change her life, clean up her act or to leave town and start anew. That would destroy the opportunity in front of them. Part of the profile analysis is about understanding how to make sure she stays put. To put it at most cynically: She has changed one pimp for another. This one may not beat her up—but they are not above threats. It becomes quite clear to her that they hold her life in their hands. If they are careless about the fact that she's working for them, she's as good as dead. That's a pretty powerful lever. If the woman has a child—and a great many do—they're even more stuck. One phone call and she could lose the kid to custody services. Am I saying they would do it? I'm saying they have the power—and in most cases that's enough.

That's not to say I would recommend these women don't get involved as informants—but I do think they should be aware of what they're getting themselves into. It's a serious game, and losers have more than their freedom at stake. She might start out as just a source; that means she should never have to testify to what she says. There are laws that protect sources. But if she proves herself valuable, they smoothly change her role from informant to source—step by step, so that she barely realizes the difference.

Another major change in my line of work has to do with informants. Whether it's the Russian mob or bikers, the informant has become the most effective tool for bringing down an organization. For guys like me, it can take months and months to get accepted enough to be brought into the action. The informant, on the other hand, is already there. All you need to do is focus your efforts on him and catch him on something that would result in a major charge, something that would lock him up for decades. Then you make him an offer he can't refuse. You'll let him go back to the nest without any charges, but now you own him. Morally, the problem is that sometimes these guys are worse than the ones they rat out. Think of the notorious Sammy the Bull. How many murders did he commit? Likely seventeen. He turned on all his friends, testified in court and served just a few years. He was released with a new identity, a huge amount of money and a comfortable new life.

When a relationship between an informant and his handlers gets that deeply involved, they end up spending more time together than they do with their own families. The coziness of the relationship can be complicated on both ends. Take biker cops. Almost all the cops I worked with on missions against biker gangs had to face the same challenges. They started by learning how to ride Harleys; on their time off, they go on short runs. It's one step into that world, but just a small one. But when it comes to real criminal activities—drugs, theft and murder—they have to maneouver very carefully. No matter what, they have to remain cops. As for myself, I never felt the lure of that side of life very strongly, even in the midst of it. I was never a real biker; the jobs just didn't get a hold on me. I haven't ridden a motorcycle since working on those cases. After the Bandidos case I was allowed to keep my bike. I put it in the garage and never touched it again. Eventually Scott Paterson called me and asked if I knew where he could get a deal on a bike. I offered him mine, and he purchased it from me on behalf of the Mounties.

A sense of fellowship often settles in between the handlers and the informant. Most of these guys never stop committing crimes while working for the cops. They might scold him, but no real attempt is made to stop him. I'm not sure what that means on the moral scale. I know from experience that the friendship between the two sides can seem real, sometimes beyond necessity. When the case eventually ends, the informer is whisked away into witness protection until it's time for the trial—maybe a year later, maybe more. No one is supposed to know where he goes or what his new name is. The cops just have to flick an internal switch to off—the guy is forgotten.

To the informant, it's a different situation: a totally new way of life, with changes across the board. When you were contributing to the case you don't have much time for relationships with your family. Now that the case is over, the distance with the wife or girlfriend vanishes. You're back together, 24/7. That might seem great for the first few days. But remember, under witness protection, you're not allowed contact with extended family or friends. Overnight, you've ended up in a new location, an unfamiliar environment. You're completely cut off. It can be devastating for a relationship. The cops you had spent so much time with—every day of the past few years—have gone on to other cases. All you've got is a pile of cash, which is no small matter, but it's not everything. The impact of the decision is huge.

And the danger remains. The bad guys don't give up just because you've vanished. They start pressuring the rest of your family and your associates to tell them where you are. Their goal is clear: to find you before the case makes it to court. No witness means no case, which is the best possible outcome for them. If they don't get you before the trial, they may still look for you—it becomes a matter of revenge. And even though you promise yourself you'll be careful, sooner or later you—or your wife or kids, if you have any—will try to contact someone from the old life. History shows it's almost inevitable. And today, with the prevalence of social media, how could you prevent your teenager from posting something online, via Facebook, Twitter or anything else? The criminals have networks that watch for signs of life. Before long, you're faced with another move, another new identity—if you're lucky. That's the reality of life under the witness protection program. And after the trial, you're cut loose from the program. You're on your own: "Have a nice life."

And what about someone like myself, a professional contracted agent—often called a "kite" by law enforcement agencies? There's no witness protection program for us—no pile of money to fall back on at the end of service. When one case is over, you get a few weeks off and then you're off to another job somewhere else, and you start all over, establishing a new character. Like many other jobs, you are only as good as your last work. It's a business relationship like any other, in some ways. You meet with the agency considering you and discuss the target and fees, the front you will use and all the other details. More often than not it's a three-month stint, subject to re-evaluation by both you and them. There is no question of you not appearing in court—you will certainly be required to testify.

Usually you're already working on another case when you're called on to act as a witness. You've been to court so many times over the years, notebooks in hand, you're pretty much a star witness at this point: no criminal record, no charges pending, you pay your taxes—there isn't much for them to use against you. That's a big advantage over the informants, who are vulnerable on the stand and tend to get mauled by the defence. Their criminal records, the deal they made with the cops, the money they made from crime: Everything is scrutinized, while just a few feet away his lifelong friends glare at him like he's the worst thing since Judas Iscariot. Court is not a pleasant experience at the best of times; for those labelled "rats," it must be hell.

The use of criminal witnesses is so fraught that it ends up undermining many cases. So why do cops rely on them? The answer is simple. Court decisions are one thing; the big media splash following the arrests is another. The praise and admiration for the authorities comes immediately after the arrests, before the drawn-out trial has outlasted the public's attention span. When they arrested over one hundred Hells Angels in Montreal and seized drugs, cash and guns, it made headlines everywhere. But where did the case end up? Seizures usually become separate charges and result in convictions; but in the case of the springtime 2001 operation, some of the accused still haven't had their day in court. The judge ended up releasing over twenty of them for violation of their right to a speedy trial. But what mattered to many involved was that the original operation had made the intended splash, and the glory would overshadow the end result.

So, informant versus infiltrator—which is the best way to go, from the perspective of the higher-ups? In my experience of typical cases, an agent infiltrating project is slow to start and expensive to run. There's absolutely no guarantee that I can succeed in the entering the crooks' world. One mistake would mean it's all over. In the end, I think that if you were a top cop evaluating your best bet, you would have to go with the informant rather than the agent. Maybe it simply comes down to the fact that we're in a tight economy.

And then there's the best-of-both-worlds option: The turncoat introduces you to the gang, says you're a friend. Voila: instant legitimacy in the eyes of the gang. But it adds a danger that is equivalent to the advantage. Suppose the turncoat has a change of heart and gets you killed by exposing you. Because of this fear, more and more seasoned agents are leaving the business to be replaced by younger guys. Cops are also increasingly relying on cops to play the role of the money guy. It affords more immediate credibility in court and requires less reliance on use of the rat.

When I retired, I felt I had completed my role and it was time to step aside. But still, when I get an offer like the recent one, I can get swept up in thinking, "Just one more case." But I know that our team was lucky not to have suffered more loss. Our over-the-hill gang rode off into the sunset and would never ride again. But things change, and that's okay. I get to relive those experiences for you—whether you enjoy the books or choose to throw them across the room!

I think back to those I've lost and those who came close: Shannon, George and Abu—and those whose story hasn't been told here, like my friend Larry, beaten to within an inch of his life in a back alley, resulting in a stroke and a heart attack that took his life. Then there are my two divorces, and three kids who had to grow up with a part-time dad. And what about the criminals whose lives I've affected? The dead, the imprisoned, locked away for years, their kids growing up on their own. What did I really accomplish? Were things changed for the better? Did I waste my life chasing shadows? I wish I could answer these questions.

My hope now is that my words reach people and inform them, to achieve things that I may not have achieved as an agent. It matters to me that the critical issues I've learned about stay in the public eye. The Aboriginal case—in my view, the worst demonstration of racism and violence against women in our country—is one of the most pressing. Maybe I will be able to share things one day that will help make someone pay for this travesty of justice, which has been going on for years. Maybe I can even help save a life or two. If I manage that, whether or not I'm around to see the end result, I think I will have done something worthwhile. For now, my work continues. I need this case as much as it needs me.

ALEX CAINE

Notes for the Conspirators Among Us

We've seen interesting revelations over recent years of secret government activities. They may account for only a small fraction of the reality. My access to information agencies and intelligence gathering has made that abundantly clear. Let's now take a look at some recent events and activities that would confirm the worst fears of those who are suspicious of surveillance—who think that Big Brother may be watching things more closely than we know.

For many years, the U.S. has eavesdropped on everybody, friends and foes alike. This has been made public by Edward Snowden, a former National Security Agency consultant, who has now found refuge in Russia. University of Toronto has already said that the NSA is collecting 25% of all Canadian Internet traffic. The most unsettling thing is how easy it is: Companies like Facebook, Yahoo, Google are American owned. The U.S. spy agency monitors 100% of the communications they transmit, and ours by default. The NSA feeds information back to our Canadian Security Intelligence Service.

And let's not fool ourselves: Our own intelligence bodies eavesdrop on us as well, and send our data south of the border. Primarily responsible for this is the Communications Security Establishment Canada (CSEC). They act with unlimited powers for primary-role cyber intelligence through a national counter-terrorism strategy launched in 2011 under the Kanishka Project.

One of the things I've learned over the years is that no government, including our own, ever tells the truth. Many of those agencies and the people who work there think that "citizens" is another word for "pain in the ass." The public should pay taxes to keep the wheels turning, vote for whom they're told, and above all stay out of the way. You don't have to go far up the food chain to notice this attitude. Even members of the Justice Department, cops and lawyers—the feeling is unanimous.

That, of course, is the main reason the U.S. is so furious with Snowden. When he started releasing the truth about how one government really feels about another: That's embarrassing but not critical. It's the wire tapping, the bugging of phones, monitoring of email accounts and even texts that are the real issue. When he revealed some of the NSA's activities such as keeping track of Americans' private mail by hacking into Yahoo and Google and picking through data from cell phone companies, things reached a new level. Let's take a look at what are considered the ten worst threats against privacy.

1. <u>NSA was secretly allowed by the Courts to scour phone records.</u>
   The NSA intercepts the communications of over a billion people worldwide and tracks the movement of hundreds of millions of people using cell phones. It has also created or maintained security vulnerabilities in most encryption software, leaving the majority of the Internet susceptible to cyber attacks from the NSA and other parties. Uproar from civil rights organizations and legal proceedings have escalated the controversy. Pressure from public opinion led President Barack Obama to make amendments to the program.

2. PRISM
    The PRISM program was described as the NSA's access key to the servers of U.S technology giants like Google, Facebook, Microsoft and Apple, among others.

    Data gathered include email, video and voice chat, videos, photos, VoIP chats such as Skype and file transfers. Another program, Boundless Informant, employs big data databases, cloud computing technology, and Free and Open Source Software (FOSS) to analyze data collected worldwide by the NSA, including that gathered by way of the PRISM program, including Canada and the UK.

    According to the Washington Post, "every day, collection systems at the National Security Agency intercept and store 1.7 billion e-mails, phone calls and other types of communications. The NSA sorts a fraction of those into 70 separate databases."

    The truth is that the NSA doesn't have direct access to the servers but can request user data from the companies. The result remains the same, but no illegal hacking is required. At first, operators were quick to deny any knowledge of PRISM, but over tense negotiations behind closed doors they obtained the right to be more transparent about government data requests.

3. British hackers are busy on the global internet version of the NSA taps fiber optic cables around the world.
    The Government Communications Headquarters (GCHQ) in the UK taps fiber optic cables all over the world. Under the codename Tempora, the GCHQ exchanges, data and intelligence files with the NSA.

    Tempora allows the two entities to collect and exchange extensive data from across the world. A German newspaper revealed the names of the companies that collaborate in the framework of the program: Verizon Business, British Telecommunications, Vodafone Cable, Global Crossing, Level 3, Viatel and Interoute. Well, that's just too bad for subscribers!

4. <u>NSA spying has no borders.</u>
    At a G7 official dinner in Brussels, political observers noted a profound discomfort between U.S. President Barack Obama and German Chancellor Angela Merkel. For several weeks, their relationship had been tense over reports revealing that the NSA tapped Merkel's phone. As a matter of fact, Snowden declared that several heads of states had their phone conversations and meetings tapped. The German newsweekly *Der Spiegel* reported that targets of the NSA included at least 122 world leaders, among them German Chancellor Angela Merkel, Brazil's President Dilma Roussef, and Mexico's former President Felipe Calderon, the French Foreign Minister, as well as leaders at the 2010 G8 and G20 summits in Toronto.

5. <u>No one can hide from XKeyscore.</u>
    XKeyscore is a worldwide interceptor, a means the NSA uses to search "nearly everything a user does on the internet." In the Snowden documents, NSA describes it as the "widest-reaching" system to search through internet data.

6. <u>NSA operations have secretly succeeded at cracking "fool proof" encryption and undermining internet security.</u>
    Firewalls, trick sites, encryption: An array of tools exists to block content from potential hackers. Consequently, the NSA had to develop a set of techniques and counter-technologies. Despite its

efforts, encryption algorithms remain a challenge to the agency.

According to Christopher Soghoian, principal technologist at the American Civil Liberties Union (ACLU), this situation has generated serious repersussions:

"Even as the NSA demands more powers to invade our privacy in the name of cybersecurity, it is making the internet less secure and exposing us to criminal hacking, foreign espionage, and unlawful surveillance. The NSA's efforts to secretly defeat encryption are recklessly shortsighted and will further erode not only the United States' reputation as a global champion of civil liberties and privacy but the economic competitiveness of its largest companies."

7. A Swat Team for risky missions

The Office of Tailored Access Operations (TAO) is an intelligence gathering unit of the NSA. When other surveillance tactics fail, these experts are trained to hack into computers and, if necessary, to infect them with viruses.

In Germany, the weekly *Der Spiegel* detailed TAO's secrets, and labelled it "a squad of plumbers that can be called in when normal access to a target is blocked. TAO comes in for specific, targeted operations when the NSA can't find intelligence or needs more detailed information on a target through its bulk surveillance programs."

8. The NSA cracks Google and Yahoo data center links.

When bulk collection fails, the NSA is able to infiltrate links connecting Yahoo and Google data centers. There is no way for the companies to trace the intrusions.

9. <u>Google-Cloud exploitation</u>
   This particular story truly enraged the tech companies, which reacted with much more fury than before. Google and Yahoo announced plans to strengthen and encrypt those links to avoid this kind of surveillance, and a Google security employee even said on his Google+ account what many others must have thought privately: "Fuck these guys."

10. <u>The NSA collects text messages.</u>
    About 200 million text messages are intercepted every day worldwide through a program called Dishfire. For a spy agency with processing capabilities, this represents, as they say, a "goldmine to exploit."

So you think that the concept of privacy in keeping with your private life still exists? Well, sorry for the reality check. CIA, FBI, NSA: They're just the tip of the iceberg. In fact, there are 16 agencies active in the U.S. There are tens of thousands of the smartest minds working and watching you, hiding behind the flag. Here's but a small sample.

Unlike the Defense Intelligence Agency (DIA) and the Central Intelligence Agency (CIA), both of which specialized primarily in foreign human espionage, the NSA referred to as "No such Agency," has no authority to conduct human-source intelligence gathering. Instead, the NSA is entrusted with coordination of SIGINT (general information) components of otherwise non-SIGINT government organizations, which are prevented by law from engaging in such activities without the approval of the NSA via the Defense Secretary. As part of these streamlining responsibilities, the agency has a co-located organization called the Central Security Service (CSS), which was created to facilitate cooperation between NSA and other U.S. military cryptanalysis components. Additionally, the NSA Director simultaneously serves as the Commander of the

United States Cyber Command and as Chief of the Central Security Service. Confused yet? You are supposed to be. It like shell companies put together to hide money and fuck with the IRS (tax people).

Ironically, if you enter an informational query into a web search engine, for instance "national security agency",* you'll find a tremendous amount of material made of recent history and facts about those organizations that have been spying on us for decades. Intentionally, I put together a montage of excerpts that you may find interesting.

— A secret operation code-named "MINARET" was set up by the NSA to monitor the phone communications of Senators Frank Church and Howard Baker, as well as major civil rights leaders including Dr. Martin Luther King, and prominent U.S. journalists and athletes who criticized the Vietnam War. However, the project turned out to be controversial, and an internal review by the NSA concluded that its Minaret program was "disreputable if not outright illegal."

After the Church Committee hearings, the Foreign Intelligence Surveillance Act of 1978 was passed into law. This was designed to limit the practice of mass surveillance in the U.S.

— Trailblazer Project ramped up in 2002. SAIC, Boeing, CSC, IBM, and Litton worked on it. Some NSA whistleblowers complained internally about major problems surrounding Trailblazer. This led to investigations by Congress and the NSA and DoD Inspectors General. The project was cancelled in early 2004; it was late, over budget, and didn't do what it was supposed to do. The Baltimore Sun ran articles about this in 2006 to 2007. The government then raided the whistleblowers' houses. One of them, Thomas Drake, was charged with violating 18 U.S.C. § 793(e) in 2010 in an unusual use of espionage

---

* https://en.wikipedia.org/wiki/National_Security_Agency
  http://www.revolvy.com/main/index.php?s=National+Security+Agency

law. He and his defenders claim that he was actually being persecuted for challenging the Trailblazer Project. In 2011, all 10 original charges against Drake were dropped.

— "Turbulence" started in 2005. It was developed in small, inexpensive 'test' pieces rather than one grand plan like Trailblazer. It also included offensive cyber-warfare capabilities, like injecting malware into remote computers. Congress criticized Turbulence in 2007 for having similar bureaucratic problems as Trailblazer. Its goal was information processing at higher speeds in cyberspace.

— The massive extent of the NSA's spying, both foreign and domestic, was revealed to the public in a series of detailed disclosures of internal NSA documents beginning in June 2013. It appeared that the scope of surveillance has become clearly beyond our grasp.

The new revelations confirmed the total break-in of our private lives by the NSA intercepting telephone and internet communications of over a billion people worldwide, on a yearly basis. The official motive for this operation was the gathering of vital information on terrorism as well as foreign politics, economics and "commercial secrets." In a declassified document it was revealed that 17,835 phone lines were on an improperly permitted "alert list" from 2006 to 2009 in breach of compliance, which tagged these phone lines for daily monitoring. Eleven percent of these monitored phone lines met the agency's legal standard for "reasonably articulable suspicion."

— A dedicated unit of the NSA locates targets for the CIA for extrajudicial assassination in the Middle East. The NSA has also spied extensively on the European Union, the United Nations and numerous governments including allies and trading partners in Europe, South America and Asia.

— The NSA tracks the locations of hundreds of millions of cell phones per day, allowing them to map people's move-

ments and relationships in detail. It reportedly has access to all communications made via Google, Microsoft, Facebook, Yahoo, YouTube, AOL, Skype, Apple, and others, and collects hundreds of millions of contact lists from personal email and instant messaging accounts each year. It has also managed to weaken much of the encryption used on the internet (by collaborating with, coercing or otherwise infiltrating numerous technology companies), so that the majority of internet privacy is now vulnerable to the NSA and other attackers.

— Domestically, the NSA collects and stores metadata records of phone calls, including over 120 million US Verizon subscribers, as well as internet communications, relying on a secret interpretation of the Patriot Act whereby the entirety of US communications may be considered "relevant" to a terrorism investigation if it is expected that even a tiny minority may relate to terrorism. The NSA supplies foreign intercepts to the DEA, IRS and other law enforcement agencies, who use these to initiate criminal investigations. Federal agents are then instructed to "recreate" the investigative trail via parallel construction.

Let's say you get information from an illegal tap that you want to use in court or to get warrants. The solution commonly used is to reconstruct a situation where you would get the same info from another source, sort of a fabricated informant. I've seen it done several times.

However:

— According to a report in The Washington Post *in July 2014, relying on information furnished by Snowden, 90% of those placed under surveillance in the U.S. are ordinary Americans, and are not the intended targets. The newspaper said it had examined documents including emails, message texts, and online accounts, that support the claim.*

And:

— *Despite President Obama's claims that these programs have congressional oversight, members of Congress were unaware of the existence of these NSA programs or the secret interpretation of the Patriot Act, and have consistently been denied access to basic information about them. Obama has also claimed that there are legal checks in place to prevent inappropriate access of data and that there have been no examples of abuse; however, a secret panel secret court charged with regulating the NSA's activities admitted its incapacity to assess how often the agency breaks even its own secret rules. It has since been established that the NSA violated its own rules on data access thousands of times a year, many of these violations involving large-scale data interceptions. It was also revealed that NSA officers have even used data intercepts to spy on love interests. The NSA has "generally disregarded special regulations for disseminating United States person information" by illegally sharing its intercepts with other law enforcement agencies. A March 2009 opinion of the panel, released by court order, states that protocols restricting data queries had been "so frequently and systemically violated that it can be fairly said that this critical element of the overall ... regime has never functioned effectively." In 2011, the same panel members noted that the "volume and nature" of the NSA's bulk foreign internet intercepts was "fundamentally different from what the court had been led to believe." Email contact lists, including those of U.S. citizens, are collected at numerous foreign locations to work around the illegality of doing so on U.S. territory.*

Legal opinions on the NSA's bulk collection program have differed. In mid-December, 2013, U.S. District Court Judge Richard Leon ruled that the "almost-Orwellian" program likely violates the Constitution of the United States, and wrote:

"I cannot imagine a more 'indiscriminate' and 'arbitrary invasion' than this systematic and high-tech collection and retention of personal data on virtually every single citizen for purposes of querying and analyzing it without prior judicial approval. Surely, such a program infringes on 'that degree of privacy' that the Founders enshrined in the Fourth Amendment. Indeed, I have little doubt that the author of our Constitution, James Madison, who cautioned us to beware 'the abridgement of freedom of the people by gradual and silent encroachments by those in power,' would be aghast."

On the opposite, and just a few days later, U.S. District Judge William Pauley ruled that the NSA's collection of telephone records is legal and valuable in the fight against terrorism. In his opinion, he wrote, *"a bulk telephony metadata collection program [is] a wide net that could find and isolate gossamer contacts among suspected terrorists in an ocean of seemingly disconnected data"* and noted that a similar collection of data prior to 9/11 might have prevented the attack.

In October 2014 a United Nations report condemned mass surveillance by the U.S. and other countries as violating multiple international treaties and conventions that guarantee core privacy rights.

The official response to this report got the authorities into trouble: It involved a series of contradictions that destroyed all credibility:

On March 20, 2013 the Director of National Intelligence, Lieutenant General James Clapper, testified before Congress that the NSA does not "wittingly" (the key word) collect any kind of data on millions or hundreds of millions of Americans, but he retracted this in June after details of the PRISM program were published, and stated instead that metadata of phone and internet traffic are collected, but no actual message contents. This was confirmed by the NSA Director, General Keith Alexander, before it was revealed that the XKeyscore program collects the contents of millions of emails from U.S. citizens without warrant, as well as *"nearly everything a user does on the internet."* Alexander later admitted that "content" is collected, but stated that it is *"simply stored and never analyzed or searched unless there is a nexus to al-Qaeda or other terrorist groups."*

Regarding the necessity of these NSA programs, Alexander stated on June 27 that the NSA's bulk phone and internet intercepts had been instrumental in preventing 54 terrorist "events," including 13 in the U.S., and in all but one of these cases had provided the initial tip to "unravel the threat stream." On July 31, NSA Deputy Director John Inglis conceded to the Senate that these intercepts had not been vital in stopping any terrorist attacks, but were "close" to vital in identifying and convicting four San Diego men for sending US$8,930 to Al-Shabaab, a militia that conducts terrorism in Somalia.

The U.S. government has aggressively sought to dismiss any legal challenges based on the Fourth Amendment of the Constitution, and has granted retroactive immunity to ISPs and telecoms participating in domestic surveillance. The U.S. military has acknowledged blocking access to parts of *The Guardian* website for thousands of defense personnel across the country, and blocking the entire newspaper website for personnel stationed throughout Afghanistan, the Middle East and South Asia.

Today, the NSA maintains at least two watch centers:
1) The National Security Operations Center (NSOC), which is the NSA's current operations center, "the nerve center" and focal point for time-sensitive SIGINT (significant intelligence) reporting for the United States SIGINT System (USSS). This center was

established in 1968 as the National SIGINT Watch Center (NSWC) and renamed into National SIGINT Operations in 1973.

2) NSA/CSS Threat Operations Center (NTOC), which is the primary NSA/CSS partner of the Department of Homeland Security response to cyber incidents. The NTOC establishes real-time network awareness and threat characterization capabilities to forecast, alert, and attribute malicious activity and enable the coordination of Computer Network Operations. The NTOC was established in 2004 as a joint Information Assurance and Signals Intelligence project.

In 2012, the NSA said more than 30,000 employees worked at Fort Meade and other facilities. Adding humor to a statement, John C. Inglis, the Deputy director, said that the total number of NSA employees is "somewhere between 37,000 and one billion" making the agency "probably the biggest employer of introverts." In 2013, the German magazine *Der Spiegel* stated that the NSA had 40,000 employees. More widely, it has been described as the world's largest single employer of mathematicians. Some NSA employees form part of the workforce of the National Reconnaissance Office (NRO), the agency that provides the NSA with satellite signals intelligence.

— The NSA received criticism early on in 1960 after two agents had defected to the Soviet Union. Investigations by the House Un-American Activities Committee and a special subcommittee of the House Armed Services Committee revealed severe cases of ignorance in personnel security regulations, prompting the former personnel director and the director of security to step down and leading to the adoption of stricter security practices. Nonetheless, security breaches recurred on July 23, 1963 when *Izvestia*, a Russian magazine and news wire service, put on its headline that a former NSA employee published several cryptologic secrets.

On that very same day, an NSA clerk-messenger committed suicide as ongoing investigations disclosed that he had sold secret information to the Soviets on a regular basis. The reluctance of Congress to look into these affairs had prompted a journalist to write, "If a similar series of tragic blunders occurred in any ordinary agency of government, an aroused public would insist that those responsible be officially censured, demoted, or fired." David Kahn criticized the NSA's tactics of concealing its doings as smug, and Congress's blind faith in the agency's right-doing as short sighted, and pointed out the necessity of surveillance by Congress to prevent abuse of power.

Counter measures against moles and whistleblowers

The NSA conducts polygraph tests of employees. For new employees, the tests are meant to discover potential enemy spies who are applying to the NSA and to uncover any information that could make an applicant pliant to coercion. As part of the latter, historically EPQs or "embarrassing personal questions" about sexual behavior had been included in the NSA polygraph. The NSA also conducts five-year periodic reinvestigation polygraphs of employees, focusing on counter-intelligence programs. In addition, the NSA conducts periodic polygraph investigations in order to find spies and leakers; those who refuse to take them may receive "termination of employment," according to a 1982 memorandum from the director of the NSA.

There are also "special access examination" polygraphs for employees who wish to work in highly sensitive areas, and those polygraphs cover counterintelligence questions, and more about behavior. NSA's brochure states, the average test length is between two and four hours. A 1983 report of the Office of Technology Assessment stated that "It appears that the NSA [National Security Agency] (and possibly CIA) use the polygraph not to determine deception or truthfulness per se, but as a technique of interrogation to encourage admissions." Sometimes applicants in the polygraph process confess to committing felonies such as murder, rape and selling illegal drugs. Between 1974 and 1979, of the 20,511 job applicants who took polygraph tests, 695 (3.4%) confessed to previous felony crimes; almost all of those crimes had been undetected. How strange is that?

Arbitrary personnel selection

There is no tolerance for malcontents. Arbitrary firing of possible whistleblowers about the agency's operations is common practice at the NSA.

The number of exemptions from legal requirements has been criticized. When in 1964 Congress was hearing a bill giving the director of the NSA the power to fire at will any employee, the *Washington Post* wrote: *"This is the very definition of arbitrariness. It means that an employee could be discharged and disgraced on the basis of anonymous allegations without the slightest opportunity to defend himself."* Nevertheless, the bill was adopted with an overwhelming majority. So if you start asking too many questions or raise legal issues, you're gone. They don't even need a reason. If you happen to be trouble, then you become history.

Boomerang routing of information

While it is assumed that foreign transmissions terminating in the U.S. (such as a non-U.S. citizen accessing a U.S. website) subject non-U.S. citizens to NSA surveillance, recent research into boomerang routing has raised new concerns about the NSA's ability to survey the domestic internet traffic of foreign countries. Boomerang routing occurs when an internet transmission that originates and terminates in a single country transits another. Research at the University of Toronto has suggested that approximately 25% of Canadian domestic traffic may be subject to NSA surveillance activities as a result of the boomerang routing of Canadian internet service providers.

A document included in NSA files released with Glenn Greenwald's book *No Place to Hide* details how the agency's Tailored Access Operations (TAO) and other NSA units gain access to hardware. They intercept routers, servers and other network hardware being shipped to organizations targeted for surveillance and install covert implant firmware onto them before they are delivered. This was described by an NSA manager as "some of the most productive operations in TAO because they preposition access points into hard target networks around the world."

It's fascinating—a very deep wormhole. Information monitoring is accelerating, privacy eroding. What we need is leadership in both Canada and the U.S. that is honest and transparent. The problem is, only the collaborators get the backing needed to fund a campaign, so there's no threatening the status quo. Look at what happened with the Obama presidency, which started with a promise for change. Voters fell for it, hook, line and sinker.

Master craftsmen at the storyboard
This next segment deals with people who invent stories, entire scenarios with no resemblance to the truth, and with real people in the cast and fabricated roles. We've all been exposed to it—some of us have even made up our own. It all seems pretty harmless until it hits the outside world as fact, as truth. Then it can have untold consequences.

I'm talking about one of the most feared and dangerous types of professional in the intelligence world: the fabricator. Wikipedia's definition: An intelligence agent or officer that generates disinformation, falsehoods or bogus information, often without access to authentic resources. It's rarely talked about publicly. To admit having been fooled by one of these sociopaths is a major embarrassment and shows a weakness in the system. The only recourse is to issue a "burn notice," to all friendly countries and to cut off all ties with that individual.

Only the Russians actively seek them out for use and re-use. The Russians will put them to work in a low-level job for a year. The F1 (the designation for the fabricator) will familiarize himself with the factory layout. He then has the framework in which to construct his fantasy. They then make him a low level spy and send him somewhere he can do some damage, like the Middle East or the U.S. How harmless can it be, you wonder? So the guy has a creative imagination. Creative, definitely. But harmless? Not a chance.

Here's one such story. It's about an F1 with the code-name Curveball. He was responsible for the death of over 100,000 people. Dangerous enough?

Rafid Ahmed Alwan, born in 1968, known by the Defense Intelligence Agency as "Curveball," is an Iraqi citizen who defected in 1999. He claimed that he had worked as a chemical engineer in laboratories of an Iraqi plant manufacturing mobile biological weapons for mass destruction.

U.S. and British Governments utilized the information to build a rationale for military action in the lead up to the 2003 invasion of Iraq. In his State of the Union address, in 2003, President George W. Bush said, "We know that Iraq, in the late 1990s, had several mobile biological weapons labs," and Secretary of State Colin Powell pushed the envelope even further by presenting to the UN Security Council a computer generated image of a mobile biological weapons laboratory. They were later found to be mobile milk pasteurization and hydrogen generation trailers. On 24 September, 2002, the British government published its dossier in the matter of WMDs (weapons of mass destruction) with a personal foreword by Prime Minister Blair, who assured readers that Saddam Hussein had "beyond doubt" continued to produce WMDs. One of the main tactics for a successful F1, is the fabrication of a story that runs in the same direction as the target. It has to be what they want to hear to justify their own agendas.

In a February 2011 interview with the *Guardian*, Blair "admitted for the first time that he lied about his story, and recognised that it was used in the end as a justification for entering into war."

Curveball's story began in November 1999 when Alwan, then in his early 30s, arrived at Munich's Franz Josef Strauss Airport with a tourist visa. Upon entering the country he applied for political asylum. That began his story of having worked in laboratories for the creation of WMD. This was a gift to German Intelligence and put them in the driver's seat with a new spy file. So, as long as they could keep this guy away from others, the CIA and MI6 would have to come to them for intelligence.

In 2003, inspectors led by David Kay conducted additional investigation into Curveball's credibility. They found among other things that he placed last in his university class when he had claimed to place first, and that he had been jailed for embezzlement before fleeing to Germany. The former point is relevant because Curveball claimed to have been hired out of university to head Iraq's bioweapons program. That he had placed last in his class would cast considerable doubt on this claim.

When the lie became public someone had to be blamed for such a failure by the security agency. In response to public criticism, U.S. President Bush initiated an investigative commission that released their report on March 31, 2005. This commission came to many conclusions including:

Curveball's German intelligence handlers saw him as "crazy and ... out of control," his friends called him a "congenital liar," the Germans wrote him up as a "blue source," that's one that is not shared with any other country. A red source is shared. The Germans did not want to give up their source and wanted to keep control.

The Bush administration laid blame on the CIA, criticizing its officials for "failing to investigate" doubts about Curveball, which emerged after an October 2002 National Intelligence Estimate. In May 2004, over a year after the invasion of Iraq, the CIA concluded formally that Curveball's information was fabricated. Furthermore, on June 26, 2006, *The Washington Post* reported that *"the CIA acknowledged that Curveball was a con artist who drove a taxi in Iraq and spun his engineering knowledge into a fantastic but plausible tale about secret bioweapons factories on wheels."*

On April 8, 2005, CIA Director Porter Goss ordered an internal review of the CIA in order to determine why doubts about Curveball's reliability were not forwarded to policy makers. Former CIA Director George Tenet and his former deputy, John E. McLaughlin, announced that they were not aware of doubts about Curveball's veracity before the war. However, Tyler Drumheller, the former chief of the CIA's European division, told the *Los Angeles Times* that *"everyone in the chain of command knew exactly what was happening."*

In February 2011, Rafid Ahmed Alwan admitted for the first time that he lied about his story regarding Iraq's secret biological weapons program. He also admitted to being shocked that his false story was used as a justification for the Iraq War but proud that the fabrications helped topple Saddam Hussein.

My perspective? That last part's a bunch of crap. Sociopaths do not have the ability to empathize with anyone—they just don't care. It remains a bit of a mystery that he was never charged or pursued for his lies. Apparently he is now living a "normal" life, still protected by Germany.

This of course is an extraordinary case and not the norm. But fabricators also work at much lower levels such as in drug enforcement, lobbying and other areas, within the bounds of the law or beyond it. Professions such as acting and writing even painting are fertile grounds for these people. The scammers and fraudsters of Wall Street, those who milked the system for hundreds of millions of dollars—maybe they deserve the title as well. Maybe, when it comes down to it, we've all met the type: The person who can't tell the truth to save their life.

When President Bush and British Prime Minister Tony Blair made the big push for war because of WMD, the information came from Curveball. When they said they had "eye-witness proof," they were talking about Curveball. Were they totally duped? That's going too far, I'd say. It was widely know by then in the intelligence community that he was almost a "fabrication artist." The leaders needed a reason, and Curveball provided one—so they ran with it.

There's a certain point at which we all do that. Confirmation bias. We start with an opinion, research it, and pick and choose the information that best suits our point of view. Only when we have no set opinion—almost impossible—do we consider both sides and let the facts dictate what we "know."

It's a world of truth and lies and so many permutations of both. What is the truth? Does the question "Who shot Kennedy" have the same meaning as "Who shot J.R."? Who's to say where fiction ends and reality begins?